Praise for *Bond Portfolio Investing and Risk Management*

Bonds are—to borrow from Friedman—always and everywhere a quant's domain. Vineer has done a masterful job of creating *the* reference for risk management in the bond world. This book is deep, thorough, and well written. We already view it as a "go-to" reference for our own investments.

Robert D. Arnott
Chairman, Research Affiliates, LLC
Jason Hsu
CIO, Research Affiliates, LLC

Excess returns or yields do not come without risk. *Bond Portfolio Investing and Risk Management* delves comprehensively but intuitively into the various risk factors and delivers the tools to understand, measure, control, and take advantage of risk premiums in practical fixed income investing. As the financial crisis has made all too clear, this book's unifying treatment of risk and return is essential for all bond investors.

Andrew Ang
Ann F. Kaplan Professor of Business, Columbia Business School

If financial theory broke during the crisis, then this book shows how to fix up fixed income finance.

Peter Carr, Ph.D.
Global Head of Market Modeling, Morgan Stanley
Executive Director, Masters in Math Finance, NYU

This moves instantly to the top of my recommended list of important reading for concept-oriented fixed income investors. Profit by learning how a true expert makes risk-return tradeoffs when constructing portfolios of bonds and related derivatives.

Darrell Duffie
Dean Witter Distinguished Professor of Finance
Graduate School of Business
Stanford University

Bottom line: This book will be valuable for all bond managers by providing fresh and important insights for the postcrisis market, which in our biz is the highest compliment a competitor can offer.

Bennett W. Golub, Ph.D.
Chief Risk Officer
BlackRock, Inc.

This well-written book provides an excellent guide to the fundamental economic factors driving fixed income portfolios. In a masterful way, Bhansali is able to provide deep insights and intuition about key issues such as optionality, convexity, systemic risk, and tail risk using both his extensive knowledge of fixed income markets and many real-world examples drawn from his long trading experience. This is a must-read book for anyone navigating the postcrisis fixed income markets.

Francis Longstaff
Allstate Professor of Insurance and Finance, Area Chair
UCLA

Vineer Bhansali combines the mathematical rigor of a trained physicist with the commonsense wisdom of a school-of-hard-knocks practitioner to deliver a unique prism into the world of bond investment and risk management after the financial crisis. The book is not just valuable but extremely timely. You won't want to read it quickly, but slowly and thoughtfully, because it is an analytical mosaic, not simply a well-written narrative, even though it is indeed that. Bravo, Vineer!

Paul McCulley
Managing Director
PIMCO

Drawing on his years of experience as a portfolio manager, his knowledge of and contributions to the academic literature, and his quantitative training, Bhansali bridges the gap between book knowledge and the practicalities of successful long-term investing. By focusing attention on big-picture questions that are often forgotten in the course of portfolio "optimization"—Which options are you short? Who else is in the trade? What will happen in a liquidity-stress scenario?—this book will help asset managers to improve the risk-return characteristics of their portfolios and to avert disasters.

Bruce Tuckman
Author of *Fixed Income Securities* and Director of Financial Markets
Research Center for Financial Stability

How has the recent crisis changed the true value of bonds? One of PIMCO's brightest provides the answer.

Jack Treynor

Bond
Portfolio
Investing
and Risk
Management

Bond Portfolio Investing *and* Risk Management

POSITIONING FIXED INCOME PORTFOLIOS FOR ROBUST RETURNS AFTER THE FINANCIAL CRISIS

VINEER BHANSALI

New York   Chicago   San Francisco   Lisbon   London
Madrid   Mexico City   Milan   New Delhi   San Juan
Seoul   Singapore   Sydney   Toronto

For Beka

Contents

Foreword

Every once in a while, a major shock leads people to review the continued relevance of "conventional wisdom," and every once in a while, the result is an evolution in thinking that anchors the emergence of a new conventional wisdom. Those who understand and prepare for such a possibility may gain important first-mover advantages in portfolio management, risk mitigation, and conceptual analysis.

The 2008–2009 global financial crisis surely meets the test of a major shock. It exposed weaknesses at virtually every level of society—from the individuals who bought homes they could not afford, to the banks that took on risks they did not understand, and to regulators who fell asleep at the wheel. The crisis disrupted entire sectors and economies around the world. In the process, the previously unthinkable and highly improbable became both thinkable and probable. The consequences have been and will continue to be material, having an impact on both Wall Street and Main Street.

At its most basic level, the 2008–2009 crisis reflected a massive failure of risk management, again at every level of society. The size and composition of numerous balance sheets were allowed—indeed enabled—to get to unsustainable levels, and risk identification and mitigation were diluted, lulled into a sense of complacency by all the prior talk (in 2006–2007) of "the great moderation" and "Goldilocks."

Vineer Bhansali has been among the leaders in showing a willingness and an ability to espouse a fresh new perspective on both fixed-income investing and risk management. His perspectives were born well before the financial crisis, based on forward-looking analysis and the courage to question the conventional way of doing and thinking about things. They evolved dynamically in the midst of the crisis and are now acting as a magnet for other forward-looking analyses.

I first came across Vineer when he joined PIMCO in 2000. My PIMCO colleagues and I were attracted to the quality of Vineer's thinking and his willingness to question and debate. And we were not the only ones. His repeated ability to publish papers in respected academic and industry journals confirmed what we saw in Vineer.

In 2006, Vineer embarked on the intellectually demanding task of thinking about portfolio positioning and risk management in terms of risk factors rather than just asset classes. By then, I had left PIMCO for a 22-month stint at Harvard Management Company (HMC), the entity responsible for managing the university's endowment. And coincidently, my HMC colleagues and I were dealing with the same analytical challenges.[1]

In every investment made, investors underwrite a distinct combination of risk factors—whether they know it or not. For simplicity, the industry has bundled these risk factors into asset classes that can be elegantly presented in model portfolios and benchmarked and followed using relatively simple indices.

This shorthand makes sense in an "equilibrium" state that is characterized by stable correlations and little, if any, structural change. But it is severely challenged in a changing world, with national and global regime shifts—such as the reality that we live in today. Correlations among asset classes become unstable, and the very definition of asset classes may blur. In such a world, investors must go beyond asset classes and ask about their risk factor exposures—an important yet far from simple requirement.

---

[1] See El-Erian, Mohamed A., *When Markets Collide: Investment Strategies for the World of Global Economic Change.* New York: McGraw-Hill, 2008.

This is just one of the many insights offered by Vineer Bhansali in this valuable and timely book. His analysis elegantly speaks to the what, how, and why. For example, risk factor analysis is explained in detail. Vineer shows how and why it contributes to better portfolio management and more responsive risk management. As a result, the tradeoffs between risk and return become clearer, as does the interaction between cyclical and secular forces and between bottom-up and top-down factors.

This book will be of interest to many and of particular use to two groups of readers—those of you who are involved in portfolio construction and analysis and those who are interested in how analytical advances make their way from the minds of people to the day-to-day reality of portfolio and risk management. I hope that you will all benefit from this book as much as I did.

Mohamed A. El-Erian
CEO and co-CIO, PIMCO
Author of *When Markets Collide*

Acknowledgments

I would like to thank numerous colleagues and collaborators at PIMCO, Credit Suisse First Boston, Salomon Brothers, and Citibank, as well as researchers and coauthors from academia with whom I have worked over the years. Thank you for educating me and for your insights and comments.

The major impetus for writing this book was PIMCO's clients, with whom my interactions over the last ten years have required constant refinement and precision of thought. Many PIMCO colleagues who were part of our presentations suggested that I write them up as a book. A special thanks to our clients for the opportunity to be of service.

My special thanks to Mohamed El-Erian and Bill Gross, who by their example of clarity, depth, and perception continue to raise the bar for investors. No author can even come close to explaining their investment acumen and perception. One rarely gets the privilege of observing such brilliance at close quarters. I learn every day from them.

The inspiration for my writing remains my parents, whose mantra of "strive for excellence" points my inner compass. The voyage has only begun.

My sons Zane and Kieran have been sources of unbelievable joy and affection. This provided the all-important balance of perspective.

Most importantly, this book could not have been completed without the unwavering love and support of my wife Beka. Thank you for your support and for letting me to go on those long runs where most of the thinking "work" was done.

Preface

The title of this book suggests that there is or will be a state of the world *after* the financial crisis. Whether this new state is different from anything we have ever seen or the same as we have always seen with new twists will be hard to tell definitively until it's too late. We also know that there will be more crises in the future. But a bond investor should not be held to the too-high standard of being able to forecast beyond doubt what regime of the world we are in now and how and when we will switch to another one. Bonds are conservative investments, and bond portfolios ought to be structurally positioned to both add value over the riskless rate (at essentially 0 percent today) and not lose substantial value over cycles.

Audience

This book is targeted toward professionals involved in institutional fixed income investment. I visualize the user as a specialist (trader, portfolio manager, financial engineer) involved in one of the mainstream fixed income areas who is eager and prepared to use a source from which to learn practical investment techniques and tools for investment decision making. I have had the privilege of meeting clients over the years who have planted the seeds for many of the ideas and thoughts in this book. I found myself refining the ideas I have learned and invented over the years to a degree where I could present the coherent whole in a manner that made sense. The ultimate purpose of this clarity is to provide the tools for making better investment decisions. While I tried to keep this book free of stochastic calculus and graduate-level math (the curious reader can learn those techniques from my other recent book with Mark Wise entitled, *Fixed Income Finance: A Quantitative Approach*, published by McGraw-Hill in 2010), I had to lean on simple mathematical arguments to make some points concisely. I hope they do not distract the reader too much from the conceptual thrusts of this book. For many, who have seen and heard this discussion before, seeing it all laid out in paper might answers questions not answered in our meetings.

History of the Book

The hardest part is to think about what to put in and what to leave out, and over the last three to five years I have refined the outline to what I consider are the essential and most important parts for real investments. Much of the book was written three or four years ago, but then the crisis happened, and not only did I not get a chance to finish, but I also learned so many new things that I considered waiting to write a more relevant book the best choice. But authors have deadlines, so at some point I had to turn the screens off, quit working on new research (and reading the copious academic literature), and just write what I could. I am happy to report that despite all the new *facts* that have emerged, the *concepts* have not changed over the last few years and through the crisis. So I could easily have titled the book *How to Construct Robust Portfolios through and after Crises* instead of what you have on the cover. I also think that the best books are short, with a very compact and direct discussion of the relevant topics with examples, so I have tried to provide as many examples as I could. To make the principles more user-friendly, I use Bloomberg screens (which in my view is the major public, nonproprietary tool used by participants) to illustrate quantitative concepts. I find the ability of users to "touch" the numbers makes a big difference in their faith in using the concepts and tools.

How This Book Is Different

There are, of course, a number of excellent books on fixed income topics (such as the survey ones by Fabozzi), as well as books on modeling (Tuckman) and risk management (Golub et al.). In addition, there are a number of excellent MBA-level books that survey the broad markets and principles of asset allocation. In my view, most books do not give a unified, simple treatment of how fixed income investors actually think about risk and return, especially principles that focus on crisis resistance. They do not include most recent research from tightly attended practitioner conferences and workshops on topics of current interest whose content has not yet reached the printed page.

Why This Book?

I think there are a number of things my book has to say that are hard to find in traditional books written by academics or by practitioners with a more specialized focus. For instance, topics discussed here include incorporation of economics in financial modeling, measurement of liquidity and stress risks, asset allocation, discussion of the state of the art macro models, anomalies in markets such as munis, cross-market (e.g., FOREX and fixed income) relationships, forecasting of cyclical returns and risks, tail-risk measurement, and so on. I thought hard about especially simplifying the concepts and unifying and separating the facts that matter from the facts that are irrelevant.

The Key Idea

If there is one idea that carries more relevance than any other, it is that excess yield usually comes with excess risk, and this excess return and excess risk can be qualitatively explained as a short option position. While any individual option might trade cheap or rich from period to period, a portfolio of sales of such options, well diversified, properly scaled, and hedged against catastrophic risk, has odds tilted in its favor.

Outline of the Book

Chapter 1 starts with a summary of key risk factors in fixed income and the predictability of risk and return. In my view it is most important to start with risk, with a focus on the risk factors that matter. The chapter concludes with a look back at the crisis of 2007-2008 and what one can do to create a robust portfolio construction process. Chapter 2 discusses the basic building blocks of fixed income investing. Instead of beginning with a survey of the different types of securities that comprise the fixed income investment universe, we dig a layer deeper to focus on risks, and to examine how optionality plays a key role in risk and return computations. The chapter emphasizes keys to the understanding of financing and repo markets (even for a non-levered portfolio). We also discuss swaps and asset swaps, which are essentially liability transformation mechanisms. Finally, we discuss scenario analysis as the imperfect but essential tool for the evaluation of complex mortgage linked securities that consist of heterogeneous underlying cashflows that are highly sensitive to initial conditions. Chapter 3 gets to the root of structural investing, that is, the approach to harvesting fixed income risk premia across a wide variety of markets. It is the ability to evaluate these opportunities that makes fixed income investing so special, and creates the necessary mix for a portfolio for all seasons. I am indebted to the education I have received from Bill Gross in this area over the last twenty years of following his writing and more recently working for him. Chapter 4 digs into the relevance of a macroeconomic framework for model building. I think this is a topic that is ignored in most classic fixed income and even broad finance books, partly because it is so hard to make concrete statements that can be quantified. I take the risk of trying to wade the treacherous waters of macroeconomics as relevant to investing, only because it is so critical to making robust decisions. In Chapter 5 we discuss replication and use of derivatives to create risk and return profiles of key "betas" that we find in fixed income markets. ETFs have become the rage in the markets recently, because they allow investors to create asset allocation mixes at low costs. This replication is based on matching risk factors as we have discussed in the introductory chapters of the book. Chapter 6 discusses risk management from a stress testing approach. Instead of using Value at Risk, where aggregation results in loss of information, I find it easier to manage and measure risks using concentrations in "risk silos," i.e., disaggregate risk limits. This chapter discusses the practical aspects of designing and implementing a robust risk measurement platform. Finally, in Chapter 7 we bring in asset allocation—it is not sufficient to understand how bonds behave in isolation from other assets. Investors want to know how to include bonds in the context of their broader asset allocation portfolio. This requires understanding of the common risk factors, such as the equity factor, that pervades both bonds and other risky asset classes, and incorporation of forward looking views in a robust fashion into investment allocations. The book concludes with a recap and an epilogue of the key principles. My purpose in writing this book is to tell a unified story which evolves in a way that shows the connection of all the pieces. If I succeed in communicating what I have learned from so many others and from my own research in these few hundred pages all the work will have been worth it!

Bond Portfolio Investing *and* Risk Management

I

Risk and Total Return

"There is nothing new under the sun but there are lots of old things we don't know."
—Ambrose Bierce, *The Devil's Dictionary*, U.S. author and satirist, 1842–1914

The financial world changed in 2008. Many brokers become banks, and a large portion of the global financial system is owned or controlled by governments. Many fixed income markets that were "rates" markets, such as municipals, have become "credit" markets, and many credit markets have disappeared into a morass of defaults. What is an author supposed to do to relay principles of fixed income when the best he can do is to take a snapshot of a path-dependent process that is transmogrifying[1] every day? Consider the yield on Treasury bills:

---

[1] *Transmogrify:* to change into a different shape or form, especially one that is fantastic or bizarre. *Source:* Free Online Dictionary.

1

U.S. One-Month Bill Rate Negative for First Time Since December 2009-03-26 14:04:13.765 GMT

By Dave Liedtka, March 26 (Bloomberg)—Treasury one-month bill rates were negative for the first time since Dec. 26. The rate on the one-month bill was negative 0.0152 percent in New York, compared with 0.03 percent yesterday.

The only reason a person would accept a negative return *and* part with his or her money would be if the holding of the asset conferred some risk-mitigating benefit to the holder. In the case of the T-bill with negative yields, this benefit was the protection of capital. Investors were so scared of not getting their principal back that they were willing to give up return on their principal (actually they were willing to pay the federal government to keep their money safe).

The reason I start with this example is because return cannot be separated from risk. Unless a fixed income investor understands the inherent risks of an investment, it makes little difference where the return is coming from. To understand risks, we build models. Models are simply analytical tools that make sense, and they should not be confused with mathematical symbols or computational ability.

Model builders have lots of choices. What differentiates a good model from a bad model? My view is that it is the relevance to the markets and the ability to be robust to structural changes. A Wall Street trading desk that intermediates risk between two different counterparties uses its models as an inventory management system for important risks that do not impact the bottom line for short time intervals. So the models can be relatively simple and coarse. At the same time, a proprietary desk for the same dealer requires a more sophisticated set of models, especially if derivatives are involved, to ensure that there is no mispricing between similar or fungible assets. An asset manager who holds securities for longer time horizons requires even more truth in the models used because most of the reward for holding risks is through the risk premium realized. Valuation of risk premia, which is ignorable for a short-term trading desk, is the key issue for longer-term holders of risk. So, while a short-term trading desk can get away with risk-neutral valuation, another way of saying that the market is efficient in the short term, longer-term holders of securities and risk can hardly exploit short-term mispricing. For *investors*, the class that covers most of us, it is more important to be able to position portfolios to take advantage of risk premia than to arbitrage short-term mispricing.

To understand risk premia, we need to understand risks. A convenient way to describe the risks of securities is by using risk *factors*.[2] For any security, we can postulate that the return is proportional to the return on some factors, and the exposure of the security to those factors, plus some idiosyncratic return. In other words, let us assume that we can write the returns of a security r_i as

$$r_i = a_i + \sum_{j=1,N} \beta_{ij} f_j + \epsilon_i \tag{1.1}$$

where the N variables labeled $f_i \cdots f_N$ are the return on the fundamental variables we call factors that can influence the price of the security. Typically, we also impose the condition that the expected value of the noise term is zero, that is, $E(\epsilon_i) = 0$, and that the factor movements are orthogonal to the noise term.

Now suppose that the mean return on the asset is $\bar{r}_i$. Then the excess return is $r_i - \bar{r}_i$ and can be written in terms of the excess factor returns:

$$\tilde{r}_i = r_i - \bar{r}_i = \sum_{i}^{N} \beta_{ij}(f_j - \bar{f}_j) + \epsilon_i \tag{1.2}$$

---

[2]Much of this was discovered in the work of Stephen Ross almost a half cetuty ago in the guise of arbitrage pricing theory (APT).

As long as the factor set is complete, this equation holds true for all assets. In this chapter we will identify and explore the factors that are relevant to the management of fixed income portfolios. Since the excess returns on securities can be expected to be proportional to the excess returns on the factors, the risk on securities is also linked to the risk on the factors.

Indeed, with the introduction of new types of securities, many exotic and really invented in the last decade, traditional risk factors are far from sufficient. This demonstrates the limitation of the factor approach. For such securities, current technological expertise does not allow much more than a rudimentary valuation of the security in various hypothetical but reasonable scenarios.

The power of the risk-based approach becomes apparent when we apply it to portfolio construction from the ground up. Suppose that we were to forecast that equity volatility over the next five years (our investment horizon) would average 20 percent a year (the long-term average or close to it). An equity exposure of 60 percent in our portfolio would translate this to a 12 percent volatility (0.60 times 20 percent) from the equity risk factor. This means an approximately 5 percent chance, of a drawdown of 1.6 times the volatility, that is, a 1 in 20 chance of a drawdown of more than 19.2 percent. Clearly, having this estimate as a rough starting point allows us to scale the *big* bets properly. Too frequently investors get focused on what to buy and not on how much risk to take. Similarly, for interest-rate risk, if we forecast a volatility of 100 basis points per year, then a 5-year-duration portfolio leads to approximately 5 percent volatility per year and a 1 in 20 chance of a drawdown of more than 8 percent over a year. However, if yields are high enough, the coupon income might subsidize the risks from negative mark-to-market, that is, the embedded carry can smoothen price-based return volatility. This observation highlights something that we will discuss in detail later—that *carry*, or *structural return*, is an integral part of robust portfolios.

Fixed Income Risk Factors

For fixed income securities, risk measurement is fundamentally a more complex task than it is for securities such as equities. There are a lot more moving parts. To name a few:

- Shifts of the yield curve lead to duration and convexity risk.
- Yield curve reshaping leads to what is called *curve risk*.
- Various kinds of spreads can change without the yield curve changing. These result in spread durations.
  - Mortgages
  - Corporates
  - Municipals
  - Emerging
  - Treasury Inflation Protected Securities (TIPS)
  - Converts
- Currency-rate movements result in exchange-rate risk.
- Volatility and prepayment risk result in negative convexity (especially in mortgage-related securities).
- Liquidity risk creates additional spread risk and possibly tail risk (to be described later).

The relevance of measuring these risks carefully is not simply for risk management and control but also for active alpha generation. Sustainable alpha is generated from exploiting attractive sources of risk premia. Risk management is simply the other side of the coin—it means systematically managing the risks from the sources of risk premia.

Perhaps the most important idea is that by managing investment portfolios using the factor approach, we can achieve dual objectives of *efficient* risk management and alpha generation. If we can match the factor exposures of a portfolio using cheap securities and derivatives (if allowed), then there is a built-in bias toward outperformance. Many active bond funds have almost as many independent securities as are in their indices (such as the Barclays/Lehman Brothers U.S. Aggregate), but only a few hundred nonmortgage securities overlap (the mortgage pools make up the bulk of the line items in the portfolio as opposed to generic mortgage pools in the index). But the risk exposures, as measured by the risk factors described earlier, are very close to the index risk factors. Such a portfolio replicates the index risk factors but has built-in "alpha" from not holding each index security. Index securities typically trade richer due to holding by passive indexers who are required to purchase these securities in order to minimize tracking error to the indices.

Of course, in and of itself the reduction in overlap is not a sufficient objective. We have to make sure that the reduction in overlap actually improves the portfolio's risk-return characteristics. In the example portfolios we mention, the reduction of idiosyncratic risk requires a larger holding of common corporate bonds, nonagency mortgages, and other credit-sensitive securities. This makes sense because bonds subject to default risk carry idiosyncratic risks, which is harder to justify using just factor exposures.

Different Ways of Measuring Risk

There are a number of ways that the risk statistics, once computed, can be used for analysis of the risk-return potential in a portfolio. The first one is simply stress testing or scenario analysis. We can take each factor that can affect the value of a security and move it by some large magnitude. The impact of the factor shock on the percentage change of the security's price is the *factor duration*. For example, if we change the level of the yield curve by a parallel shift, the resulting impact (in percentage) on the price of a bond is simply the interest-rate duration relative to the Treasury curve. We could proxy the change in the yield curve by taking one or many points as reference.

However, this methodology does not say anything about the possibility that many of the risk scenarios can be realized simultaneously, that is, that the yield curve shifts up and flattens simultaneously. The approach also does not use any input on the probabilities of the particular scenarios. To tie in the correlations between the simultaneous movement of risk factors, we need to estimate a covariance matrix of the factors, either historically or ex ante, and compute the total risk as one number. The value of having one risk number is that different portfolios with different mixes can be compared. The shortcoming of this approach is that whenever disparate sources of risk are aggregated, there is a loss of information—aggregation done wrongly can lose more relevant information than the gain in simplicity from having one number for stating risk.

Finally, instead of estimating the total risk using a covariance matrix, one can estimate the risk by running actual simulations. You simply take the change in the factors over a predefined interval and see how the change affects the portfolio value.

The "Big 4" Risk Factors for Active Fixed Income and Total Return

A yield curve theoretically has an infinite number of maturity points that can fluctuate. However, to capture most of the risks of the yield curve, we do not need to describe the movement of each and every point in the curve. A simple analysis, for example, the one originally proposed by Litterman and Scheinkman [42] using principal components analysis, shows that three dominant movements—yield-curve shifts, twists, and curvature—capture approximately 85 percent, 10 percent, and 5 percent of all the volatility in the yield curve. Of course, this is a backward-looking statistical conclusion that says nothing about the future movements of the yield curve. To forecast the future movements requires much more thought and needs to draw on macroeconomic conditions, technical conditions, flows, and so on. Much of this will be discussed in a later chapter. For now, note that a framework of stylized factors is sufficient for us to construct the foundations for risk-factor allocation.

Duration is the risk factor that captures the response of a portfolio to the parallel shifts of underlying yield curves. For instance, a typical intermediate-term bond index has a duration of approximately five years.[3] Of course the question immediately arises, why would anyone take duration exposure? The answer lies in the fact that taking duration-factor risk is compensated in terms of excess risk-premium return. Since extending duration requires tying up money for a longer period and giving up access to it, the compensation is in terms of higher yields. Every source of excess return is compensation for some option that is sold to someone else. In the case of duration, the option that is sold is the ability to rebalance to higher yields if yields rise in the interim.

Curve duration is the the risk measure that captures the impact on the portfolio from a steepening of the yield curve by 100 basis points. To describe the steepening, we need to pick a point that remains fixed (the *pivot*). We can use the 10-year point on the U.S. yield curve as the pivot. The reason for this is simple: We are trying to describe independent movements of the yield curve in terms of three or so factors, so it makes sense to pick factors that capture individually most of a particular type of risk actually observed in the market and that are consistent with the intuition of practitioners. The 10-year point is the benchmark for most global bond markets; hence parallel shifts are best described using the 10-year point as a proxy. Then the steepening factor should be constructed so that the parallel shift is as independent of the steepening movement as possible.

Spread durations are the percentage change in the portfolio from a change in the spreads of the bonds, not changes in the levels or shape of the yield curve. In practice, to compute spread durations, we have

---

[3] The Barclays/Lehman Brothers U.S. Aggregate Index for the United States is one of the most common bond indices used in the market.

to compute the option-adjusted spread of a bond, hold the yield curve fixed, shift the option-adjusted spread, and then recompute the new price.[4] We will have much to say about what option-adjusted spread really means, how it is computed, and whether it is a good measure for valuation in later chapters.

Convexity, or the concept that duration does not remain unchanged as the yield curve moves around, is what makes fixed income different and interesting. There are different types of convexities that arise in the bond markets, but the most fundamental type is the one that arises from the fact that prices and yields are related through a nonlinear relationship. To compute the convexity of a bond portfolio, we first need to compute the convexity of individual bonds or their derivatives. To compute the convexity of a bond, we can use analytical methods, but in most cases we need to do the computation numerically. For securities such as mortgages, this is achieved by simulation first for a shifted yield curve and then recomputation with shifts from the already shifted yield curve. Ultimately, the output is something that we can call *bull duration* and *bear duration*, where bull duration is the duration for a 50 or 100 basis point parallel yield curve shift downward (lower yield), and bear duration is the mirror-image shift. To give an idea of the magnitudes, for a typical benchmark such as the Barclays/Lehman U.S. Aggregate Index, the baseline duration is approximately 4.5, and for a 50 basis point shift up, the duration increases by 0.20 year to 4.7. Similarly, for a 50 basis point shift down, the duration falls by 0.20 to 4.30. As we can see, this indicates that this index is negatively convex (a typical, positively convex Treasury bond would lose duration when yields rise and pick up duration when yields fall). Where is the negative convexity coming from? The answer is almost completely from mortgages. Note that

---

[4]For floating rate bonds, the interest-rate duration, as well as the curve duration, is small, but the spread duration equals roughly the duration of the equivalent maturity fixed rate bond.

almost 35 percent of total market value and 30 percent of interest-rate duration risk of the Barclays/Lehman Index is from mortgages. Since mortgages are negatively convex securities (owing to the embedded prepayment option), the index picks up the negative convexity.

Extra yield is the reward for incurring the negative convexity risk. Mortgages compensate the investor for the negative convexity via a higher yield than a comparable-duration Treasury bond. If time passes and markets come to a standstill, positive convexity is a waste. Flipping the argument on its head, if markets come to a standstill and only time passes, then the yield compensation an investor received for selling the prepayment option and incurring the negative convexity results in excess return.

Broadly speaking, the risks, and thus the returns, of a fixed income portfolio originate from the sum of *things that change* and *the passage of time*. Let's explain what this means in some detail. When a portfolio is positioned to take advantage of changes in the exposure to some market factor, say, duration, the return is simply the duration times the change in yield. But, even if the market does not change, the portfolio has some excess positive or negative return simply because time passes.

We break down the total return of the portfolio in terms of these two different pieces:

$$\text{Total return} = \text{return due to factor changes} \qquad (1.3)$$
$$+ \text{return from passage of time}$$

So far we have described risk measurement using separate factor exposures. However, we know that factor exposures may be correlated; for instance, a parallel shift in yield up is accompanied by a flattening of the yield curve. To estimate the impact on the portfolio from both the parallel shift and the twist of the yield curve, we can apply an appropriate covariance matrix to the factor exposures. This portfolio variance then can be converted to a standard deviation or tracking error metric.

Finally, instead of estimating the portfolio risk for hypothetical scenario shocks, we also can run the portfolio for actual historical scenarios. A complex fixed income portfolio can be described by its factor exposures plus the exposure to convexity (positive or negative). Once the change of the factors for the starting and ending points is measured and the carry per unit time is summed up for the interval of the period under scrutiny, we can estimate the actual performance of the portfolio. Note that this is nothing but an attribution model in disguise and, hence, is limited in its scope to the capturing of the idiosyncratic risks of particular securities.

To reiterate, if there is one concept that is common to all the sources of risk, and hence return, it's that *risk for securities almost always can be traced to one or many embedded options.* These options may be implicit or explicit, but the expected return depends strongly on the pricing of the option in different real-world scenarios. For instance, the excess yield that was being earned on many subprime-related securities was due to embedded options of illiquidity and default (the buyer of the securities essentially received the excess return for giving up access to liquidity and the option to default to the seller). On the other hand, securities such as Treasuries that pay lower yields than almost anything else (like the T-bill example at the start of this chapter) are useful exactly because they perform better in periods of crisis. The liquidity that Treasuries provide is compensation for the yield giveup.

"Structural" Approach to Investing

Investors can behave like insurance companies if they sell options that collect premiums while statistically likely to not pay off.[5] It is well known in the practitioner community (though perhaps not in academia) that markets are rarely in equilibrium, and hence prices are frequently

---

[5] I am indebted to Bill Gross for the insights in this section.

distorted. These "insurance" risk premia can be earned in many different ways.

The general idea is to sell mean-reverting volatility within the context of long-term secular trends. Such volatility premia may appear in the form of mortgages, explicit option sales, and yield-curve exposure. For absolute-return portfolios, it can appear in terms of long-short strategies. For portfolios measured relative to indices, this can be by being long or short the basis against benchmarks and in some cases substituting out of index securities that are cheap. Additionally, liquidity sales backed by the investor's balance sheet by purchasing less liquid paper is a potent source of structural "insurance" premia. Typically, new security or asset types that do not have a wide following also confer the opportunity for excess returns to the investor willing to take the informational risk (of course, one has to be careful in doing all the excess due diligence that this requires).

But the structural returns are also deeply tethered to structural risks, as many levered hedge funds find out. Capturing mean reversion is risky because markets can trend for extended periods of time, or they may take longer to mean revert than the seller can endure. Since markets can remain irrational for long periods of time, the structural approach to investing requires that the investor take only as much risk as will enable him or her to withstand underperformance for a period where such investing does not work. Typically, the reason that the "insurance" model fails is not because markets do not mean revert; rather it is because the investor overlevers the mean-reverting bets and cannot remain solvent when the inevitable break occurs.

In a later chapter we will discuss tail risk management. The reason such an approach is complementary to the structural approach to investing is because there are episodes in which the total return from a particular type of risk premium bet can be tilted to have negative expected returns. In such periods, it is important not only to reduce the risk posture of portfolios but also to actively search for cheap "insurance" on the tails. This is rooted in the observation that leverage can be differently priced in different markets.

Relative Value

Relative value can be characterized as

- More expected return for same amount of risk
- Less risk for the same expected return

An investor might correctly argue that since markets clear, for every buyer who perceives a security as relatively cheap, there is a seller who perceives the security as relatively expensive. So the concept of richness and cheapness implicitly depends on the preferences and investment horizons of buyers and sellers. Investors may give up return in order to mitigate the risk of their total portfolio. For example, even though there are states of the world in which inflation-linked bonds yield less than nominal bonds (i.e., when inflation is low), for a long-term pensioner who has inflation-adjusted return as his or her objective, inflation-linked bonds may be preferable to short-term T-bills even if the T-bills yield more than the inflation-linked bonds.

The central and unfinished task of absolute asset pricing is to understand and measure the sources of aggregate or macroeconomic risk that drive asset prices. Of course, this is also the central question of macroeconomics. The risk premia of assets is proportional to the correlation between the asset payoff and consumption. In states of high consumption (as in expansions), assets such as stocks tend to pay off well. In states such as recessions, stocks tend to pay off badly. So the correlation between stock payoffs and consumption is positive and leads to a positive risk premium to stock returns. For bonds, the risk premium is lower because the correlation is negative. Thus risk premia are not static but change over time and lead to opportunities for excess return for investors who are willing and able to take risks. Thus it is impossible to talk about investing without reference to the macroeconomic background that has resulted in current prices for securities and the macroeconomic evolution that one expects in the future.

Predictability of Asset Excess Returns

The efficient-market hypothesis says that excess asset returns are not predictable. (The expectations hypothesis that long yields are the average of future expected short yields is equivalent to the statement that excess returns should not be predictable.) This statement is closely related to the statement that any opportunities for obtaining excess returns will be quickly arbitraged away. However, recent research shows that over macroeconomic cycles, asset returns are indeed predictable. We can always write the expected excess return on any asset as the negative of the product of the risk-aversion level, macroeconomic uncertainty, and the correlation between the prices of "risk-free" bonds and the asset. Typically Treasuries are considered the risk-free asset as they are backed by the U.S. Government. Although the recent crisis has brought sovereign risk to question, highlighting that all investments contain some level of risk. So, in periods of high risk aversion or high macroeconomic uncertainty, all risky assets in general are expected to yield higher expected returns. What differentiates one type of risky asset from another is that some assets are bondlike and thus have a higher correlation with the riskless asset than others and subsequently lower returns. Assets such as stocks, which are inversely proportional to the riskless asset, are expected to yield positive excess returns under this model.

Now, from day to day, the risk-aversion level and the correlation are fairly stable, so asset volatility is the main source of excess return. Over economic cycles, though, the risk aversion can change and can lead to different expected returns for assets against each other and against other periods. Indeed, the Federal Reserve can influence each term in the equation. The Federal Reserve can affect the risk-aversion parameter and the volatility of the "risk-free" term rate by following specific monetary policy rules. By setting rates to a target short-term rate, the Federal Reserve affects the actual level of the term "risk-free" rate (since market participants "transmit policy") across the yield curve if the central bank's policy is credible. For investors, the behavior of government authorities begins to take a central role in asset pricing after the crisis, as we will discuss in Chapter 4 on macro modeling.

There has been considerable recent research to find fundamental or yield-curve variables that have predictive power for excess returns for long-term holding periods. Other than financial variables such as term premium, default premium, dividend and price ratios, and stock market volatility, some recent work concludes that there is sufficient information in the term structure itself to predict excess returns. Cochrane and Piazzesi [19] find that a linear combination of five forward rates explains approximately 35 percent of the variation of next year's excess returns ranging up to five years. While their research has not been conclusively accepted, the idea that there is sufficient information about the markets in the markets themselves is worthy of investigation. Another area of work that was driven by the seminal paper of Ang and Piazzesi [2] constructs a term-structure process that combines the latent variables from the market (i.e., captures the statistics) while including macro variables.

To summarize the research concisely, let us discuss how these results are empirically tested. First write the identity for the continuously compounded zero-coupon bond price

$$P_t^n = e^{-y_t^{(n)} n} = e^{-f_t^n 1} e^{-y_t^{(n-1)}(n-1)} \tag{1.4}$$

We define the log forward rate at time t for the loan between time $t + n - 1$ and $t + n$ in terms of the log price $p_t^{(n)}$ of an n-period bond at time t as

$$f_t^n = y_t^{(n)} n - y_t^{(n-1)}(n-1) \tag{1.5}$$
$$\equiv p_t^{(n-1)} - p_t^{(n)}$$

The log holding period return from buying an n-period bond at time t and selling it as an $n - 1$-period bond at time $t + 1$ is

$$r_{t+1}^{(n)} \equiv p_{t+1}^{(n-1)} - p_t^{(n)} \tag{1.6}$$

so, the excess log returns are

$$rx_{t+1}^{(n)} \equiv r_{t+1}^{(n)} - y_t^{(1)} \tag{1.7}$$

which basically looks at the difference between the 1-period return on an n-period bond and a 1-year bond.

The Cochrane-Piazzesi result is basically that one linear combination of forward rates determines the excess return for all maturity bonds. In other words,

$$rx_{t+1}^{(n)} = b_n(\gamma \cdot f) + \epsilon_{t+1}^{(n)} \tag{1.8}$$

so the excess returns for different maturity bonds can be forecast by scaling their return forecasting factor $\gamma \cdot f$ by a maturity-dependent number b_n (γ is a vector of coefficients). Their coefficients are $\gamma_0 = -3.24$, $\gamma_1 = -2.14$, $\gamma_3 = 0.81$, $\gamma_3 = 3$, $\gamma_4 = 0.80$, and $\gamma_5 = -2.08$, and the maturity-dependent scalars are $b_2 = 0.47$, $b_3 = 0.87$, $b_4 = 1.24$, and $b_5 = 1.43$. Cochrane and Piazzesi also make the strong conclusion that their return-forecasting factor, while it is correlated with the slope factor, is independent of the level, slope, and curvature factors. They conclude that while the classic factors are sufficient to capture the variance of the yield curve, they are not sufficient to capture expected returns from the yield curve, and the return-forecasting factor is required to forecast returns with any degree of accuracy. One of the limitations of this work is that it is limited to the very short end of the yield curve (the really interesting dynamics resulting from inflation risk are in the long end greater than five years).

While the jury still might be out on the full economic content of this new factor, it is clear that ex ante returns are driven by more than the statistically observed factor movements of the yield curve. For instance, we can empirically observe that when volatility is high, asset prices are depressed because market participants require a high compensation to take risk. Hence ex ante return expectations should be higher during the height of market crises or when volatility is high (assuming that partcipants can survive the periods of high market volatility). Figure 1.1 shows a simplified version of the Cochrane-Piazzesi factor using Eurodollar contracts regressed versus the one- into seven-year swaption volatility that is a proxy for forward-looking risk of the 10-year sector for one year. We see that the two time series are indeed correlated, suggesting that structural positioning indeed has the potential to result in substantial ex ante high returns.

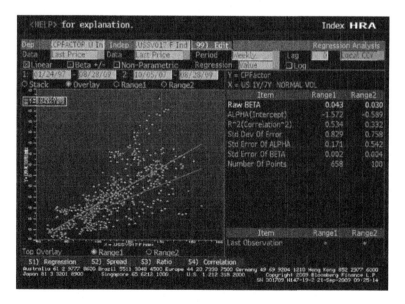

Figure 1.1 Eurodollar contract–based Cochrane-Piazzesi factor and one-into seven-year swaption volatility in basis points.

Predictability of Risk

While considerable effort has been spent in research on prediction of returns (because this is where the "money is"), little has been said about risk prediction. Market participants frequently will look at what is priced into options markets or credit curves to anticipate how much risk lies ahead. The Treasury Inflation Protected Securities (TIPS) to nominal spread (known as the *breakeven inflation rate*) is used as a handy tool for prediction of future inflation expectations. However, market-based forecasts can be biased because in periods of falling risk aversion, the market measures understimate risk at all horizons.

For corporate bonds, the major risk is one of default. We can approach default-risk forecasting in three broad different ways. First, we can look at the history of defaults and extrapolate from history (this is behind the cumulative default-rate tables published by Moody's, etc.). Second, we can build a model: The model can be structural, such as the Merton model [31] or its enhancements, which think of equity in firms as call options on underlying assets. Third, we can use the market to forecast defaults. Altman's approach shows that regressing default rates for the following year on spreads for this year is significant with a coefficient of approximately 1.3 and a 0.70 r^2.

Looking Back, Looking Forward

To end this chapter, I will take a quick look back at the lessons learned from the crisis of 2007 and 2008. This crisis was different in its details but very similar in general features to past crises in its symptoms and effects. Again there was rapid fall in asset values, increased correlations, increased volatility, risk aversion, and bonds behaving badly, that is, bonds tracking equity risks more than what one would have thought.

- *Lesson 1: Common risks drove portfolio performance.* Assets are more similar than they look. Asset class diversification does not necessarily mean risk reduction. One hallmark of the investment environment prior to the crisis was that there was excessive asset class pollution. One major theme we will keep coming back to is that macro risk-factor sensitivity is more important than idiosyncratic risk for a large class of investments. For instance, the exposure to the housing market was key in the last crisis, and the sensitivity to the related risk factor would have kept investors from building large positions in mortgage-backed securities. Very few stress-tested their portfolios to significant housing market shocks, focusing rather on "arbitrage" opportunities. One key lesson learned is that when it comes to portfolio construction, getting the big things right is more important than getting the little things wrong.

- *Lesson 2: Liquidity must be liquid.* There was a false sense of security in illiquid/liquid instruments, such as tranches from collateralized debt obligations (CDOs) that were sold as cash equivalents. Liquidity premium was mispriced because there was a general desire to boost returns by selling "lottery tickets" (securities with carry from low probability/high severity) in levered form. Many investors ran an implicit carry trade, with a mismatched horizon of assets and liabilities. Having grown up in an equity bull market, systemic risk and its damages were underestimated. For an investing style trained on mean reversion, it was a surprise to realize that systemic risk distortions can last for a long time and that doubling down by increasing the bet does not always pay.

- *Lesson 3: Leverage was everywhere.* There was explicit leverage through outright borrowing made easy as lending standards were relaxed. But there also was hidden leverage in complex, opaque structures. This was a packaged way for those who could not easily lever to get the leverage "built in" to the assets they were buying. Vendor financing that provided incentives to take more risk enabled dealers to distribute product and purchasers to obtain leverage. The CDO industry came up with new ways to leverage to deliver higher yields, and either voluntarily or involuntarily, the rating agencies who are supposed to be able to limit such abuse were taken along for the ride.

- *Lesson 4: Risk modeling assumed ideal conditions.* The creators of models know that models are idealizations, not reality, and that models can and do fail. The outputs are only as good as the idealized inputs. However idealized inputs such as the normal distributions, low transactions cost, and the unquestioning belief of printed matter (e.g., financial statements) led to a collective failure to evaluate the proper risks. Investors were using a similar modeling framework. Most important, the role of government and its potential influence on asset prices was ignored (we discuss this more in a later chapter).

- *Lesson 5: Fat left tails happen.* We can think of the increased volatility in the financial markets as partly a consequence of the increased participation and the "tight coupling" ([40]) of markets and participants. Just as the warming of the sea surface temperature has resulted in more frequent and more severe hurricanes, which cause more damage owing to the increase in coastal populations, the markets have gone through their own global warming. There are more low-probability events with higher-severity outcomes. There were plenty of opportunities to bring excessive risk under control, but investors voluntarilty chose not to do so because of a belief in short-term mean reversion.

- *Lesson 6. Systemic shocks exposed heterogeneity.* In a period of extreme financial stress, traditionally fungible micro risk factors did not produce similar results (heterogeneous risk) leading to a wider range of performance. This heterogeneous risk was exacerbated by government intervention in the financial system, market participants with limited capital, and the liquidity needs of investors. The performance of different parts of the capital structure (i.e., subdebt versus senior debt) shows this inhomogeneity. Capital structure positioning has been important as heterogeneous risk has exposed the dissimilarity between different parts of a firm's debt obligations.

So what can we do about these risks looking forward? How can we learn from the lessons and construct more robust portfolios for the inevitable next crisis that will happen? Here is a short list of things we absolutely need to do, knowing well that the list is probably not sufficient.

- *Identify and limit key risk factors and concentrations.* We need to differentiate risk-factor diversification from asset-class diversification. As we will discuss, it is easy to take false comfort in asset-based diversification, which does not work owing to common risks.

- *Evaluate the need for real liquidity.* Manage cash balances aggressively; that is, keep liquidity or defensive instruments available not only to weather rare events but also take advantage of the opportunities they provide. Imagine rare events that might not have happened in the past but are possible though improbable. To do this, the best approach is stress testing. One way to simulate the impact of stresses is to construct a combination of the worst of all historical shocks plus imagined supershocks. Allocate sufficient reserves against the stresses, but opportunistically deploy cash where liquidity is being egregiously priced. Pay attention to the severity more than to the ability to forecast probabilities.

- *Back to basics.* Understanding risk deeply requires transparency. Structural complexity can be the enemy of transparency. Excessive layering or hedging typically obfuscates hidden risks. An investor needs to ask honestly: Do esoteric strategies and structures really help me meet investment objectives?

- *Build in tail "insurance".* It is almost always possible to buy cheap hedges or hedge instruments against some tail risk in creative ways. Tail "insurance" reduces "black hole" or principal risk. We should think of tail hedges as a separate asset class because normal assets behave differently in periods of stress. Every portfolio should allow for some exposure to "insurance" like instruments. As we discuss later, while investors usually think of tail hedging as a cost, it really should be considered offensive risk management because the opportunities that become available can improve the long-term performance of portfolios. Thus it offers short-term catastrophe mitigation and long-term opportunity. The key idea here is that when correlations rise, basis risk becomes less important than having the right macro hedges. Use forecasting ability to find "insurance" that others are overlooking. Market dislocations and incentives create inefficiencies in the long-dated financial catastrophe "insurance" market, as was witnessed in the recent crisis.
- *Manage counterparty risk.* Be aggressive with collateral management and dynamically evaluate counterparty credit. Other than diversification of exposures to counterparties, aggressive collateral standards can mitigate many of the risks in this area.

Lest it may sound that risk management leaves no room for investment, an important point I should make is that effective risk management actually helps to focus on the proper opportunities. These pockets of opportunity need to be seized! Effective investment management balances risk and reward rather than attempting to drive risk to zero. The tools in this book hopefully will help in the identification of such "good risks."

Is the crisis "over"? If there is one poster child of the crisis, it is the so-called LIBOR-OIS (London Interbank Offer Rate–Overnight Indexed Swap) spread. The spread between the 3-month LIBOR and an overnight fed-fund swap (for three months) is a good indicator for the recent liquidity/credit crunch as any. The OIS (Overnight Indexed Swap) is a fixed to floating swap, where the floating index is a published overnight index rate. The two parties in the swap agree, at repayment date, to exchange the agreed fixed rate plus accrued interest for the geometric average of the floating overnight index on a given notional amount. Thus they allow the mitigation of short-term funding risk by providing an ability to lock-in the average of that rate for a fixed tenor. The recent credit crisis which made LIBOR less reflective of actual borrowing costs (note LIBOR is a survey and not a traded rate) made the OIS, which is based on actual transactions more relevant. This is especially true for the OIS based on the overnight fed-funds rate set forth in the Fed H.15 release, which reflects the trading of excess reserves funds between financial institutions. Since the OIS captures the

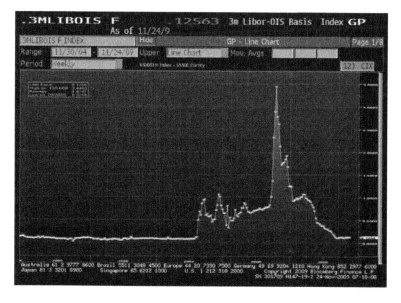

Figure 1.2 Three-month LIBOR-OIS spread.

© 2009 Bloomberg L. P. All rights reserved. Used with permission.

(*Source*: Bloomberg)

term-premium of the fed-funds market, the LIBOR-OIS spread measures both the credit quality (of the banking sector which sets LIBOR) and the term premium simultaneously. It can thus be used as a barometer of the credit quality of financial institutions. Further, if one implements a forward-starting LIBOR-OIS swap, the variable is the difference, between, say, 3-month LIBOR and 3-month OIS rates, and can be used to hedge banking sector credit risk.

As Figure 1.2 shows, this spread moved out from close to 0 to a peak of almost 350 basis points near the end of 2008. Since then, a rapid inflow of liquidity globally by central banks has driven this spread back to its precrisis levels. At first blush, it would appear that the crisis is "over," but the question might be more complicated. If the inflow of liquidity is used to attack the symptom (the spread), then there might be serious doubts as to whether symptomatic tightening is really indicative of the financing system's recovery. With this in mind, turn next to the building blocks of fixed income pricing to equip the reader with the critical tools of valuation.

2

Building Blocks

There are four key practical insights for pricing that are critical to security valuation and hence to portfolio management. First, all extra return is due to embedded optionality; second, it is not the price today that matters but the distribution of prices at the investment horizon that matters; third, we can build intuition for complex securities by scenario analysis; fourth, we can try to aggregate different types of assets into a portfolio with the concept of a risk or "beta" adjustment. This chapter will use examples to highlight these four critical items in a practitioner's toolkit.

Option-Based Approach to Risk and Relative Value

Asset markets are at the end of the day "insurance" markets. In other words, the primary reason for the markets to exist is that they allow transfer of unwanted risks in exchange for wanted risks. I will find it convenient to discuss the valuation of securities in terms of a framework that assumes that *all excess risk and reward in a security relative to a benchmark arises from embedded options*. Some of these options are explicit, and others are implicit. However, the key to understanding fixed income valuation and risk management is an understanding of practical option-pricing theory.

Black's famous paper [14] goes as far as to characterize even nominal short rates as options. Since the nominal short rate cannot go below zero (except for technical reasons), we can think of the nominal short rate as an option whose underlying are the real short rate and inflation. When the sum of real rates and inflation is negative, the nominal rate gets stuck at zero, but as the real rate or inflation rise such that their sum is larger than zero, the nominal rate rises above zero. Black calls this negative nominal rate when the short rate is stuck at zero the "shadow nominal rate." Some recent studies of the Taylor rule estimated that this shadow short rate might have to be as low as -6 percent! Since long-term nominal rates are nothing but the sum of real rate expectations and inflation expectations plus risk premium, long-term rates can be larger than zero if the sum of these three quantities is larger than zero. Thus, as long as there is a possibility that short rates might ever be positive in the future, no long-term rates can be lower than zero. Since even forward rates are options (the payoff is $\max[0, f_s]$, where f_s is the shadow forward rate), an increase in the volatility of the shadow forward rate will make the yield curve steeper.

Within this framework, the difference in returns and risks arise from embedded options in the payoff functions of securities. The design and purpose of valuation and risk measurement tools is to value and measure the risks of the embedded options. When an investor makes investment choices, he or she prefers to buy options for risk factors to which he or she has aversion and prefers to sell options for which he or she is risk-neutral or risk-loving. It is this transaction in embedded options that makes relative value possible. Arbitrage possibilities arise owing to the ability of certain investors to reconstitute options in ways in which the composite security is transacted at a price that is different from the fair reconstitution price. The advantage of this framework is that all value can be understood relative to a benchmark that is option-free for a convenient risk-neutral investor. But the benchmark itself becomes irrelevant other than as a convenient measurement unit.

We can also use this approach to understand the risk premium in the yield curve. Suppose that short rates are at 2 percent today and at 3 percent implied in the forward market in 1 year (using traded Eurodollar futures prices). So the expected future rate in the market is 1 percent higher than the spot rate now. How much of this extra rise is rational, and how much is a risk premium? A risk-neutral lender would be willing to lend at some forward point in time for the actuarially fair value of the interest rate. For him or her, everything excess of the future rate is free money, that is, a risk premium that he or she can earn. However, when a risk-averse investor meets a risk-neutral investor, they transact at a price equal to the expected rate plus a market value for the risk. We can approximate the market's risk aversion by looking at the price of traded options.

Heuristics of Options

Options can be characterized by the following features:

- Options allow for bets to be placed on discrete portions of the return distribution of the underlying.
- Option prices depend on the passage of time.
- Options are more basic than the underlying (the underlying can be replicated in terms of options).
- Options allow for leverage of the underlying exposure.
- Options can theoretically be combined with the underlying to remove all reference to the movement of the underlying—leaving only the variance of the underlying as the relevant variable.

The pricing of hedgable financial securities does not depend on the preferences of the investors trading them. This is the key intuition behind risk-neutral pricing. When we look to exploit risk premia in the market, we are really looking at transference of risks. The risks that can be readily hedged using a set of underlying securities do not provide any risk-premium return.

Option-Adjusted Spread

While susceptible to dangers from overdependence, the concept of option-adjusted spread (OAS) is essential to the understanding the risk and return tradeoff of fixed income securities. Simply put, OAS is the extra spread that an investment is expected to yield over the life of a security after accounting for embedded options.

Mortgage-backed securities (MBSs) traders have been using OAS as a summary measure for the value of securities for many years. When mortgages are taken out by home owners, the banks that are making the mortgage loans pool many of these loans together into mortgage-backed securities. The home owners typically have the ability to prepay these loans for any number of reasons. If rates fall, or if a home owner sells the home, he or she may choose to voluntarily prepay the loan. On the other hand, if the mortgage becomes delinquent, or if the home owner defaults on the loan, the bank may take possession of the mortgage and enforce an involuntary prepayment. In either case, the owner of the MBS is short a prepayment option and is compensated for this option in terms of an excess spread or extra expected return. Suppose that we run various macroeconomics-based projections on the mortgage rate for the future and on each one of these scenarios evaluate the potential cash flows to the mortgage. If we discount all the cash flows back to present day and average them, theoretically, we should obtain the price of the mortgage that is trading in the market. If the MBS price is different from the traded price, we can shift each interest rate path by a constant amount and find the value of the shift for which the market price of the mortgage equals the theoretical model price. This is the OAS. Note immediately that the OAS valuation should be expected to be highly sensitive to the model used to project the rates forward into the future. If the model is inaccurate, then the OAS obtained could be erroneous as well. In practice, to avoid having an arbitrarily specified model, most research desks calibrate the model by matching OASs of some liquid securities to actual prices and then use this model for other securities.

The price of a callable bond is simply the price of a noncallable bond minus the value of the option. Suppose that we estimate the price of the call option to be 4 points (on a redemption price of 100). We can convert this into yield terms by dividing by the duration of the bond. Suppose that the OAS duration is estimated to be 8. Then the yield equivalent of the OAS is 50 basis points. If volatility rises, the call option becomes more valuable. For instance, if the true value of the option is 8 points, then at the same price as before, the callable bond is expensive relative to its fair value. Thus, all else being equal, higher option value or volatility reduces the OAS of a callable or prepayable security. To compare the richness or cheapness of different types of securities, we have to choose common benchmarks versus which way the cash flows are computed, and assume that market volatilities are used to price the embedded options. Given that the swap or LIBOR (London Interbank Offer Rate) curve is the natural reference instrument used by market participants to hedge their portfolios, it has become common to use the swap curves and their volatilities as the calibration instruments versus which OASs are computed.

To illustrate this with a simple example, Figure 2.1 shows the OAS of the current 5-year Treasury note against the Treasury curve, and Figure 2.2 shows the same security's OAS versus the swap curve. Since this security has no call option, we expect the option premium to be zero and the OAS to be effectively the swap spread of the security (the spread to the two curves in simple yield terms). This trivial but illustrative example shows that the −44 basis points of the swap spread for the Treasury is a measure of the implicit option content of the Treasury that arises

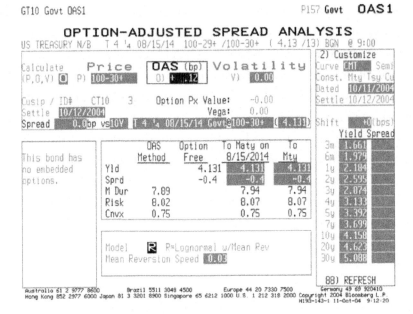

Figure 2.1 OAS versus Treasury curve analysis.

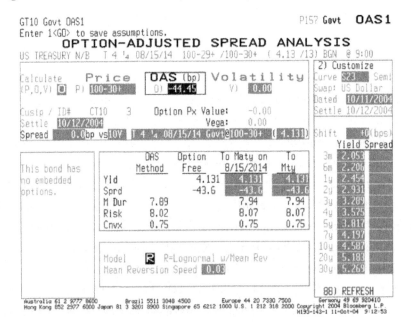

Figure 2.2 OAS versus swap analysis.

from it being a safer security than the swap. In other words, an investor who holds this security is effectively paying 44 basis points of "insurance" premium (in terms of a lower yield) to receive the additional benefits that arise from holding a Treasury note. Whether this amount of excess yield premium is too much or too little needs to be determined by the investor based on his or her portfolio risk management considerations.

Forward Pricing

A repo contract is essentially a contract to exchange a physical security for cash. This naturally can be stated as a forward purchase or sale of the security at the delivery date for a fixed price. The repo rate is the rate that takes the spot rate and translates it into a forward price. Suppose that there is an n-period zero-coupon bond that pays 1 at maturity. If we purchase it today for one period at p and fund it at the repo rate r, then, including the cost of carry, the forward price is $F = (1 + r)p$.

Repos, Reverses, and Specials

The study of fixed income investments has to start with a thorough understanding of the financing markets—also known as the *repo markets*. The simple arithmetic of financing, when cast in an option framework, forms the basis for the valuation of more complex securities.

First, the definitions. When an investor buys a bond and lends it out, he or she is doing a repo (repoing the bond out). In exchange, the investor receives an interest rate for the term the security is lent for cash. This collateralized rate is the *repo rate*. On the other hand, when an investor shorts a security and borrows them to deliver, he or she is reversing them in (reverse repo) and lends out cash.

Since specific bonds are repoed or delivered, the rate that applies to the funds that are exchanged for the bond can be different. Sometimes the funds that are lent in exchange for the security can carry a lower rate of interest than a generic security. This is known as a *special* repo rate. A more plain-vanilla or older security commands the *general collateral* repo rate (the GC rate). The specialness is measured as the difference between the GC rate and the special repo rate. In option language, the difference is the option premium paid to have access to a more liquid/special security. The investor (typically the short) is willing to have access to the security in exchange for lending cash at a lower than market rate. The investor who holds the security in his or her inventory can lend the security for a cheaper access to funds. The crisis in 2008 showed the option premium earned for this option sale sometimes can go in the money if the borrower defaults and cannot return the borrowed securities. There is a life-cycle of repo-specialness in the Treasury market that coincides with issuance. Specialness for Treasuries builds up after an auction because new holders do not make the security easily available in the repo market. The specialness peaks near the next auction, after which it declines as shorts start to use the when-issued (WI) market to place their shorts.

Repo rates are characterized by the rate and the maturity. Typically, the most common maturity is overnight, although they can extend to many months. When markets are volatile, or the counterparty is deemed risky, the party lending the cash might require additional security as a buffer against the movements of the price of the security, called the *haircut*. Also, as the mark-to-market value of the security changes, the lender of funds might require the borrower of funds to post additional collateral or cash via a *margin call*. The crisis of 2008 demonstrated that this risk is not negligible. Most broker-dealers used to run their business using a matched book—they would purchase securities by borrowing money short term and then lend out the same money long term (with the reverse side on the security). As availability of funds became scarce during the liquidity crisis, this way of financing inventory became unfeasible, and dealers were either forced to sell their securities off their balance sheets or, in cases where this was not possible, have to seek (successfully or not) other sources of funding. This embedded default option on a levered position creates the positive spread between the term repo rate and the overnight repo rate.

Many dealers also naturally get into the classic liquidity selling trade between the on-the-run and the off-the-run Treasuries. Note that since the on-the-run is the more recently issued Treasury, it is more liquid; hence, shorting it is essentially a sale of liquidity. Assume that a dealer buys an off-the-run security. To do so requires lending the security out and borrowing funds. To hedge the risk of the securities, the dealer shorts the on-the-run Treasury. Assume that he or she does this by matching the factor exposures we talked about (level, curve, convexity, etc.). To deliver this security when the delivery date comes, the dealer has to accquire it somewhere. If there is general risk aversion and liquidity fear in the market, no one will be willing to sell their on-the-run securities or lend them out for fear of not being able to get them back. In this case a short squeeze can develop, where the price of the security in demand can shoot up. We also thus can see that, all else being equal, there should be a tendency for the repo rates for the on-the-run securities to be lower than the GC rate. The difference between the GC rate and the special rate is the *repo spread*. In an anomalous situation, it is actually possible for the repo rate to go to zero (if the need for the special security is high enough).

The repo spread (GC special) is determined by the relative quantity of longs (doing repos) and shorts (doing reverses). Whenever the spread is positive, the holder of the special securities can earn a spread by lending them out. On the other hand, if the spread is small enough, then there might not be the incentive to give away the *liquidity option* in exchange for the spread. Some holders (such as sovereign funds and some pensions) are also restricted from lending them out. In the recent environment, large secured lending programs that used to generate significant amounts of income from the lending of securities have become fearful about getting the collateral back and thus will not lend out specific collateral under any circumstance. Typically, when a new bond is issued, there is plenty of supply for the bond, and the repo spread is close to zero. As time passes, the bonds are purchased by holders who do not lend them out, resulting in an increasing spread. As the next bond is issued and starts to trade in the when-issued (WI) market, the repo spread again starts moving close to zero. Sometimes, when rates are low and the penalty to fail to deliver a security is low, the market starts to suffer from *repo fails*. In the late part of 2008, interest rates were extremely low as the Fed pushed the target fed-funds rate down to 1 percent. There was a whopping 5 trillion worth of Treasuries that were not delivered or received.

Note that there are other variants of the repo trade such as buy/sellbacks and securities lending. In a classic repo, the legs of the repo transaction are marked-to-market, whereas in buy/sellbacks, the mark-to-market is not conventional. Securities lending is used by many ETF providers to earn extra income from passive portfolios by lending out securities in exchange for repo driven income.

A major risk in repo trades is counterparty credit risk. If the value of the collateral falls, the cash lent in exchange for the securities might be larger than the market value of the securities if they have to be liquidated. On the other hand, if the value of the securities rises, the failure of the party holding the securities can result in a mark-to-market loss for the securities lender. Tight thresholds for the posting of additional collateral in the form of less volatile securities or cash is used in the market to minimize some of this counterparty risk. Most repo transactions are arranged in a triparty format, where the custodian bank stands between the lender and the borrower to mitigate operational and counterparty credit risks. A handful of banks play the role of the triparty repo intermediary, and recent discussions in the aftermath of the crisis are investigating the systemic risks posed by such concentration of settlement risks.

Haircuts

Haircut is the difference between the face amount of the security purchased and the amount of money borrowed, expressed as a percentage of the security's par amount. In other words, it is the percentage of the security's par amount that the borrower is putting down to purchase the security. Since the amount is much smaller than the par amount, the haircut is basically the way the investor creates leverage.

Suppose that the par value of a floating rate bond is P, and the bond pays a floating rate of $L + r_b$. Then the gross return on the bond is $P(L + r_b)$. If the bond is funded at a rate of r_r (the subscript r is for repo), and the investor puts up a fraction, say, h as a haircut, then he or she has to pay the interest cost on $(P - h)$, and the cost is $(P - h)(L + r_r)$. So the total gross return on the position is $(L + r_b)P - (P - h)(L + r_r)$. The return on equity is the gross return divided by h, the haircut. So the gross return is $P(r_b - r_r) + h(L + r_r)$, and the return on equity (ROE) is $P(r_b - r_r)/h + (L + r_r)$.

To do an example, say the haircut is 7 percent, the asset returns $L + 200$, and the funding rate is $L + 100$. Using $P = \$100$, we obtain $100(200 - 100)/7 + (L + 100) = L + 1529$. Thus a low-return security's return is levered up via the repo market.

Repo Failure During the Crisis

The two Bloomberg articles that follow document in real time the relationship between the repo market and need for liquidity and safety.

The first article describes the failure of participants to deliver Treasury securities even when they were contractually obligated to do so in a repo agreement. When rates are low, the penalty cost of failing is so low (of late, this rule has been modified to make the penalty more substantial; see the second article) that people would rather fail on the delivery than make the delivery and lose access to the liquidity. The articles highlight the broader context in which rates and yield curve valuation have to be evaluated.

Treasury Trading Failures Surge to Record Amid Credit Freeze

Oct. 2 (Bloomberg)[2]—Failures to deliver or receive Treasuries in the $7 trillion-a-day market for borrowing and lending securities surged to a record as investors sought the safety of government debt. Failures, an indication of scarcity, rose to $3.545 trillion in the week ended Sept. 24, from $578 billion the prior period, according to the Federal Reserve. The prior record of $3.244 trillion was in August 2003. Fails averaged about $181 billion a week since July 1990, data on the Federal Reserve Bank of New York's Web site show. "Fails reflect fears about counterparty risks, incurred both directly and from those incurred indirectly through the chain . . . as when one counterparty fails and it affects numerous other counterparties." Demand for the relative safety of government securities surged in the last week after the U.S. House of Representatives failed to get sufficient votes last week to pass a $700 billion government bailout package of the banking system intended to revive lending and unfreeze credit markets. The House is expected to vote on the bill tomorrow. Dealers often let trades in the repurchase agreement, or repo, market go uncompleted when it is difficult to obtain the securities or the cost to get the securities becomes too expensive. Since dealers typically use repurchase agreements to finance their holdings, movements in the rates affect the cost of holding the securities in inventory.

(*Continued*)

---

[2]October 2, 2008.

Interest Free Loans: Treasuries were in such demand this week that traders were willing at times to lend cash at virtually zero interest overnight to obtain the securities as collateral. The difference, or gap, of the general collateral repo rate below and the Fed's target rate, which widens when collateral becomes scarce, averaged 1.12 percentage points since Sept. 15. That compares to an average gap of 0.06 percentage point for the 10 years prior to August, when subprime mortgage losses began to spread. Securities that can be borrowed at interest rates close to the Fed's target rate are called general collateral. Notes and bonds that are in the highest demand are called "special" by traders because rates on loans secured by these securities are lower than the general collateral rate. "Some fails will continue for weeks, but the magnitude of fails will overall be less," as cash and securities are likely to return to the market given that quarter-end has passed.

Treasury Traders Paid to Borrow; Fed Examines Repos

Nov. 24 (Bloomberg)—Owners of Treasuries may soon get paid to borrow as the U.S. tries to break a logjam in the $7 trillion-a-day repurchase market. Treasuries are in such high demand that investors are lending cash for next to nothing to obtain the securities as collateral through so-called repos, which dealers use to finance their holdings. The problem is many parties involved in repos aren't delivering the bonds because there is no penalty for not doing so, causing fails to exceed $5 trillion, according to the Federal Reserve Bank of New York. Now, an industry group

(Continued)

is trying to fix the mess, which New York Fed Executive Vice President William Dudley said could cause U.S. borrowing rates to rise if not rectified. The Treasury Market Practices Group wants to impose a penalty on failed trades, a move that may result in borrowers who put their Treasuries up as collateral for loans effectively receiving 2 percent interest. This is an extraordinary thing to perceive for a market of the size and significance of the U.S. repo market. . . . Failures to deliver or receive securities climbed to a record $5.311 trillion in the week ended Oct. 22. While the amount fell to $1.26 trillion by Nov. 12, that's still above the average of $165 billion before credit markets seized up in August of last year, based on Fed data that goes back to 1990.

Negative Consequences: The disruption in the repo market comes as the Treasury steps up debt sales to finance a record budget deficit and the bailout of the nation's banks. Gross issuance of Treasury coupon securities will rise to about $1.15 trillion in fiscal 2009 from $724 billion last year, according to New York–based Credit Suisse Securities USA LLC, one of the 17 primary dealers that are obligated to bid at the government's auctions. The more chronic fails disrupt the Treasury market, the more it reduces its liquidity and efficiency, Dudley said in a Nov. 12 interview. Over time, this could have some negative consequences for the ability of the U.S. Treasury to raise money at the lowest cost possible. Reduced liquidity also affects other markets as the Treasury market is used to hedge positions in other security classes. . . . Treasury's acting assistant secretary for financial markets strongly urged dealers, traders and investors on Nov. 5 to find a way to reduce the number of failed trades. Otherwise, he said, regulators would step in.

Financing Holdings: In a repurchase agreement, one party provides cash to another in exchange for a security, and vice versa.

(Continued)

Repos are typically used to finance holdings, meaning movements in the rates affect the cost of holding the securities in inventory. As of the end of June, primary dealers reported financing $4.22 trillion of fixed-income securities with repo agreements, according to the Fed. Since the bankruptcy of Lehman Brothers Holdings, Inc., in mid-September traders, investors and dealers have been willing to lend cash to obtain Treasuries at almost zero interest. The lowest overnight repo rate on Nov. 21 was 0.05 percent for the five-year note maturing in October 2013, according to London-based ICAP, PLc, the world's largest inter-dealer broker. Repo trades go uncompleted when it's difficult to obtain the securities or the cost to get them becomes too expensive. Fails aren't usually considered a breach of contract and the parties involved typically keep re-scheduling delivery.

Treasury Review: A day after . . . warning, the Treasury said it was reviewing the trading of two- and five-year notes after a scarcity in the securities led to rising fails. The Treasury has conducted at least nine such reviews, known as large position reports, to monitor against market manipulation since 1997. A week later the Treasury Market Practices Group recommended imposing a penalty rate that equals either 3 percent minus the Fed's target rate for overnight loans between banks or zero, whichever is greater. The central bank's target is 1 percent. The TMPG said it plans to discuss by Jan. 5 a potential plan to implement the measures. A negative rate repo is somewhat counterintuitive as basically, a lender is not only lending money, but paying a borrower to take that money, said . . . managing director of the Securities Industry and Financial Markets Association, a New York–based trade group. The borrower has something, in this case a particular security,

(Continued)

that the lender really wants. It's essentially paying a premium to get a particular security.

Japan Precedent: Negative repo rates have happened before. The Bank of Japan's decision to adopt a zero interest rate during the Lost Decade of the 1990s because of deflation and a protracted banking crisis triggered the phenomenon for Japanese government debt. Rates less than zero surfaced in the U.S. in 2003, when the Fed's target interest rate fell to 1 percent and traders sought to cover bets against 10-year Treasuries after their yields jumped more than a percentage point in about a month. Demand for short-term Treasuries may increase if repo rates turn negative as investors would receive interest, as opposed to typically paying it, for money they borrow to finance their holdings. Credit Suisse expects the two-year Treasury note's yield to fall to 0.5 percent by the end of the first quarter from about 1 percent last week.

Significant Kick: For certain sectors of the Treasury curve, such as the short end, the implementation of negative repo rates would provide a significant kick to the market, said . . . an interest-rate strategist at Credit Suisse in New York. Yields have room to fall further, with the front end outperforming the long end. Treasury yields tumbled to record lows last week, with two-year notes dropping below 1 percent for the first time, as deepening recessions in Asia, Europe and the U.S. and signs of deflation drove investors to the safest assets. The yield on the 1.5 percent note due October 2010 slid 9 basis points to 1.11 percent, according to BGCantor Market Data. The price, which moves inversely to the yield, rose 5/32, or $1.56 per $1,000 face amount, to 100 24/32. Five-year note yields dropped as low as 1.87 percent, the least since the Fed first started keeping records in 1954. Yields rose for a second day in New York. Like in Japan in the 1990s, traders have

(Continued)

increased bets that the Fed will cut the target federal funds rate as the economy sinks deeper into recession, further increasing the chances of negative repo rates. JPMorgan Chase & Co. economists forecast a reduction to zero percent.

Investors purchasing a coupon-bearing fixed income instrument receive carry income from the coupon. Suppose that instead of buying the Treasury today, we were to forgo the income and contract to buy it at a future date, say, in a month. The price of the security "drops" in the forward market to compensate us for the loss of the coupon. Of course, if we were financing the position via the repo market, the interest rate we would pay on the financing would change what the breakeven forward price should be. In Figure 2.3, the Treasury note maturing in August 2014 is priced for a cash price of 99-20/99-20+, which corresponds

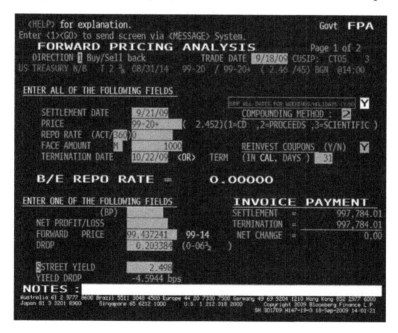

Figure 2.3 Forward pricing analysis with zero repo rate.
© 2009 Bloomberg L. P. All rights reserved. Used with permission.

to a yield of 2.45 percent. If we borrow money at zero percent repo rate against this collateral, the fair price of the Treasury on a 1-month forward basis is 99-14. This 6.5-tick "drop" of the price is equivalent to approximately 4.5 basis points of yield pickup on the forward trade.

If we now change the repo rate to 1 percent from 0 percent (Figure 2.4), we see that the same Treasury has a drop of only 3.75 ticks (or 2.6 yield basis points pickup). The best way to think about this is that the effective income is the difference between the coupon income and the repo cost; thus, as the repo cost rises, the advantage from giving up the income decreases. We also can see that movement of repo rates lower can increase the prospective returns from buying the security on a forward basis, hence creating a pressure for the security to rise in price.

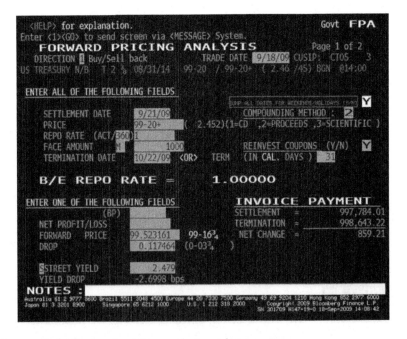

Figure 2.4 Forward pricing analysis with 1 percent repo rate.
© 2009 Bloomberg L. P. All rights reserved. Used with permission.

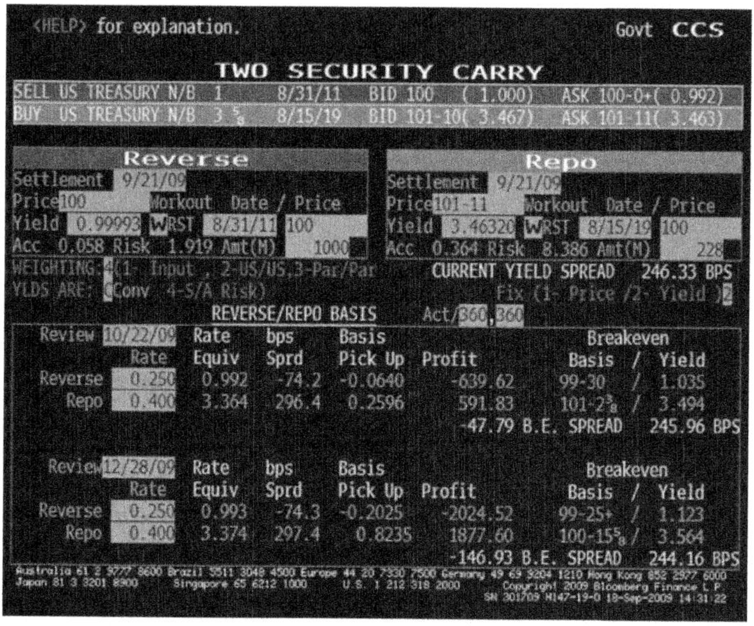

Figure 2.5 Two-security carry analysis for a 2- and a 10-year note.
© 2009 Bloomberg L. P. All rights reserved. Used with permission.

Figure 2.5 shows the carry considerations one faces when implementing duration-neutral yield-curve flattening and steepening trades. In this example, we are buying the 2019 Treasury (10-year note at the time of this writing) and selling the 2011 Treasury (2-year note). The nominal yield spread is 3.463 percent minus 0.992 percent. Now the long-side (the 2019 Treasury) position is funded at a repo rate of 0.40 percent, and the short position is reverse repoed ("reversed") at 0.25 percent. Note that this means that for a 1-month horizon, the spread breakeven has to be below 245.96 basis points for the trade to start making money. The point of the exercise is to emphasize that the attractiveness of a position such as this cannot be judged without going into the forward space and taking into consideration the impact of funding costs on each leg of the spread trade.

Asset Swaps

An *asset swap* is a synthetic package that allows an investor to swap the fixed coupons of a bond for floating rate, thus reducing most of the interest-rate exposure but keeping the credit exposure. We will use the asset swap concept in Chapter 3 when we discuss the credit default swap basis trade.

In the most common par-for-par asset swap, there are two simultaneous trades: (1) The asset swap buyer purchases a bond from the asset swap seller in exchange for the full price of the bond, and (2) the asset swap buyer enters into a swap to pay a fixed coupon to the asset swap seller that equals the coupon on the bond. In return, the asset swap buyer receives regular payments of LIBOR plus or minus an agreed fixed spread. The maturity of the asset is kept the same as the maturity of the bond. Note that if the bond defaults, the asset swap buyer loses principal and interest but is still required to pay the coupon on the interest-rate swap. Thus the asset swap package really is a bet on the credit of the bond.

Figure 2.6 shows the asset swap for a Treasury 10-year note. The price of the bond is higher than par, so the asset swap buyer pays higher than par for the bond. This is an immediate "profit for the asset swap seller" and has to come out of the cash flows from the swap. If the swap curve is higher than the Treasury curve, we will obtain a price for the bond that is lower than the traded price. The shift of the swap curve that makes the traded price equal to the market price is the gross spread. The gross spread can be computed in two steps. First we compute the value of the bond on the swap curve (instead of on the Treasury curve). This shows that the bond price implied by the swap curve is 100.305. This price subtracted from the traded price can be turned into the spread of -10.3 by dividing by the duration of the bond. (Another measure known as the Z-spread, on the other hand, is the continuously compounded constant spread to the swap curve to reprice the bond. In

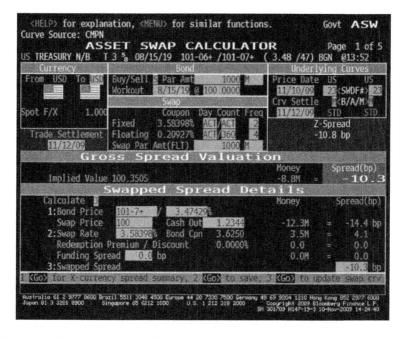

Figure 2.6 Asset swap for Treasury note.
© 2009 Bloomberg L. P. All rights reserved. Used with permission.

other words, if the Z-spread is z, then it solves $P = c \sum_{i=1}^{n} d(t_i)e^{-st_i} + d(t_n)e^{-st_n}$, where $d(t_i)$ is the discount factor for the time t_i.

The asset swap spread in a par-for-par asset swap solves the equation

$$100 - P + c \sum_{i=1}^{n} d(t_i) - \sum_{i=1}^{n} D_i(L_i + A)d(t_i) = 0 \qquad (2.1)$$

where D_i is the day-count fraction, L_i is the LIBOR rate for the ith time, A is the asset swap spread, and $d(t_i)$ is the ith discount factor.

Since the par asset swap creates counterparty risk for the buyer of a discount bond, an alternative version of the asset swap is the market asset swap, where the bond is purchased at full price of the bond and not at par. Compared with the par asset swap, in a market asset swap, the counterparty risk for a premium bond shifts from the seller to the buyer. In a par asset swap, the counterparty risk is maximum at the initiation of the package and falls to zero at maturity if there is no default. On the other hand, in a market asset swap, the counterparty risk is zero at intitiation but rises to its maximum value close to maturity as the par value of the bond has to be exchanged.

In a cross-currency asset swap, the investor buys a bond in one currency, pays fixed on the swap in this same currency, but receives the floating leg in the base currency. All the cash flows are exchanged at some fixed exchange rate, and there is an exchange of principal at the end. This structure reduces the currency and the interest-rate risk but keeps the credit and cross-currency basis swap risk in the structure.

Valuation Using Scenario Analysis

For many securities, the underlying cash flows are highly variable and depend on contingencies in the contractual specification of these securities, that is, the underlying collateral characteristics and the structures into which the collateral flows are directed. For instance, nonagency mortgage-backed structured securities are exposed to the prepayments and defaults of many thousands of loans. To model the risks of such securities properly, one needs to project how individual loans that form the collateral will perform in the future. Individual loans are exposed to various macro factors such as housing price appreciation assumptions that impact the loan's current combined loan to value (CLTV) of each loan which drives delinquencies and defaults, as well as interest rates, geography, government subsidies, modification plans, and so on. Other variables that affect the likelihood of defaults include the credit score of the borrower, based on credit scoring stats such as the FICO (Fair Isaac Corporation), whether the loan is for investment or habitation, whether it is multifamily or single family, and so on. Companies such as Loan Performance have become market standards for the underlying collateral data, and almost every fixed income investor has his or her army of technologists and financial engineers working on default, severity, and prepayment forecasting models to capture the effect of the underlying loan-specific and macro variables in forecasting the performance of the collateral using these data. While it would be desirable to have the technology to iterate over all possible probability weighted future scenarios, computation limits the state of the art to discrete scenario analysis. First the analyst generates prepayment and default vectors, as well as severity curves, using some combination of econometric and forward forecasts. These vectors are fed into a cash-flow engine (such as Intex or Bloomberg) to estimate the yields and simple risk factors such as spread durations. The typical asset backed security (ABS) trader looks at the "yield table" under many combinations of these forecasts to estimate the risk and reward of a particular structure. Critical to this analysis is an understanding of the structure of the bonds and what type of credit enhancement is present. Typically, credit enhancement is internal (through subordination or lower bonds in the structure, over-collateralization, excess spread, etc.) or external (via " insurance" from third parties).

Case Study: Mortgage Credit

Let's look at the CUSIP 07384M7CO, which is the class A1 tranche issued by Bear Stearns Adjustable Rate Mortgage Trust (Figures 2.7 through 2.10). I believe that the only way to understand pricing is to look deeply inside the prospectus of the security (this is usually available from the underwriter), read all the fine print, and understand the details of the collateral. This tranche is the supersenior and, when originally issued, had a face value of $1,661,650,700. On July 9, 2009 reporting, it had a remaining balance of only $653,505,203 (for a pool factor of 0.403). The formula for the coupon (floating rate) is 1-year Treasury plus 245 basis points. There also were caps of 9.185 percent and floors of 2.45 percent. The tranche resets monthly. Since this is the supersenior tranche, it suffers principal loss after all the other tranches are wiped out

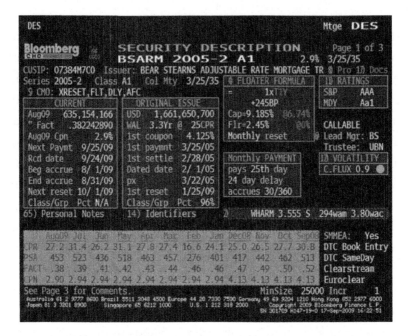

Figure 2.7 CUSIP 07384M7CO.

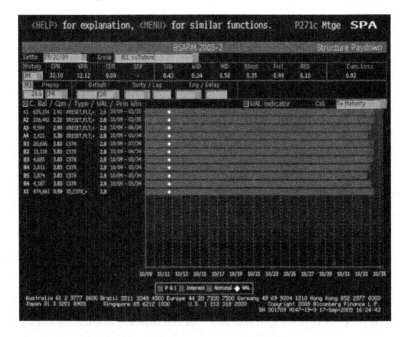

Figure 2.8 CUSIP 07384M7CO structure details.

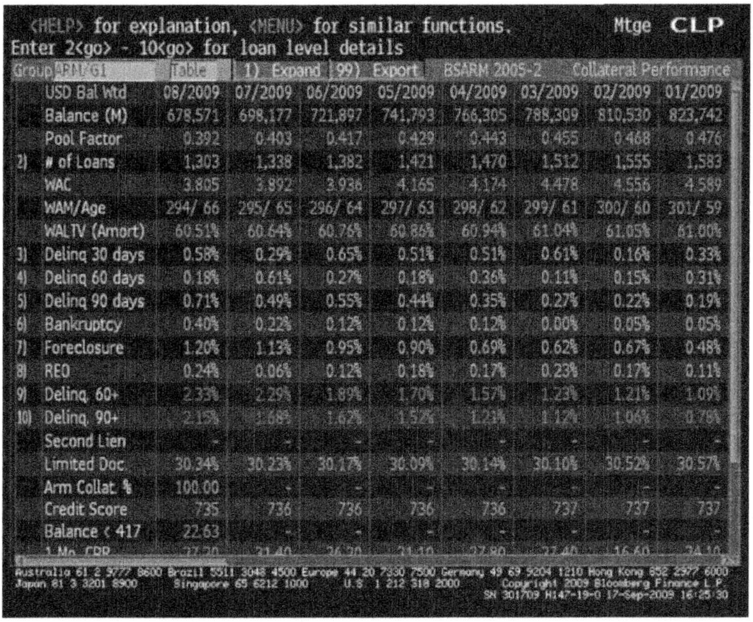

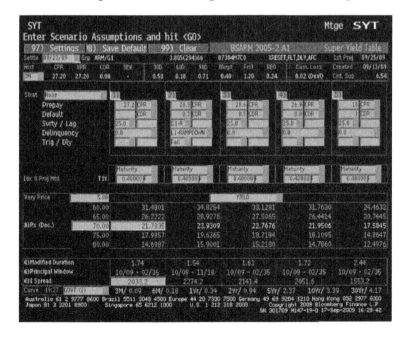

Figure 2.9 CUSIP 07384M7CO collateral performance.
© 2009 Bloomberg Finance L. P. All rights reserved. Used with permission.

Figure 2.10 CUSIP 07384M7CO collateral performance.
© 2009 Bloomberg Finance L. P. All rights reserved. Used with permission.

(hence it is most protected and has the least yield). This is a classic option pricing consequence—because the default option is the most out of the money, the tranche has the lower premium for the default option. Thus the primary protection comes from the type of credit enhancement known as *subordination*; that is, it has lower tranches that will absorb losses first.

This tranche has a collateral that currently has over 1,300 loans. Of these loans, 0.29 percent were 30 days delinquent, 0.61 percent were 60 days delinquent, 0.49 percent were 90 days delinquent, 0.22 percent were in bankruptcy, 1.13 percent were in foreclosure, and 0.06 percent were real estate owned (RED). Over 30 percent of the loans were issued with limited documentation. The average FICO credit score was 736, although there was lots of dispersion about this mean. Highly relevant was the percentage of loans in California (60 percent). The pool of loans was prepaying at a conditional prepayment rate (CPR) of 31 percent, and on the 0.76 percent default rate, 10.40 percent was the average severity of the loss.

As one can see, there are so many features of each loan that can vary, and predicting the performance of the security is tantamount to predicting the performance of each loan in the future. This is next to impossible, so the best one can hope to do is to create some simple techniques to predict the average behavior of the loans and the dispersion about the average behavior.

Two tools are critical in doing this. The first one is a yield table. Given different assumptions for the prepayment rate, default rate, and severity, what is the yield at different prices? This is akin to scenario analysis. If the security is being sold at a price where under most feasible scenarios the yield is high enough, then the bond becomes a good investment opportunity. As an example, inputting a CPR of 31 percent, CDR of 0.76 percent, and severity of 10 percent at a price of 85, this bond has a discount margin (spread over the index) of over 1,000 basis points. Most analysts use INTEX for performing the cash-flow analyses.

Their cash-flow engine basically attempts to translate a wordy set of rules from the prospectus into precise rules that can be run repeatedly under various prepayment, default, delinquency, and interest-rate assumptions.

The more idiosyncratic the security (which is usually a given for mortgage-structured products), the more critical it is that the investor do thorough due-diligence by reading the legal materials that describe the strucure. Issuers and underwriters provide prospectuses, which are required to disclose any material facts about the bonds. Typically, most prospectuses have a large amount of extraneous cookie-cutter, information, but there is indeed relevant information on a few pages. The investor has to develop the skill to hone in on relevant pages. For the security under discussion, page S-18 of the prospectus describes the mortgage pool, page S-22 describes the delinquency experience (to be followed with periodic updates), pages S-26 to S-29 describe the structures and the waterfalls, and especially page S-34, which describes the allocation of losses and subordination of the various bonds. It is also important to know who the servicer is because the servicer is repsonsible for collection of interest and principal and management of the borrowers' escrow accounts.

Most structured ABSs have features that can be classified under the following categories:

- *Credit enhancement.* Typically senior/subcapital structure, over-collateralization, and excess spread are designed to provide the protection to bondholders of different layers.
- *Coverage tests and triggers.* Passing or failing grades on overcollateralization or interest coverage tests affect the allocation of cash flows.
- *Priority of payments.* Every structure has rules on how cash flows are allocated to bondholders. This is usually a function of status of performance triggers, deal age, and prepayments.

- *Optional calls.* Some transactions, with call features, can allow for liquidation of assets and return of principal.
- *Other features.* There is a plethora of other features, such as "turbo" features, timing of triggers, and swaps and reserve accounts.

The section on macro modeling will revisit the issue of how to project the prepayment, default, and severity rates. These rates are driven by both the internal features of the deal (the quality of the borrowers, services, and incentives) and the macroeconomic conditions. The point to be made at this stage is that the more complex a security, the more critical it is that it's robustness be evaluated under stress-scenario assumptions that might not have occurred in the past. It is tedious to do so but can spell the difference between a security that is a good investment and one that is not.

Betas: Risk Adjustment and Portfolio Aggregation

Investors in fixed income instruments typically have a heterogeneous mix of bonds. Many of these bonds carry risks that at first blush should not be aggregated; for example, the spread duration of an investment-grade corporate bond should not be added to the spread duration of a high-yield bond because the underlying risks are actually different. In practice, though, most investors do benefit from some level of aggregation. To achieve this aggregation, we basically need to evaluate the correlation between the securities and the ratio of their volatilities.

In other words, the beta between security a and b is

$$\beta_{a,b} = \rho_{a,b} \frac{\sigma_a}{\sigma_b} \tag{2.2}$$

There are three different ways to compute betas. First, however, let's clarify how beta is used.

- Define a reference spread with reference to which betas will be measured, for example, investment-grade spreads. Call this the *independent spread.*
- Second, define what spread whose movement we are interested in estimating, for example, bank spreads. Call this the *dependent spread.*
- Finally, figure out what the beta is by figuring out the value for beta in the relationship:

$$\text{Change in dependent spread} = \text{beta} \times \text{change in independent spread} + \text{error term}$$

The purpose is to forecast the beta with maximal accuracy; this is, the error term should be as small as possible and with a mean of zero.

The approach should be simple enough that we can comprehend what we are doing over long-term holding horizons and that we are not at the mercy of a black box that can quickly become hard to decipher. We basically have three choices:

1. *Forward-looking betas.* We start by assigning the default beta using internal or external ratings that are overlaps of ratings agencies and our own estimates. Then we override these default betas where we believe that the ratings are erroneous; for example, there was good reason for believing that history-based betas for banks and brokers in July 2007 were off by a large margin. As for all forecasts, this methodology has its shortcomings because it depends on the best opinions of human agents.
   Pros: Specialty traders forecast risks in their areas, and the overall investment process validates these opinions. Where we do not have strong opinions, we use the ratings as the standard. This approach is stable and simple. *Cons*: This approach is too static; it assumes that betas only change infrequently and do not depend

on level. It also depends on human opinion for overrides and thus potentially suffers from biases.

2. *Empirical betas.* This is the historical approach. We can regress the dependent spread changes on the independent spreads.

   Pros: This is a mechanical approach and does not require any forward-looking input. *Cons*: Using history to forecast volatilities and correlations (beta is the product of correlations and the ratio of the volatilities of the dependent and independent spreads) is fraught with disaster. For instance, once a bond has gone down in price by a lot, it will show zero empirical beta because its spread barely moves (e.g., BBB- ABX tranches after the mortgage market meltdown which showed almost zero empirical beta). Where empirical betas are handy is in calibrating the forward-looking views so that we know we are not completely arbitrary in our forecasts. We can use this approach to validate forward-looking views. But we still need to come to some agreement on what the window of history to use is, and this shifts opinionating from the direct forecasts of betas to forecasts of window period and size.

3. *Market-implied betas.* This approach says that the market spread is the best forecast of betas. Lehman/Barclays has been promoting this under the name *duration times spread* (DTS) [22].

   Pros: This is another mechanical approach and assumes that the market is the best forecaster of risk as spreads change. *Cons*: The market may not be the best forecaster of risk. Again, if we had looked at banking-sector spreads during the crisis, the market would have said that financials have no risk. The biggest objection here is that it assumes that risk premia over and above the fair risk are relatively small in the total spread.

There is no single mechanical measure of risk that will be robust under all situations. To make the beta computation robust requires work and thought. A risk-manager needs to understand that making forecasts of beta, is an implicit forecast about the future risk of that asset class relative to other asset classes. While limited in accuracy, various asset classes can be brought to a common denominator and compared for value using this approach.

In this chapter we have highlighted the major building blocks for analysis of fixed income investments. We next turn to the backbone of robust portfolio construction.

3

Portfolio Structure

"Long-term secular strategy is critical, but equally important is our perhaps almost unique ... focus on structure."
—Bill Gross, in "Thoroughly Modern Billie,"
PIMCO *Investment Outlook*, 2005.

Fixed income markets provide investors the opportunity to take advantage of the difference in liquidity and risk of various instruments. Long-term investors can harvest the risk-premium benefits "left on the table" by shorter-term investors or by the behavior of indirect market participants. For example, home owners' prepayment rights are in fact options that frequently are valued too high relative to their fundamental value. Or market segmentation in the yield curve might occasionally lead to higher-than-usual forward rates that can be exploited by an investor systematically betting against "the market." Another example of systematic mispricing is that due to the use of margin products such as futures contracts, by hedgers who might systematically richen or cheapen the contract in relation to the futures' deliverable basket. This chapter builds on the fundamentals introduced in the last chapter to create a strong scaffolding for bond investments.

Understanding Carry

Let us first calculate the return on a bond for a holding horizon in more detail. Let us look at a 10-year note (Figure 3.1) with a coupon of 5 percent at a yield of 4.75 percent. The price is 101.9718. Now, if we wait for 1 year, the 10-year note becomes a 9-year note, and if the current yield curve is upward sloping, the 9-year yield will be lower than the 10-year yield. Let us assume that current 9-year yield is 4.65 percent. Changing the maturity and the yield, we obtain the price of the 9-year 5 percent coupon note at 4.65 percent to equal 102.5501.

Now the coupon return of the note is simply coupon divided by initial price; that is, $5/101.9718 = 4.9$ percent. Also, since the price itself rises, the price return is $(102.5501 - 101.9718)/101.9718 = 0.5671$ percent. So the total return equals the coupon return plus the price return $= 4.9$ percent $+ 0.5671$ percent $= 5.4671$ percent.

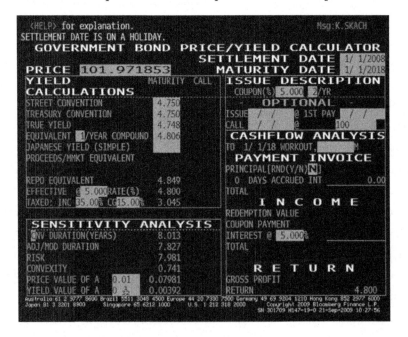

Figure 3.1 Treasury bond carry.
© 2009 Bloomberg L. P. All rights reserved. Used with permission.

We can approach this computation using a forward purchase analysis. We know that if we agree to buy the bond forward, we can invest the cash currently for one year at the money-market rate. The total return then will be simply the return on this cash plus the "pickup" from buying the bond at the forward price. Suppose that LIBOR is 1 percent. Then we know that the cash will return 1 percent, so the return from the forward purchase should equal 4.4671 percent. This has to solve:

$$\frac{(102.5501 - F)}{101.9718} = 4.4671 \tag{3.1}$$

so that $F = 97.9947$ is the fair forward price of the bond. Of course, we can turn the argument upside down and start in terms of the forward price to extract the expected return.

The fact that the 10-year note becomes a 9-year note means that in an upward-sloping yield curve, the bond will have positive "roll down." Since the cash is invested at better rates, the return on investment is an additional contribution to the carry. If the bond were trading cheap to the benchmark curve, as in having an option-adjusted spread (OAS) that was positive, then we would expect to earn additional return from the OAS converging to its fair value. Also, as we discussed earlier, Treasuries actually can trade special in the repo market; that is, owning a security that is in demand can result in the ability to obtain additional financing advantage. Finally (see below), we lose some of the roll-down carry from the loss of embedded convexity premium. The net result of adding all these components is that we can judge the value of the security to our holding horizon from looking at all the different pieces. Structural investing means balancing between all these different sources of carry.

Let us formalize this intuition. The change in price of a bond is given in terms of its yield y, spread over benchmark s, value of embedded options, and time t by [32]

$$dP = \frac{\partial P}{\partial t}dt + \frac{\partial P}{\partial y}dy + \frac{\partial P}{\partial s}ds + \frac{1}{2}\frac{\partial^2 P}{\partial dy^2}(dy^2) \qquad (3.2)$$

Substitute

$$\frac{1}{P}\frac{\partial P}{\partial y} = -D \qquad (3.3)$$

$$\frac{1}{P}\frac{\partial P}{\partial s} = -D_s \qquad (3.4)$$

$$\frac{1}{P}\frac{dP}{dt} = (y - c) \qquad (3.5)$$

where c is the continuously compounded coupon. This leads to

$$\frac{\Delta P}{P} = -D\Delta y + (y - c) - D_s\Delta s + \Delta t + \frac{1}{2}C(\Delta y)^2 \qquad (3.6)$$

Taking expectations,

$$E\left(\frac{\Delta P}{P}\right) = -DE(\Delta y) + -D_s E(\Delta s) + y - c\Delta t + \frac{1}{2}C\sigma^2\Delta t \qquad (3.7)$$

So the change in value of a bond, assuming no change in interest rates, can be attributed to

- The change in the yield times the duration of the bond
- The change in the spread times the spread duration of the bond
- The difference in yield versus the implicit rate of financing times the time
- The change in the value of the bond as the yield curve moves forward (For example, in one year's time, a 2-year bond is a 1-year bond. Assuming that the shape of the yield curve is unchanged,

the change in price of the bond equals the difference between the 1-year forward 1-year rate and the 1-year spot rate times the duration of the 1-year bond.

How does this risk premium manifest itself in the yield of the bond? Note that to avoid arbitrage opportunities, the return over an instantaneous period Δt on any bond has to be equal to the short rate plus the additional risk assumed. To linear order,

$$\frac{dP}{P} = r\Delta t - D\lambda_y - D_s\lambda_s \qquad (3.8)$$

where λ_y is the risk premium owing to interest-rate risk, and λ_s is the risk premium owing to spread. For positive returns from extending duration, we should find that λ_y is consistently negative.

Solving the set of equations above, we find that

$$y = r + D[E(\Delta y) - \lambda_y] + D_s[E(\Delta s) - \lambda_s] - \frac{1}{2}C\sigma^2 \qquad (3.9)$$

or in other words, the yield of a bond is equal to the short rate plus the expected return from a bond owing to yield changes minus the interest-rate risk premium plus the expected change in the spread of the bond over the risk-free rate minus the risk premium for spreads minus the advantage of convexity.

If the bond is callable or has other sources of optionality, that is, $P_c = P_{nc} + O$, then we need to add another term proportional to dO to the price of the noncallable bond to account for the change in the value of the option.

We also can write down the price in terms of forward rates:

$$\frac{1}{P}\frac{dP}{dt} = \frac{1}{P}\frac{dP}{dy_f}\frac{dy_f}{dt} \qquad (3.10)$$

which equals

$$\frac{1}{P}\frac{dP}{dt} = -D_f R \qquad (3.11)$$

where D_f is the forward duration of the bond, and R corresponds to the carry and roll-down components as the forward rate moves in for a small instantaneous period. One can use this to compute the carry of any security once the forward key-rate durations are known. A simple application is to Eurodollar contracts that mature at 3-month intervals. As time passes, the longer-term Eurodollars roll down to shorter ones. One simply can take the difference in the implied yield of such contracts to quantify the carry in the forward yield curve.

Understanding the Butterfly Strategy

In the preceding section we showed the computation of total return as arising from the sum of "things that change" and the "passage of time." We can combine multiple securities to isolate structural value in the yield curve. Perhaps one of the simplest fixed income strategies that expresses a structural investing style is the classic "butterfly" strategy. This strategy is implemented by purchasing the "body," say, the 5-year note, and selling the "wings," say, the 2- and 10-year notes, as displayed in Figure 3.2. Conceptually, there are many ways of implementing the butterfly because the weights for each of the positions can be determined in many different ways. The simplest implementation is to make sure that the duration of the wings matches the duration of the body and at the same time the proceeds from selling the wings match the cost of purchasing the body. In the example in Figure 3.2, each unit of the 5-year note requires a short position in 0.572 unit of the 2-year note and 0.419 unit of the 10-year note. This is obtained by requiring that the total duration of the 5-year note matches the weighted-average

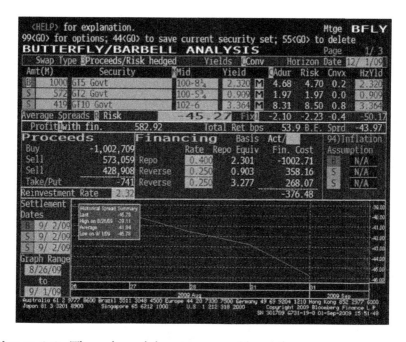

Figure 3.2 The cash- and duration-neutral butterfly strategy.
© 2009 Bloomberg Finance L. P. All rights reserved. Used with permission.

duration of the 2- and 10-year notes and also that the proceeds from sale and purchase match and there is no net cash outlay. Looking across the top box, we can see that investing in this type of butterfly creates a lot of duration risk from the 10-year note. Since the position is a short 10-year position, we would expect this type of butterfly to do well when the curve steepens and do badly when the curve flattens (it has "curve duration risk exposure"). Thus, even though this butterfly is cash- and duration-neutral, it has a curve-steepening bias. Also see that selling the 10-year note creates a negatively convex position relative to the purchase of the 5- and 2-year notes. So the butterfly is negatively convex overall. Since the premium to convexity (we will discuss this more below) rises when volatility rises, this butterfly is a net short of volatility or convexity.

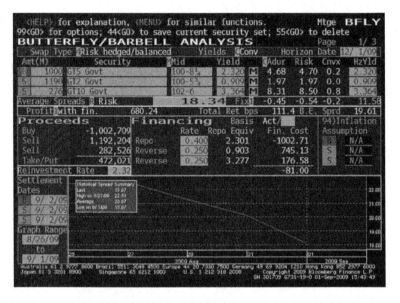

Figure 3.3 The risk-neutral butterfly strategy.
© 2009 Bloomberg Finance L. P. All rights reserved. Used with permission.

Compare this butterfly with the butterfly in Figure 3.3. This butterfly is risk-neutral; that is, the short wing (2 to 5 years) risk is matched by the long wing (5 to 10 years). Hence this butterfly requires more concentration in the 2-year note. This butterfly is neutral by construction to equal amounts of pivoting around the 5-year point. The performance of this type of butterfly is very different because it has less convexity risk associated with it.

Convexity and Time Decay

Option-free bonds express positive convexity. Mathematically, this means that for an expected outcome of rates exactly equal to zero, the expected outcome of prices may be nonnegative. Assume two states of the world, one in which yields can move up or down by 1 percent. Owing to positive convexity, the fall in price for a 1 percent rise in yields is less than the rise in prices for a 1 percent fall in yields. Hence the average, or the expectation of bond prices, is positive, even though the expectation of yield changes is zero. Now assume two other states in which yields can either rise by 20 percent or fall by 20 percent. Again, the expectation for rate changes is zero, but the expectation of price changes is positive and higher than the case where yields can change only by 1 percent. In other words, the change in the expected value of the bond increases as the outcomes become more volatile. To a good approximation, we can convert convexity into basis points of time decay per year by using the relationship of option gamma and option theta that is standard in the option pricing literature. First, the result:

$$\text{Time decay} = \theta \approx -\frac{1}{2}\sigma^2 \left(\frac{D^2}{100} + \Delta_- - \Delta_+ \right) \qquad (3.12)$$

where θ is the *one-year expected time decay* in percentage points of return, D is the duration, Δ_- is the duration for a large downshift of the yield curve (*bull duration*), and Δ_+ is the duration for a large upshift (*bear duration*). The downshift and upshift can be taken to be 50 basis points for convenience (so the difference is 100 basis points, or 1 percent). Also, σ is the normalized yield volatility of the yield of a bond with the same duration as the portfolio.

For instance, a typical value for the Barclays/Lehman Aggregate U.S. Index (assuming interest-rate volatilities of 100 basis points per year) would be

$$D = 4.3 \qquad (3.13)$$
$$\Delta_- = -0.5 \qquad (3.14)$$
$$\Delta_+ = 0.45 \qquad (3.15)$$
$$\sigma = 1 \qquad (3.16)$$

which would imply

$$\theta = -0.5 \times [(18.49 \times 0.01) - 0.5 - 0.45] = -0.38 \quad (3.17)$$

that is, over the next 1-year horizon, the time decay of the portfolio is roughly 38 basis points. Here we chose normalized yield volatility to be equal to 1 percent, or 100 basis points, for a 5-year note that has the same duration as the total return fund. In principle, as the volatility increases, so does the magnitude of time decay. σ has to be chosen with reference to the expected yield volatility of each bond over the time horizon—in practice, the swaption volatility that is closest to the duration of the index (with 1-year maturity) might be a good proxy.

Note that when a portfolio has positive convexity, that is, $\Delta_- > 0$, and $\Delta_+ < 0$, then θ is less than zero; that is, the portfolio is effectively long an option and should lose money over the 1-year horizon from time decay if nothing changes. Also, for zero-coupon-like portfolios, the bull and bear duration deltas are zero, so the time decay simply equals $\frac{-1}{200}\sigma D^2$. For example, if one bought a 30-year zero-coupon bond portfolio, one would lose roughly 100 basis points of yield per annum as premium for the convexity (a very expensive option if the markets come to a standstill).

In order to see how this result is derived, the first step to note is that locally the portfolio change for a portfolio P is

$$dP = \frac{\partial P}{\partial t}dt + \frac{\partial P}{\partial y}dy + \frac{1}{2}\frac{\partial^2 P}{\partial y^2}dy^2 \quad (3.18)$$

Assuming that the portfolio value remains static over time and that yields do not change (in equilibrium, the first one has to be the case, so there is no ability to make free money, and the second one has to be true because we are assuming that all the portfolio return is coming from structural time decay and not from yield change), we can write in terms of expectations

$$E(dP) = 0, \; E\left(\frac{\partial P}{\partial y}dy\right) = 0 \qquad (3.19)$$

which implies, that for any time horizon t,

$$E\left(\frac{\partial P}{\partial t}dt\right) = -\frac{1}{2}CP(\sigma^2 t) \qquad (3.20)$$

where C stands for the convexity. Now $dp/dt = \theta$, the time decay, so

$$\theta = -\frac{1}{2}CP\sigma^2 t \qquad (3.21)$$

To derive the value of C in terms of Δ_+ and Δ_-, note that

$$\frac{dP}{P} = \frac{1}{P}\frac{\partial P}{\partial y}dy + \frac{1}{2}\frac{1}{P}\frac{\partial}{\partial y}\left(\frac{\partial P}{\partial y}\right) \qquad (3.22)$$

Using

$$D = -\frac{1}{P}\frac{\partial P}{\partial y} \qquad (3.23)$$

$$C = \frac{1}{P}\frac{\partial^2 P}{\partial y^2} = \frac{\partial D}{\partial y} + \frac{D^2}{100} \qquad (3.24)$$

$$\frac{\partial D}{\partial y} = \Delta_- - \Delta_+ \qquad (3.25)$$

we can show, using the preceding expression for θ, that

$$\theta = -\frac{1}{2}\sigma^2 tP\left(\frac{D^2}{100} + \Delta_- - \Delta_+\right) \qquad (3.26)$$

which for $t = 1$ and $P = 1$ reduce approximately to the results given above.

Extracting Risk Premium

Earlier we mentioned that structural investing exploits attractive sources of risk premium. But before we start to construct such investment strategies, there are a few questions that need to be answered:

1. Is there risk premium in the interest-rate markets?
2. What is the source of this risk premium?
3. Is the risk premium constant or time-varying? If time-varying, are there systematic sources that are responsible for the time variation?
4. What is the least risky way to extract the risk premium?

Let us work through an example to understand the meaning of risk-neutral pricing [10]. Assume that the 6-month rate on a bond is 5 percent and that the 1-year rate is 5.15 percent. Next, assume that the 6-month rate 6 months from now can be 4.5 or 5.5 percent with equal probability of 1/2. The price of the 1-year zero today is $1000/(1 + 0.0515/2)^2 = 950.4230$. On the other hand, the expected (average) present value of the zero using the uncertain outcomes of 5.5 and 4.5 percent forward rates is 951.82. The difference of 1.4 is the premium the buyer charges for buying a risky security. Thus, under the assumed real-world probability of 1/2, the price of the zero-coupon bond does not equal its expected present discounted value. If the upstate probability is changed to 0.8 (with the downstate probability of 0.2), then the price of the bond indeed does equal the expected discounted value. Under this probability, though, the expected value of the rate in 6 months is not equal to the spot rate for 6 months but a higher number (0.80 times 5.5 percent minus 0.20 times 4.5 percent). An investor is risk-neutral if he or she computes the prices of bonds using the expected discounted value.

We can make this formal using utility functions. Assume that there are two investors, both with power utility functions. We recap [39] that

$$E[U(W + \tilde{\epsilon})] = U(W - \Pi_i) \qquad (3.27)$$

which states that the expected utility of a risky gamble is equal to a riskless wealth level that is less than the expected wealth. $W - \Pi_i$ is the *certainty-equivalent wealth*. Π_i is the compensatory risk premium to avoid taking the risky gamble. By Taylor expansion,

$$\Pi_i \approx -\frac{1}{2}\left[\frac{U''(W)}{U'(W)}\right]\sigma_\epsilon^2 \qquad (3.28)$$

where the quantity in the brackets is called the *absolute risk aversion*. When

$$U(W) = \frac{W^\gamma}{\gamma} \qquad (3.29)$$

the investor has constant relative risk aversion $1 - \gamma$ and decreasing absolute risk aversion. This investor bets increasing dollar amounts as his or her wealth increases, but the same proportion of his or her wealth. When γ is 0.2, the investor has constant risk aversion (CRA) of 0.8; when $\gamma = 0.5$, he or she has CRA of 0.5. Thus a larger gamma means less constant risk aversion.

To compute the expected utility, we integrate over all possibilities

$$E(U_\gamma) = \int_0^\infty U_\gamma(\tilde{W})\phi(x)dx \qquad (3.30)$$

where $(\tilde{W}) = W_0 \times (1 + x)$ is the uncertain wealth when the investor invests in a security with random outcomes x. We can check that when $\phi(x)$ is the normal density, then

$$E(U_{0.2}) > E(U_{0.5}) \qquad (3.31)$$

Thus, when the payoff is restricted to be positive (x integral only done over positive values), then the more risk-averse investor has a much higher payoff. Obviously, these two investors, when they meet in the market, will trade this payoff with each other only if the expected value of the payoff was equal. We can add a drift term such that the expected value of the less risk-averse investor (with $\gamma = 0.5$) equals the expected value to the more risk-averse investor (this is the upfront compensation received by the less risk-loving investor to do the trade. For some large upfront drift, the risk-averse and the risky investor will trade the option.

A security's risk premium is proportional to the risks to which the bond is exposed. As an example, assume a short-term bond yielding x percent. Now, the expected return from a long-term bond that yields $2x$ and 0 percent is equal to x percent. But an investor is not indifferent to these two bonds. As shown in [39], the risk premium is proportional to the interest-rate risk to which the longer-term bond is exposed. If the bond is exposed to risk factors beyond interest-rate risk, then the risk premium is a weighted average of the risk premia from these sources and the loadings to the risk factors. In Chapter 4 on macro risk factors, we list some of the risk factors to which typical fixed income portfolios are exposed.

The Risk Premium Embedded in Eurodollar Futures

When one looks at the shape of the forward curve implied by Eurodollar futures, one finds the curve to be uniformly upward-sloping. The natural question is whether the curve embeds a risk premium. Note that if the short-term rate is lower than a longer-term forward rate, then, on average, the market expects rates to go up (owing to Fed policy, etc.). Can one make money betting against the forwards? For example, take the spot 3-month rate at 1.5 percent and the 3-month rate 1 year out at 2.5 percent. Does the difference of 100 basis points have any exploitable value in it? Mathematically, we want to know α and β in the following equation:

$$R_{\text{actual}} = \alpha + \beta R_{\text{forecast}} \qquad (3.32)$$

where R_{actual} is the return from buying a deferred Eurodollar contract and holding it to the (1-year) horizon, and R_{forecast} is the difference between the deferred Eurodollar contract and spot rates.

Here are some possibilities:

- $\beta = 1, \alpha = 0$. Forward rates are perfect predictors of spot rates; that is, in a year, the short rate will become what is implied by the forwards. Then there should be no money to be made if one got into an investment to lend at a higher rate (equal to the forward rate) in the future. This is so because when the future date arrives, the spot rate will be exactly equal to the forward rate now. Graphically, if one were to draw the ex ante roll-down (difference between forward rate and spot rate) on the x axis and the realized ex post return on the y axis, for history, one should find a flat horizontal line.
- $\beta = 1, \alpha \neq 0$. The forwards are imperfect predictors, and they would predict the direction but not the magnitude. If $\alpha > 0$, then there is a risk premium to be had by betting against the forwards.
- $\beta = 0, \alpha = 0$. The forwards have no predictive ability. Then the return from the roll-down exactly equals the steepness of the curve.

The analysis is muddied by the fact that the size of the risk premium in the outright contract might come from a large amount of directionality. To take the directionality out, one needs to subtract the drift. But the average drift is not constant and depends on the macroeconomic environment. To take out the drift, one needs to create locally hedged portfolios that are level and curve-reshaping-neutral.

This analysis can be done rigorously, and academic work spawned by Fama and French has created a veritable industry around this topic. We find that indeed the forward curve, on average, has not been a good forecaster of realized short rates. This risk premium or anomaly has been exploited over the years by investors with longer-term horizons. Why might this structural value continue to exist? We focus on the fifth Eurodollar contract, the ED5.

Here are some possible candidate explanations, and the truth is most likely a combination of all these explanations:

1. The ED5 point is the shock absorber for Fed policy changes. Since information ratio by definition is the ratio of return to standard deviation, it does not capture the fat tail risk from monetary policy. Hence the excess compensation is for taking tail risks.

If this explanation is correct, we should be able to measure the skewness and kurtosis of duration-adjusted excess ED5 returns and see if they are actually higher. By running a statistical analysis of the skewness and kurtosis of duration-adjusted excess returns, we indeed find that the ED5 contract has one of the highest negative skewnesses and kurtoses of all the other assets over short periods. Over longer periods, the differences are more moderate.

2. Market segmentation creates opportunities. In other words, some investors flock to long-term instruments, and some stay close to cash. Owing to various regulations on money-market funds, the region around the 1-year sector (where ED5 lives) becomes the orphaned contract. Like other market-segmentation hypotheses, this one almost assumes the conclusion and is harder to test. One approach is to watch flows into duration and see whether the performance of ED5 is correlated. We find that even after adjusting for duration, ED5 actually does tend to outperform in periods when duration falls; that is, there is residual duration risk in the ED5 contract. More generally, assets that are bondlike tend to outperform when rates fall even after adjusting for duration.

3. ED5 is a momentum asset. Central banks want stability, and hence their policy is one of gradualism. Statistical behavior of the Fed shows that since 1971, the Fed has changed rates in the same direction 195 of 250 times; that is, the probability of consecutive changes in the same direction is 80 percent. This explanation, if true, would show that, all else being equal, the ED5 should both outperform and underperform more than the forwards encapsulate. Item 7 below might explain why positive (lower rate) momentum may provide a relatively higher payoff.

4. ED5 is a tail-risk hedging asset. We observed last year that as the economy ran into trouble, ED5 outperformed. If the economy is structurally more prone to disasters (owing to leverage, etc.), then being long ED5 on balance should be profitable, as long as the market does not price the "insurance" premium into the contract price. Indeed, the test for this is straightforward: We regress the ED5 price performance versus the VIX index, $/yen, credit spreads, or our new systemic tranche index, and in all cases we find the correlation to be significant. Thus, structurally, the ED5 is a cheap "insurance" asset, especially close to turning points in the economy.

5. ED5 is underpriced owing to hedging activity. In a other words, short-term rate exposure is a systematic risk that commands a risk premium. This argument is similar to the one used for commodities, where it is well known that hedgers pay speculators a risk premium. In the rate markets of levered economies, hedgers hedge against rising interest rates (i.e., they are naturally short the Eurodollar contracts), and hence the fair value is higher contract prices or lower rates. The test for this hypothesis is to see the balance of speculators versus hedgers. Again, it is hard to fully obtain the evidence because there are so many large over-the-counter (OTC) transactions, but on balance, it is not hard to argue with the fact that the risk lies toward rising rates, and hence, hedging activity would be skewed toward more hedgers being short the contract.

6. Futures/forwards bias. A mark-to-market long futures position has to borrow margin at higher rates when the contract falls in price (rates rise) and invests at a lower rate when contract rises (rates fall). This embedded convexity makes the fair value of the contract lower (assuming balance of hedgers and speculators). For a hold-to-horizon investor who does not hedge the margin flows, the convexity premium is a gift.

7. Inflation trends create ED5 trends. Taylor rules create overshoot that gets corrected when the need for tightening goes away. It is well known that inflation is autoregressive, both statistically and on fundamental principles. As shown by Clarida et al., a policy rule to counter increasing inflation has to have a higher than 1 coefficient; that is, nominal rates need to rise faster than the anticipated inflation gap. If this is true and is built into the forward curve, then the eventual turnaround will create excess premium in rates from which a long can benefit.

Structural Value in Mortgage Rolls

We have already spoken about repo transactions earlier. In a repo transaction, two parties get into an agreement where one party sells a security to another for cash with a simultaneous agreement to repurchase the same security at a specific agreed-on price at a later date. In a repo transaction, the ownership of the security transfers to the cash lender, but the interest and principal continue to be sent to the original owner.

In the mortgage market, the dollar roll is the more popular financing transaction. First, the principal and interest go to the holder of the security as of each record date; second, the returned securities do not have to be identical to the original securities (just substantially similar); and third, any prepayment risk gets reflected in the delivery of the securities. While technically the dollar roll is a sale and a purchase (i.e., two separate transactions), it is still economically a financing trade. The structural advantage comes from the fact that the holder of the roll never has to take delivery of the mortgage but can benefit from the implied financing of the roll, especially if it is attractive relative to other cash investments.[1]

Figure 3.4 displays the roll of a 5.5 percent Fannie Mae agency mortgage TBA (To Be Announced). TBAs are essentially mortgage forwards. The current price for the TBA for immediate delivery is 104-28. The traded price for the next delivery (a month hence) is 104-15+. So the "drop," which is the difference in the prices, is 12.50 32nds. Now, to calculate the structural advantage from rolling the TBA (i.e., selling the front TBA and buying the deferred TBA) requires some accounting.

First, if we sell the front TBA, then we can take the uncommitted cash and invest it in the money markets at 0.25 percent (the reinvestment rate). When the deferred date arrives, we can commit to buying the MBS. However, since prepayment rates can impact the actual amount of MBSs delivered on the deferred date (and prepayment rates are uncertain), we don't know exactly the amount of mortgages we will receive

---

[1] To derive the dollar-roll formula, assume that B_0 is the balance in the mortgage at the beginning of the roll perriod, P_0 is the mortgage-backed security (MBS) settlement price at the beginning of the roll period, A_0 is the accrued interest associated with sale price P_0, B_1 is the balance at the end of the roll period, P_1 is the settlement price at the end of the roll period, A_1 is the accrued interest associated with repurchase at P_1, r is the reinvestment or funding rate, c is the coupon, n is the number of days from the beginning settlement date to the ending settlement date, and m is the number of days from the ending settlement date to the payment date.

Then the principal paydown is $B_0 - B_1$, and the value of the roll is

$$
\begin{aligned}
\text{Roll} = \; & B_0(P_0 + A_0)\left(1 + \frac{n}{360}r\right) \\
& - B_1(P_1 + A_1) \\
& - \frac{P + B_0 c/12}{1 + mr/360}
\end{aligned}
\tag{3.33}
$$

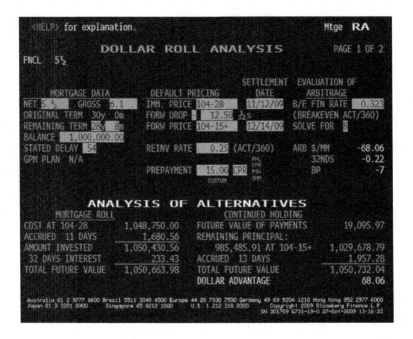

Figure 3.4 MBS TBA dollar roll.

© 2009 Bloomberg Finance, L. P. All rights reserved. Used with permission.

in the future. In the figure we assumed that the mortgages prepay at 15 CPR. Now, based on these inputs, the dollar advantage to holding versus rolling the MBS is 68 (per million). The implied breakeven funding rate is 0.323 percent. So, if we can invest cash at higher than 0.323 percent, it is better to roll. Now, suppose that we change the drop to 6/32 (i.e., hold the current TBA price fixed and raise the deferred TBA to 104-22). All else being equal, this results in a dollar advantage to holding versus rolling of $2069.83 per million and a breakeven rate of 2.467 percent. In other words, the current reinvestment rate has to be much higher for the investor to roll versus holding. What happens if prepayment rates change? Suppose that the CPR falls to 5 percent from 15 percent. Then the total amount of mortgages in the future is higher (less prepayment). This requires more dollars to buy the MBSs in the future; hence the breakeven financing rate goes up.

```
<HELP> for explanation.                                    Mtge  RAM
              DOLLAR  ROLL  ANALYSIS
FNCL  5½

 Settle   Price    PSA    Roll  Fwd Price  Horizon  Days  B/E  FINAN
11/12/09  104-28  400.00  -12    104-16    12/14/09  32      0.555 %
                  CUSTOM

       BREAKEVEN  FINANCE  RATE  SENSITIVITY
                                                        step
    Roll: -15    -14    -13    -12    -11    -10    -9    1  32nds
PSA
 340.00  -0.34  -0.01   0.32   0.65   0.98   1.31   1.65
 360.00  -0.37  -0.04   0.29   0.62   0.95   1.28   1.61
 380.00  -0.40  -0.07   0.26   0.59   0.92   1.25   1.58
 400.00  -0.44  -0.11   0.23   0.56   0.89   1.22   1.55
 420.00  -0.47  -0.14   0.19   0.52   0.85   1.18   1.51
 440.00  -0.50  -0.17   0.16   0.49   0.82   1.15   1.48
 460.00  -0.53  -0.20   0.13   0.46   0.79   1.12   1.45
 20.00 step
Net 5 ½   Gross 6.1      Term 30:0   Rem WAM 28:8   Stated Delay 54

       Reinvestment rate = 0.25          FED FUNDS = 0.11
Australia 61 2 9777 8600 Brazil 5511 3048 4500 Europe 44 20 7330 7500 Germany 49 69 9204 1210 Hong Kong 852 2977 6000
Japan 81 3 3201 8900      Singapore 65 6212 1000      U.S. 1 212 318 2000     Copyright 2009 Bloomberg Finance L.P.
                                                      SN 301709 G731-19-0 27-Oct-2009 13:35:19
```

Figure 3.5 MBS TBA dollar roll for different combinations of drops and prepayment speeds.

Figure 3.5 displays the breakeven financing rates for different combinations of rolls and prepayment speeds for premium mortgages (coupons higher than the current coupon or MBSs with prices above par). As we can see, for the same speed, a tightening drop results in higher breakeven rates (i.e., its better not to roll when the drop tightens). On the other hand, for the same drop, as the prepayment rates rise, we obtain lower breakevens (i.e., if we expect prepayments to speed up, its better to roll for the same drop). For the same breakeven financing rate, as the prepayment speeds rise, the premium mortage roll tightens and becomes less negative. For discount mortgages, the roll widens as the prepayment rates rise.

Of course, this can all be represented in terms of breakeven drops. When the market roll is trading wider than the breakeven drop, then the roll is said to be *trading above carry*, and it's better to roll long positions in the nearest TBA to the next TBA. When the reinvestment rate is close to 0 percent, then the breakeven drop represents the dollar roll *trading at fail*.

This example shows that if the roll is too wide, a structural investor in MBSs might be able to harvest extra yield in his or her portfolio by continuing to roll the MBS positions. However, we have mentioned frequently that this type of structural advantage (indeed, almost all the structural advantages) arises from an implicit option sale. What is the option that leads to structural value in mortgage rolls? First, note that the holder who does not roll takes delivery of mortgages that will season over the next month compared with the holder who rolls and commits to taking new, less-seasoned mortgages. Since seasoning can result from carry gains (from curve roll-down), as well as other improvements, all else being equal, seasoned mortgages should command a higher price than unseasoned ones. The deferred TBA also gives the seller of the TBA the option to deliver worse pools; that is, the roll implicitly is subject to adverse selection. Further, any sharp change in underlying dynamics, including a shock to the yield curve, can result in the collateral characteristics of the further-out TBAs changing more than anticipated (i.e., they carry more negative convexity risk).

We also have mentioned in the past that many structural opportunities can be evaluated in terms of option-pricing considerations, but it is critical to understand what creates these inefficiencies or options in the first place. In the case of the roll, the demand for collateral by various parties (such as collateralized mortgage obligation (CMO) "factories" or indexers) can create a substantial mispricing between the front- and the back-month TBAs. More recently, the purchase of mortgages by the Federal Reserve created significant demand for the front-end TBAs (the Fed would buy the TBAs and take delivery), creating opportunities for structural investors to sell the front TBAs and roll out to the deferred TBAs.

Structural Value in Futures Contracts

Futures contracts on interest rate instruments allow investors to get the exposure to interest-rate movements synthetically. Figure 3.6 shows the December 2009 futures contract deliverable instruments. By design, the contract can be settled by delivery of U.S. Treasury notes with at least 6.5 years of maturity but no more than 10 years of maturity from the first day of the delivery month. The invoice price on delivery equals the futures settlement price times a conversion factor (see Chicago Board of Trade Web site for more details) to convert all the deliverable bonds into comparable securities (the price of the delivered note to yield 6 percent).

The investor who is long the futures contract is effectively short a delivery option to the investor who is short the futures contract (see [17] for details on the Treasury futures basis). The futures short has the

```
<HELP> for explanation.                                      ComdtyDLV
Hit {NUMBER} <GO> to view Historical Basis/Repo
INCREASING  NET  BASIS          Trade 10/27/09 Dlv 12/31/09 p.1 / 2
US 10YR NOTE FUT  Dec09  TYZ9 117-29⁴  Set 10/28/09 Cheapest IRP= .32
                                         64 Days Act/360
PRICES AS DECIMALS    (Mid)      Conv.    Gross Implied  Actual  Net
   Order  re-sort  Price Source Yield C.Factor Basis Repo%  Repo%  Basis
                                                            .05
 1 T 4⅞ 08/15/16  111-25 BGN 2.949 .9402  29.2  -.32   .05   2.3
 2 T 4⅝ 11/15/16  110-04 BGN 3.019 .9245  35.4 -1.49   .05   9.7
 3 T 3  08/31/16   99-31 BGN 3.005 .8405  27.4 -1.82   .05  10.7
 4 T 3¼ 07/31/16  101-23 BGN 2.967 .8538  33.2 -2.59   .05  15.4
 5 T 4⅝ 02/15/17  110-02 BGN 3.075 .9223  41.7 -2.53   .05  16.3
 6 T 3¼ 06/30/16 101-25+ BGN 2.951 .8538  35.7 -3.01   .05  17.9
 7 T 4½ 05/15/17 109-02+ BGN 3.140 .9128  46.0 -3.32   .05  21.0
 8 T 4¾ 08/15/17  110-22 BGN 3.191 .9254  50.0 -3.71   .05  23.9
 9 T 3  09/30/16  99-25¾ BGN 3.031 .8354  41.4 -4.30   .05  24.8
10 T 4¼ 11/15/17 107-01+ BGN 3.248 .8927  56.9 -5.39   .05  33.3
11 T 3½ 02/15/18  101-14 BGN 3.300 .8430  64.9 -7.82   .05  45.8
12 T 3⅞ 05/15/18 103-31+ BGN 3.335 .8632  70.2 -8.15   .05  48.7
13 T 4  08/15/18  104-23 BGN 3.375 .8683  74.5 -8.70   .05  52.5
14 T 3¾ 11/15/18 102-20+ BGN 3.408 .8485  82.7 -10.51  .05  61.9
15 T 2¾ 02/15/19   94-20 BGN 3.430 .7765  97.9 -15.25  .05  82.8
16 T 3⅛ 05/15/19   97-13 BGN 3.446 .7981 105.4 -15.79  .05  88.0

Australia 61 2 9777 8600 Brazil 5511 3048 4500 Europe 44 20 7330 7500 Germany 49 69 9204 1210 Hong Kong 852 2977 6000
Japan 81 3 3201 8900    Singapore 65 6212 1000    U.S. 1 212 318 2000   Copyright 2009 Bloomberg Finance L.P.
                                                   SN 301769 G731-19-0 27-Oct-2009 14:33:09
```

Figure 3.6 Ten-year futures contract deliverability analysis.

choice (among others) to deliver any one of the deliverable notes. In practice, the short will deliver the note that has the lowest implied repo, that is, the note whose effective financing cost is the lowest.

Again, increased volatility in the markets makes it more likely that the cheapest to deliver (CTD) will switch, that is, that the option that the futures short has becomes more valuable. The risk that the futures long is taking is that the deliverable switches and the duration of the portfolio switches as well. Thus the futures long demands excess compensation for taking this risk. In effect, the option is due to the negative convexity of the futures contract (it likely switches to the higher-duration bond as CTD as rates rise and to the lower-duration bond as rates fall). Futures are actively used by interest-rate risk hedgers for controlling their duration risk. A hedge fund that is long other types of bonds will short the futures contract, in effect purchasing an option (the delivery option). If time passes and the markets are not volatile, then this option will expire worthless, and the party that is long the futures contract, in effect, will earn the option premium.

Swaps and Structural Alpha

As discussed in the last chapter on asset swaps, the spread between an interest-rate swap and an equal-maturity Treasury is the *swap spread*. The term structure of swap spreads is typically positive, but in the crisis of 2007 and 2008, longer-term swaps went to highly negative values; that is, swaps traded at a lower yield than equivalent-maturity Treasuries. The basic building block for the swap curve is the General Collateral (GC)–LIBOR spread (or more recently, the LIBOR-OIS spread displayed at the end of chapter 2). Since the long-term government curve is an average of the short-term government rate, and the long-term swap rate is the average of forward LIBOR rates, the difference between the GC and LIBOR rates evolved forward should yield the swap spread. The fair swap spread is equal to the size of the annuity that has the same present value as the expected difference of the LIBOR and the repo rates over the life of the swap. Thus, even though cosmetically it might appear that one should prefer swaps (because they are higher yielding than government bonds), this is only part of the picture. An investor is indifferent between holding swaps (funded with LIBOR) or government bonds (funded with repo) if the present value of the yield difference equals the present value of the funding difference.

If one were to look at a limited amount of data prior to the crisis, swaps would have looked like an easy structural trade. Receiving swap spreads at face value thus appears to be a profitable strategy. Liu and Longstaff [25] summarize the historical data from 1988 to 2003. Since 1988, if one had followed the strategy of receiving swap spreads using month-end closes, odds were high that the trade made money if held to maturity. For example, for the 2-year swap spread, assuming that swap spread tightening bets were put on when spreads were 10 basis points from expected LIBOR-repo spread, there were 108 actual trades since 1988, 35 of which went underwater at some point, and 11 were losers (i.e., spreads were wider than inception after 2 years passed). The average gain was 3.39 percent, and the maximum drawdown was −7.0 percent.

However, our option-based framework says that excess yield can be traced to excess risk. The excess risk in this case arises from swaps tracking OTC banking-sector risk. The excess returns from the swap-spread strategy is highly correlated with market factors. The most important factors are bank spreads and the butterfly component of the yield curve (the butterfly component is a measure of volatility, so higher volatility means wider swap spreads).

The swap spreads in 10-year maturities show a strong correlation with both net Treasury issuance and MBS issuance. Since mortgages use swaps as a proxy (indeed, agencies use the mortage swap spread to figure out the economics of MBS on their balance sheets), swap spreads should be expected to be correlated with MBS issuance. Treasury issuance has the opposite effect. The higher the expected supply, the lower is the swap spread of swaps over Treasuries. For longer-term swaps, there is another, hedging-related risk factor. Since swaps allow easy access to duration exposure (they do not require purchase of bonds with cash), in times when hedgers are net short duration, there is a tightening of swap spreads.

In the cross section there is a tight relationship between swap spreads and net government debt. On average, countries with high amounts of government debt as a percentage of gross domestic product (GDP) show tighter swap spreads than those with low amounts of government debt. As government debt quality worsens, many swap spreads have gone negative.

Since swaps are indexed off LIBOR rates, the spreads are really a function of long-term forecasts of LIBOR rates and GC Treasury repo rates. Also, based on International Swap Dealer Association (ISDA) agreements, swap mark-to-market values are collateralized daily. So there is very little direct default risk on a swap position. The bigger risk is a systemic one, where LIBOR itself comes under pressure or a whole collection of banking counterparties come under the threat of correlated defaults. In a recent paper [47] we showed that a simple two-factor term-structure model with a model that is macroeconomically driven can explain the term structure of swap spreads. The key observation is that swap spreads are quantified by a hazard rate, which is a function of observed macro variables such as yield-curve factors, deficits, and total issuance.

Structural Value in CDS Basis Trades

Chapter 1 discussed the concept of an asset swap. The aset swap is a good measure of the credit risk of a bond. The credit default swap (CDS) basis is defined as

$$\text{CDS basis} = \text{CDS premium} - \text{asset-swap spread} \qquad (3.34)$$

Thus, when the asset-swap spread is greater than the CDS premium, the basis is negative. On the other hand, when the CDS premium is wider than the asset-swap spread, the basis is positive. "Negative-basis" trades allow a bondholder to purchase a bond and CDS protection against it with positive carry. For a long-term holder, despite the fact that CDS settlement might not compensate for default losses completely, this can provide for a structural source of return. In the crisis of 2007–2008, the basis for most corporate bonds went substantially negative, that is, on the face of it, an investor could buy a bond, buy protection against default, and still take out extra "free" carry return. It behooves us to understand the reasons why these types of situations can occur.

What can drive the basis more negative? The CDS basis can turn more negative if either the asset-swap spread widens or the CDS premium narrows. In 2007 and 2008, the liquidity crisis caused many bonds to be sold at cheap prices (both because liquidity did so by selling existing bond positions and because the lack of liquidity made purchasing cash bonds difficult). In other episodes, the issuance of large synthetic transactions, especially collateralized debt obligations (CDOs) that package default spreads as synthetic baskets of credit-sensitive products, would put pressure on spreads and tighten the basis. When combined with the fact that credit default swaps have built-in leverage owing to their self-funding nature, they also put pressure on tightening basis in periods of increased participation by levered participants.

What can drive the basis more positive? Some bonds have good funding or repo characteristics. For these bonds, the repo optionality can drive the asset-swap spreads tighter and hence the basis wider. There is also a delivery option in the CDS that gives the protection buyer the option of delivering any qualifying security in return for full-par repayment under physical settlement (much of this has changed with new cash settlement protocols). However, since there is a limited supply of the cheapest-to-deliver obligations, there is frequently a demand-driven upward pressure on deliverable bonds and a tightening pressure on spreads, which can drive the basis wider.

Other features such as the definition of restructuring and default, coupon step-ups, and so on also can create systematic biases on the CDS basis, but their impact is usually not stable.

Since a seller of protection is expossed to the par amount following a credit event, a seller usually will demand a higher spread than the bond if the bond is trading at a discount (as compensation), causing discount basis to be wider. For premium bonds, this same dynamic drives the basis tighter.

Before the crisis of 2007 and 2008, the common investment lore held that negative basis beyond 20 or 30 basis points was as wide as the negative basis could get before arbitrage forces would drive it back in. This assumption of arbitrage assumes that a cash-bond buyer can either raise liquidity or buy the bond and fund it in the repo market to take advantage of it. However, the crisis essentially shut down the repo markets and enabled investors with excess liquidity to exploit the structural advantage of the illiquidity. Of course, since excess return comes from shorting an option, here the shorting of the liquidity option proved very painful for those who entered the negative-basis trades too early.

Currently an interesting area of investigation is the basis for sovereign debt, which is made possible owing to the existence of sovereign debt and credit default swaps on the sovereign debt.

Mean Reversion: Structural Value of Direct Option Sales

A very simple way to seek to generate excess returns in a portfolio is simply to sell options. We should hasten to add that this strategy is also extremely risky if applied indiscriminately. Since a short option position can cause unlimited losses, and the gains are limited to the premium, the option-selling strategy logically should be expected to outperform when markets are mean reverting and to underperform when markets trend. In the chapter on stress testing we will also see that the structural compensation for option selling has its roots in the possibility that the underlying can "jump," or have a discontinuous price movement.

The first question to answer is whether the process followed by the underlying instruments is mean reverting or trending and, if mean reverting, with what horizon? Let us discuss the estimation of a mean-reverting process using low-frequency empirical data first. In a later chapter we will also use some new techniques for measuring jump risk.

Suppose that the price of the underlying instrument is P. Then, in terms of logs, $x = \ln(P)$, and we can write a simple mean-reverting process as

$$dx = \theta(\mu - x) + \sigma dz \qquad (3.35)$$

The expectation of this at some time t is

$$E[x(t)] = \mu + [x(0) - \mu]e^{-\theta t} \qquad (3.36)$$

or written in another form

$$E[x(t)] = x(0)e^{-\theta t} + \mu(1 - e^{-\theta t}) \qquad (3.37)$$

which shows that the expectation is an exponential weighted average of the current value and the long-term value μ.

The variance of this process is

$$\mathrm{Var}[x(t)] = \frac{(1 - e^{-2\theta t})\sigma^2}{2\theta} \qquad (3.38)$$

so that as t gets large, the variance converges to a constant $\sigma^2/2\theta$.

To estimate the process, we can discretize it:

$$x_t - x_{t-1} = \mu(1 - e^{-\theta\Delta t}) + (e^{-\theta\Delta t} - 1)x_{t-1} + \epsilon_t \quad (3.39)$$

where ϵ is normally distributed with mean 0 and variance $\sigma_\epsilon^2 = [(1 - e^{-2\theta})\sigma^2]/2\theta$. Now we can run the regression of the changes on the previous levels:

$$x_t - x_{t-1} = a + bx_{t-1} + \epsilon_t \quad (3.40)$$

with the parameter estimates

$$\mu = -a/b$$
$$\theta = -\ln(1 + b)$$
$$\sigma = \sigma_\epsilon\sqrt{\frac{2\ln(1 + b)}{(1 + b)^2 - 1}} \quad (3.41)$$

Running the regressions for the 10-year futures contracts from 1990 shows that with a regression $R^2 = 0.002$,

$$a = 0.0091(0.399)$$
$$b = 0.000045(0.169) \quad (3.42)$$

In general volatility is highly correlated with the slope of the yield curve. Intuitively this makes sense. As volatility rises, there is more perceived risk, and hence yield-curve extension requires more risk-premium compensation. Thus a steeper yield curve typically is associated with higher option volatilities. This is consistent also with our approach to excess yield in terms of option premia of shorting the option to rebalance. The job of a relative-value trader who trades both direct volatility using options and volatility indirectly using yield-curve trades is to optimally mix these volatility trades.

Structural Value in Municipal Bonds

Municipal bonds in the United States come both in tax-exempt and taxable forms. The recent spate of Build America Bonds (BABs) has brought munis into the same field as corporate bonds. A relative-value investor choosing between taxable municipal bonds and taxable corporate bonds primarily makes a credit choice.

But the more interesting area is the tax-exempt municipal bond market. Naively, if the tax rate is τ, then a municipal bond should have a yield that is $1 - \tau$ of the equivalent taxable bond of the same maturity, coupon, credit risk, and callability. These close matchers are hard to find, but without much computation, we can see that long-term munis frequently trade at a yield that is much higher than the equivalent Treasury (see Figure 3.7 for the naive ratio of muni yields

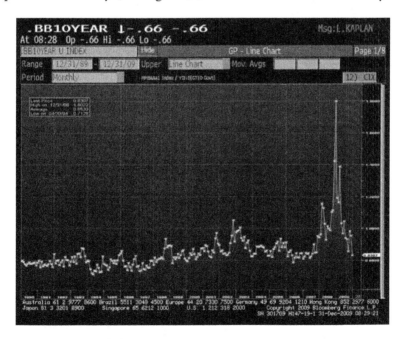

Figure 3.7 Ratio of 10-year municipal bond index yield to the on-the-run 10-year Treasury.

to Treasuries, which should be close to 1 minus the tax rate if munis are exactly similar to Treasuries). Even after adjusting for credit quality, coupon, callability, and so on, we find that there is left over extra return to munis, which structurally makes them more attractive than Treasuries for a long-term buy-and-hold investor. This excess spread can be due to the relative illiquidity of the muni market (there are a large number of CUSIPS that never trade, and despite recent efforts, price transparency is low), default risk (the recent crisis has exposed the precarious fiscal position of many municipalities, including some of the largest states in the union), tax effects (there is a real threat that taxes can be volatile, and holders require compensation for the tax risk), or embedded structural features (such as the market-discount rule that can result in grave tax consequences for certain bonds; see [3].) In the last work, we show that implicit tax rates priced in the cross section of municipal bonds are approximately two to three times as high as statutory income tax rates, with implicit tax rates close to 100 percent using retail trades and above 70 percent for interdealer trades. These implied tax rates can be identified on the cross section of municipal bonds because a portion of secondary-market municipal bond trades involve income taxes. After valuing the tax payments, market-discount bonds, which carry income tax liabilities, trade at yields around 25 basis points higher than comparable municipal bonds not subject to any taxes. The high sensitivities of municipal bond prices to tax rates can be traced to individual retail traders dominating dealers and other institutions.

Another type of inefficiency in the muni market arises from the so-called prerefunding option that the issuer of a muni bond is long. This is an additional option that is on top of the embedded call option in most long-term munis. An issuer can choose (depending on the particular state, the rules can vary) to refund a bond with a new tax-exempt issue. The older bonds are escrowed to their call date, with the cash flows defeased using Treasuries or other "risk-free" assets as backing of identical maturity. When the call date comes around, the issuer simply pays off the old (refunded) muni bond. Since we can think of the prerefunding option as an option, its exercise is efficient if all the option value is captured. For an investor, the prerefunding of a bond can result in substantial capital gains because the Treasury collateral results in an improvement in the quality of the bond and a price appreciation.

Segmentation effects can impact the pricing of the municipal yield curve. In the short end of the muni curve, money-market funds dominate and keep muni yields close to the value dictated by adjusting taxable rates down. On the other hand, the longer maturities are dominated by arbitrageurs who are betting that the implied forward tax rates will not be realized. If muni yields are close to taxable yields, the effective tax rate is zero. In other words, taxes have to be less than the implied tax rate in reality for the municipal versus Treasury trade to lose. Of course, this assumes that municipals do not have any jump to default risk, and current debacles in many states such as California have called this assumption into question.

Volatility and Currency Carry Trades

Traditional fixed income books do not include currency investing and valuation. To this author, this seems strange, since the interest-rate and currency markets are the two key macro markets that have their dynamics based on similar factors such as inflation, monetary policy, trade, and growth. It is no wonder that there are deep structural relationships between these markets.

In this section we discuss the effect of carry on volatility of the currency markets. Just as rate volatility and term premium are related, that is, steeper yield curves signify higher risk from interest-rate volatility, we can make some connections between currency carry differentials and foreign exchange volatility [51].

In the currency carry trade, an investor borrows in a low-yielding currency and invests in a high-yielding currency. Empirically, it is observed that carry trades do well when currency volatility is low. This makes intuitive sense. To realize the carry in a carry trade, investors are required to hold the position for a while. If the foreign rate is r_f and the domestic rate is r, then the return to the carry trade is proportional, to leading order, to $(r - r_f)T$, where T is the holding period. The risk to the carry trade is an adverse price movement in the level of the exchange rate. We can mitigate this risk by hedging in the currency options markets. If the spot foreign exchange market and the options market price risk differently, then one could have potential arbitrage opportunities.

To illustrate this, consider the following strategy: Suppose that we invest in the higher-yielding currency and hedge the exposure by purchasing an at-the-money forward (ATMF) put on the higher-yielding currency [51]. Then, since the delta of the out-of-the-money option is approximately $1/2$, at inception, we would be immune to the movements of the exchange rate. If we adjust the notionals correctly, then by put-call parity, this portfolio is the same as an outright ATMF call on the higher-yielding currency.

To leading order, we can easily work out the dependence of an at-the-money forward call option to implied volatility in the Black-Scholes framework. The forward foreign exchange rate F_0 can be written in terms of the domestic interest rate r and the foreign interest rate r_f as

$$F_0 = S_0 e^{(r-r_f)T} \tag{3.43}$$

where S_0 is the spot exchange rate, and T is the maturity of the option. Then the Black-Scholes option prices for the calls and puts are simply

$$c = e^{-rT}[F_0 N(d_1) - KN(d_2)] \tag{3.44}$$
$$p = e^{-rT}[KN(-d_2) - F_0 N(-d_1)] \tag{3.45}$$

where

$$d_1 = \frac{\ln(F_0/K) + \frac{1}{2}\sigma^2}{\sigma\sqrt{T}} \tag{3.46}$$

$$d_2 = d_1 - \sigma\sqrt{T} \tag{3.47}$$

Here, $N(x)$ represents the standardized cumulative normal distribution evaluated at x, and K is the strike of the option.

For at-the-money forward options, $F_0 = K$, so $d_1 = \frac{1}{2}\sigma\sqrt{T} = -d_2$, and the call option price simplifies to

$$e^{-rT} F_0 \left[N\left(\frac{1}{2}\sigma\sqrt{T}\right) - N\left(-\frac{1}{2}\sigma\sqrt{T}\right) \right] \tag{3.48}$$

But since $N(x) = 1 - N(-x)$, we can write this as

$$c = e^{-rT} F_0 \left[2N\left(\frac{1}{2}\sigma\sqrt{T}\right) - 1 \right] \tag{3.49}$$

We can expand this about σ to obtain, to leading order,

$$e^{-rT} F_0 \sigma \sqrt{\frac{T}{2\pi}} \tag{3.50}$$

which, in terms of percent premium (percent of forward), is simply

$$e^{-rT} \sigma \sqrt{\frac{T}{2\pi}} \tag{3.51}$$

Putting the carry relationship together with the leading behavior of an ATMF call option, we conclude that in equilibrium, a carry trade hedged with options would obey, to leading order,

$$(r - r_f)T \approx \sigma\sqrt{T} \tag{3.52}$$

or, in other words,

$$\sigma \approx (r - r_f)\sqrt{T} \qquad (3.53)$$

Suppose that the actual level of volatility in the market is expected to be lower; that is, $\sigma^* < \sigma$. Then the fair carry is not $(r - r_f)\sqrt{T}$ but a quantity $(r^* - r_f^*)\sqrt{T}$. If $\sigma^* < \sigma$, then $(r^* - r_f^*) < (r - r_f)$. In the extreme case, where $r_f \ll r$, $r_f^* \ll r$ (e.g., when carry trades use the yen as the funding currency), this implies that $r^* \ll r$, and the carry trade will drive investors to hold bond instruments in the domestic currency by financing them in the lower-yielding currency as a *direct bet on lower volatility*. In other words, the carry-volatility equilibrium dictates the availability of profits to investors who are willing to take interest-rate risk as foreign exchange volatility falls. Similarly, if we expect volatility to rise, investors will shed bonds in the higher-yielding currency. We will see that the simple math shown above is borne out by actual data, especially for EM currencies such as the Mexican peso and the Brazilian real (see Figures 3.8 and 3.9).

To further explore implementable strategies and their attractiveness, we will define a simple quantity to measure the relative mispricing of foreign exchange options that we will call the *true option cost*. The true option cost O as a percent of the full premium is

$$O = \frac{P - \Delta C}{P} \qquad (3.54)$$

where P is the option premium, Δ is the delta of the option (approximately 0.48 for at-the-money-forward), and C is the carry. Intuitively, what this equation says is that the true cost of purchasing an ATMF call option on a higher-yielding curency should be computed by adjusting the premium for the carry. The reason to multiply by the delta of the option is to equalize the starting notional exposure of the option posi-tion (on approximately twice the full notional) to the carry (on the full

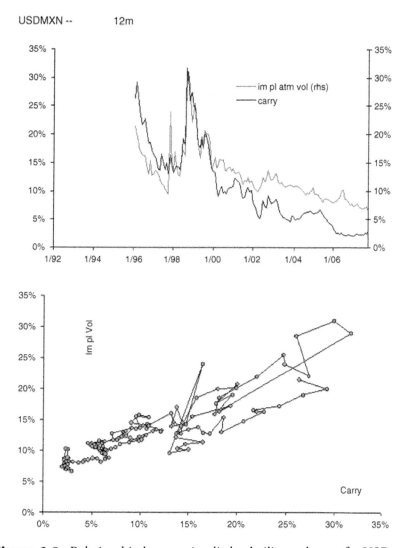

Figure 3.8 Relationship between implied volatility and carry for USD versus MXN. (*Source:* Citibank)

notional). Using the result from Eq. 3.53 we obtain

$$O \approx \left[1 - \frac{(r - r_f)\sqrt{\frac{1}{2}\pi T}}{\sigma} \right] \qquad (3.55)$$

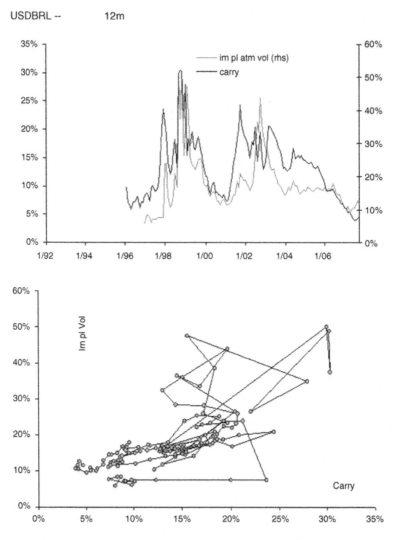

Figure 3.9 Relationship between implied volatility and carry for USD versus BRL. (*Source:* Citibank)

This simple equation illustrates the influence of volatility on the carry trade in a clear way—as the interest-rate differential widens or volatity embedded in options falls, the true fraction of option cost falls. For options of a fixed maturity, the carry per unit of volatility

$[(r - r_f)/\sigma]$ determines the relative attractiveness of entering into the carry trade. When this ratio is large, the carry trade is attractive (true option cost is low), and when this ratio is small, the carry trade is unattractive (true option cost is high).

We collected data for a number of major developed-market currencies that have been the main beneficiaries of the carry trade.[2] Typically, the JPY (Japanese yen) and the CHF (Swiss franc) have been used as funding currencies, and the AUD (Australian dollar), NZD (New Zealand dollar), and USD (U.S. dollar) have been the higher-yielding carry currencies. More recently, the improving fundamentals of the Mexican peso (MXN) and the Brazilian real (BRL) have enabled them to enter the toolkit of carry traders.

Figures 3.8 and 3.9 show that indeed for the MXN and the BRL there is a clear positive link between volatility levels and the carry relative to the USD. The relationship is somewhat weaker for the GBP versus the Swiss franc (see Figure 3.11, AUD versus the USD) and yen (Figures 3.12 and 3.14), NZD versus USD (Figure 3.13) and the weakest for the USD versus the yen (see Figure 3.10). A couple of other observations are in order.

The fact that most pairs other than the JPY show a relationship between carry and volume seems to point to an anomaly that is driven by the special relationship between the USD and the JYP. The United States historically has been a large debtor of Japan, who now, along with the Chinese, are the largest creditors of the world. To a large degree, anecdotal evidence suggests that the recycling of surplus by the Japanese and Chinese creates an effective peg of the JPY and the Renmimbi to the USD (for the RMB, the peg is actual), muting the exchange-rate volatility of these two countries versus the USD. Thus we see that even

---

[2]Data were provided by Citibank from January 1992 to October 2007.

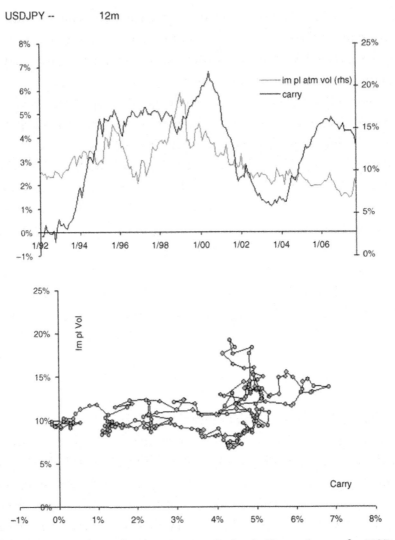

Figure 3.10 Relationship between implied volatility and carry for USD versus JPY. (*Source:* Citibank)

though carry of the USD versus the JPY has varied a fair bit (from 6 percent high in 2000 to 1 percent low in 2004), the level of implied volatility has remained on a downward trend. We also find a weak relationship of volatility with carry for the CAD (Canadian dollar)

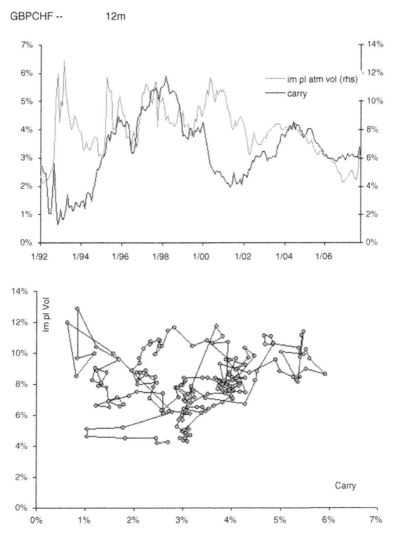

Figure 3.11 Relationship between implied volatility and carry for GBP versus CHF. (*Source:* Citibank)

versus the USD (see Figure 3.15). However, given the tight linkage via trade between the USD and the CAD, the CAD is typically not used as a carry-trade vehicle (in particular, note that the the interest-rate differential for this pair has fluctuated tightly around 0).

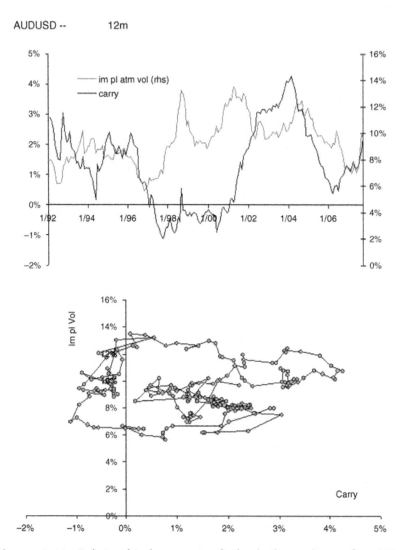

Figure 3.12 Relationship between implied volatility and carry for AUD versus USD. (*Source:* Citibank)

When we apply Eq. (3.54) to these pairs, we find that for different pairs the carry reduces the total premium cost of the options from the beneficial effects of the carry. If, as numerous studies have established, it is true that the foreign exchange forwards market biases the direction

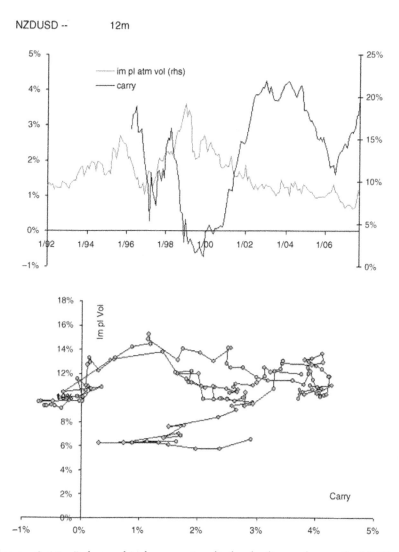

Figure 3.13 Relationship between implied volatility and carry for NZD versus USD. (*Source:* Citibank)

of the spot exchange rate, then a carry trade implemented through options when volatilies are low should have a better risk-reward profile than a carry trade done outright. We explore this in the next section. August and September of 2007 witnessed sharp increases in true options

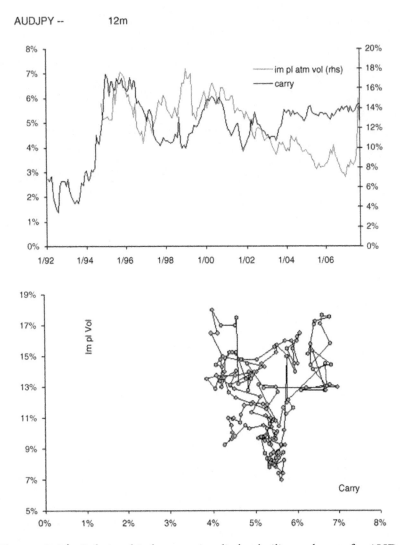

Figure 3.14 Relationship between implied volatility and carry for AUD versus JPY. (*Source:* Citibank)

costs primarily because of a rise in currency volatility accompanying the crisis.

We now discuss results of a simple backtesting of a carry strategy that uses information from both the options markets and the

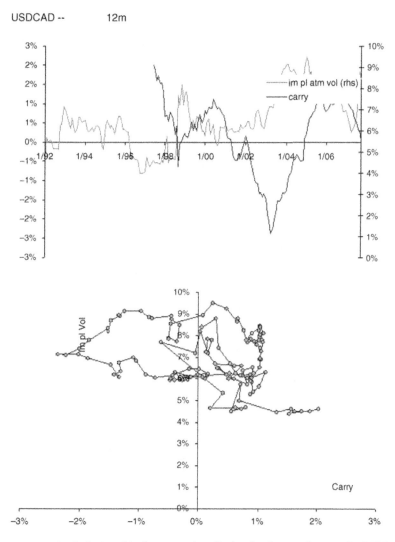

Figure 3.15 Relationship between implied volatility and carry for USD versus CAD. (*Source:* Citibank)

interest-rate differentials between currencies. The basic idea is to purchase at-the-money forward calls on a higher-yielding currency and hold them to maturity. If there is indeed a forward exchange-rate bias in the market, then simple carry strategies should result in positive returns—implementing the strategy through options, when volatility is low, would further improve the risk profile of the strategy. Another way of thinking of this is that when we typically think of option purchases, we think of the daily time decay as the cost of truncating the possibility of negative outcomes. However, if we note that as time passes the forward will "rollup" toward the current spot level, we can reduce the cost of the option by the embedded carry because the ATMF option is going into-the-money as time passes.

The strategy we explore invests in the higher-yielding currency via 1-year at-the-money forward options and rolls them every month (the results are largely similar for both shorter-dated and longer-dated options). We include transactions costs explicitly by taking the average transactions costs over the previous year. Additionally, we refined the strategies by putting optional "filters" on both volatility and carry; that is, we only enter the trade if the carry is higher than a threshold and/or if volatility is lower than a threshold.

Figures 3.16 through 3.21 show the statistics of these strategies for a variety of pairs from many different perspectives. In each of these charts, the first table on the top left shows the returns per month binned by the returns. The histogram immediately to the right and the statistics below the table show the positive skew of the option-based implementation, along with Sharpe ratios and annualized expected returns. We also display at the bottom left the carry and volatility filters (if any) used in the backtest. The charts below the histogram show the monthly performance time series of the strategy. The three charts on the right show the option-based carry strategy return versus spot levels for the pair, returns versus the carry for the pair, and returns versus the implied volatility for the pair. The AUD/JPY and NZD/JPY pairs, over the period observed (NZD/JPY data are available only from 2002), show the highest information ratio presumably because the carry over this period has been high (NZD in particular has had very high

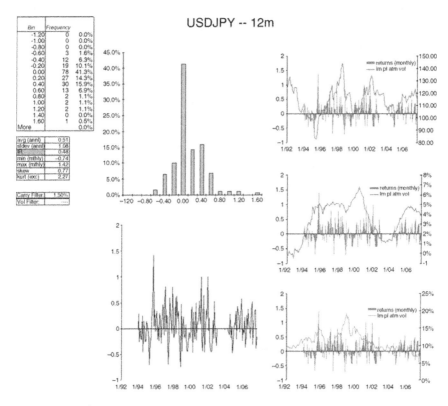

Figure 3.16 Statistics of USD/JPY carry trade with options. In this example, the carry trade is entered only if the carry exceeds 150 basis points at all implied volatility levels. (*Source:* Citibank)

short-term rates owing to the explicit inflation-targeting nature of its central bank). No wonder that as recent episodes of credit-driven risk unwind, the AUD and NZD have been the first to sell off relative to the JPY and USD.

Indeed, there is evidence that when option volatilities become cheap, levered hedge funds implement carry trades through options. Just the presence of cheap options might drive the carry trade to be a good

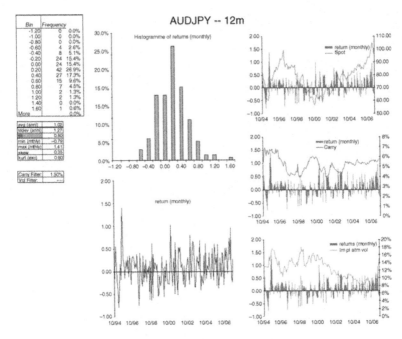

Figure 3.17 Statistics of AUD/JPY carry trade with options.
(*Source:* Citibank)

risk-reward opportunity in most states of the world, and when done through options, it creates artificial directional biases owing to the residual delta. Another possibility is the action of funds that follow dynamic option replication strategies—if, instead of purchasing options, a large number of participants set their strategy-scaling rules based on the combined inputs of carry and implied volatility, the effective deltas would affect the direction of the market.

Interaction of Foreign Exchange and Rates Markets

One of the consequences of low yields in the Japanese fixed income markets was the issuance of a particular type of exotic security whose

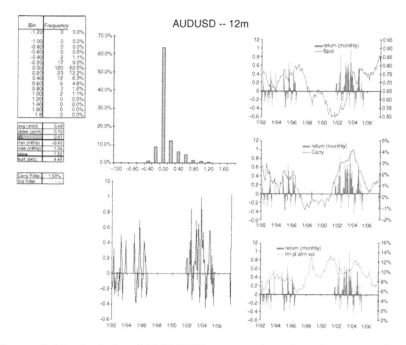

Figure 3.18 Statistics of AUD/USD carry trade with options. Note the period in the middle in the chart at the bottom where the carry filter of 1.5 percent kept investors out of the carry trade. (*Source:* Citibank)

coupon is linked to the exchange rate. A typical payoff would be:

$$\text{Max}\left(a \times \frac{X}{X_0} - b, 0\right) \tag{3.56}$$

where X is the future exchange rate and X_0 is a reference exchange rate. For instance, a typical note has $a = 0.15$, $b = 0.10$. Plugging in these numbers, when $X = X_0$, then the coupon payoff is 5 percent.

These bonds typically are long-maturity and callable. Since the investor is effectively long a call option on the exchange rate as well as short the call option on the exchange rate (the note can be called by the issuer if the value rises), his or her posture is effectively that of long a call spread. To hedge the call risk, a dealer will engage in delta hedging

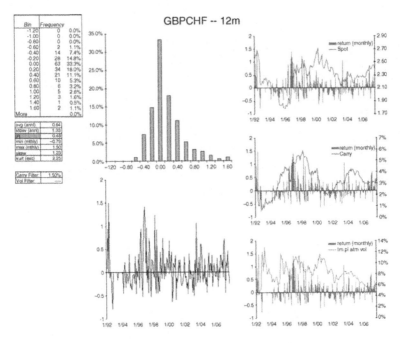

Figure 3.19 Statistics of GBP/CHF carry trade with options.

(*Source:* Citibank)

the long-dated string of options using forwards. We have seen that the forward is nothing but a long position in the spot currency and long a U.S. zero-coupon bond and short a yen zero-coupon bond, so the initial hedge is to buy the currency and receive in U.S. rates and pay fixed in yen rates. On the other hand, as the dollar appreciates (yen weakens), the probability of the note being called increases, so the dealer can reduce his or her hedges. He or she does this by selling the dollar (buying yen) and paying fixed in dollar swap rates and receiving in yen rates. As the yen rallies, the dealer has to do exactly the opposite beyond a certain point. This results in receiving U.S. rates and paying in yen rates.

When we look at a chart of the yen versus long-term U.S. rates, we see a pretty substantial correlation that seems to be driven by this dynamic since 2003, when many of these notes first became popular. Prior to 2003, the correlation was close to 0.

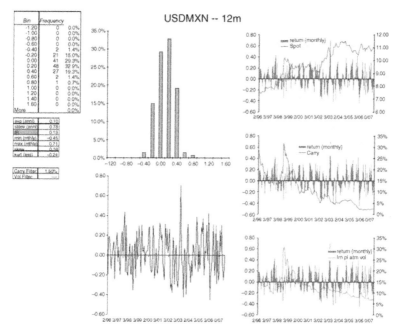

Figure 3.20 Statistics of USD/MXN carry trade with options.
(*Source:* Citibank)

Figure 3.22 shows the correlations for those two periods between the yen exchange rate and the long-term U.S. swap spread. Again, many dynamics were in play, but its quite clear that the receiving of swaps for rallying yen and paying of swaps for weakening yen has been responsible for the positive dependence of swap spreads on the level of the yen.

Caveat Emptor

The dangers of investing in assets that purportedly benefit from excess risk premia are that frequently fat tail events happen and expose the crowded nature of such strategies. This becomes even more portfolio threatening when combined with large amounts of leverage.

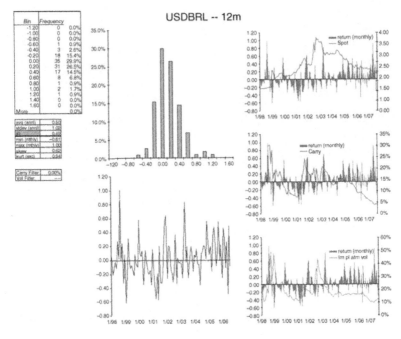

Figure 3.21 Statistics of USD/BRL carry trade with options.

(*Source:* Citibank)

The year 1998 was a watershed for fixed income arbitrage. Prior to 1998, there was a general belief that many security-specific "arbitrage" relationships were (1) immune to systematic risk factors and (2) mean reverting. The profits of legendary fixed income shops such as Salomon Brothers[3] were imitated and replicated by its founders and alumni on a massive scale. As the amount of capital deployed to take advantage of similar strategies increased ("picking nickels in front of a steamroller"), the opportunity set dwindled. To achieve high returns (which in those days meant somewhere around 20 percent and higher), arbitrage strategy sets had to extend in two directions. The first direction was an increase in leverage to magnify the already meager returns—leveraged

---

[3]The author was a member of the Salomon arbitrage desk in its last few years of existence.

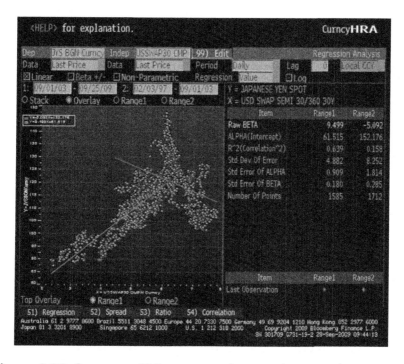

Figure 3.22 Long-term U.S. swap spreads versus the yen exchange rate. This figure shows how the dynamics of the dual currency notes have resulted in swap spreads moving with the exchange rate. (*Source:* Bloomberg)

to a degree where the size of statistically normal fluctuations in the trade easily could overwhelm the capital of any or all of the arbitrageurs. The second direction was to supplement the arbitrage strategies with "pure carry" strategies, such as emerging-market bonds, as well as closet directional strategies. Since investor portfolios are composed of different strategies (which might be uncorrelated in normal circumstances) that in sum contribute to the total capital of the portfolio, a large move in one strategy can affect other ex ante uncorrelated strategies owing to overall capital limitations. As leverage in the system increases, one generally should expect correlations of otherwise uncorrelated strategies to increase. It took the markets a decade to outlive the generation that paid for excessive leverage in 1998. However, increasing competition, increasing leverage, spread compression, and increasing correlation of what otherwise would be uncorrelated strategies show that the crisis of 2007–2008 was almost inevitable.

Fixed income arbitrage is based on the assumption that market forces of demand and supply produce relative mispricing between closely related securities that lead to exploitable risk premia. Since the risk premia themselves are time varying, a manager who believes that the risk premia mean revert will bet on the risk premia narrowing when they are too wide and widening when they are too narrow.

To illustrate this with some technical detail, suppose that we have a general affine model of the term structure with n factors $X(t)$ with dynamics (this class of models is used very commonly as the baseline for many term-structure arbitrage strategies):

$$dX(t) = \kappa[\theta - X(t)]dt + \Sigma\sqrt{S(t)}dW(t) \qquad (3.57)$$

where $W(t)$ is an N-dimensional vector of independent brownian motions, $S(t)$ is the volatility matrix for the factors, and there is a state-dependent risk premium vector:

$$\Lambda(t) = \sqrt{S(t)}\lambda^0 + \sqrt{S_X(t)}\lambda^X X(t) \qquad (3.58)$$

Then the instantaneous excess return on a τ-period zero-coupon bond is (Dai and Singleton, 2003)

$$\mu^e(t, \tau) = -B(\tau)\Sigma\sqrt{S(t)}\Lambda(t) \qquad (3.59)$$

with $B(t)$ equal to the factor loading or duration of the bond with respect to the factor. It is clear to see that if $\Lambda(t)$ is changed in form, the expected excess return can change drastically.

To capture the time-varying risk premia, arbitrage hedge funds first calibrate the market to estimate the value of the factors X_t. Once the market price of risk of each factor is estimated, appropriate factor loadings (durations) to these risk factors are implemented to capture the risk premia. If certain factor risk premia are far away from the norm owing to fundamental or technical reasons and are expected to mean revert, the hedge fund will allocate a larger portion of its capital to that factor risk premium.

Most fixed income arbitrage strategies assume that the factors X_t that drive the risk premia themselves are joint gaussian. A dominant reason for this simplistic assumption is the fact that assuming X_t to be gaussian leads to exact solutions of a large class of term-structure models. However, most arbitrageurs agree that the empirically observed factors are indeed nonnormal. In particular, if liquidity is identified as a factor commanding excess risk premia, it is easy to see why a large leveraged bet on the liquidity factor could be dangerous—liquidity "holes" appear without warning, and the liquidity factor has notoriously asymmetric fat tails.

We can think of betting on the mean reversion of factors as a short option position. Many hedge funds choose to mix long option positions in factors that they expect not to mean revert over their investment horizon, with short option positions on factors that are expected to mean revert. Buying options on liquidity is very expensive because the payoffs are notoriously short-lived. Most hedge funds are expected to have a constant stream of return. Fixed income hedge funds are expected to deliver a "coupon" every month or every quarter. Since the demand of the investor forces the manager to select strategies that generate sutainable, replicable payoffs, the manager typically chooses to be short the liquidity factor (i.e., earns premium).

The sharp meltdown in the financial markets recently has emphasized that risk management not only requires managing one's own positions in the market but also those of others who are following broadly similar strategies. Levered "crowded" trades can unwind suddenly and create a domino effect. There are a few sure signs that a particular strategy is crowded. If two securities or sectors that normally are uncorrelated suddenly begin to show increased day-to-day correlation, along with large occasional outlier moves, the strategy is probably common market knowledge with particpants at all time scales. The small-scale movements are dominated by the short-term traders who keep the markets aligned on short time horizons (effectively decreasing the opportunity set of longer-horizon investors who wait for bigger mispricings). Whenever there is information that contradicts the rationale for the comovements of spreads, traders at different time horizons can agree to not partipate in forcing short-term deviations from the mean back to the mean. This leads to larger spread movements and provides opportunities for investors who are not already completely committed to the strategy (i.e., those who have "dry powder"). Short liquidity is not the same as being short volatility, but when tail events happen (i.e., jumps), illiquidity magnifies the tails.

There is considerable evidence that many hedge fund strategies employ mean-reverting or option-sales strategies.[4] A strategy that sells out-of-the-money options will keep most of the premium from option sales if the underlying shows a higher tendency to revert to the mean than what is priced into the options. Similarly, a mean-reverting strategy will benefit if assets are purchased when the asset price falls below some mean (such as a moving average) and sold when they rise above the moving average. The difference in the asset price from the moving average is analogous to the out-of-the-money-ness of the short strangle

---

[4]With the notable exception of managed futures managers and a few macro funds. However, since managed futures managers are a small fraction of the universe of hedge fund managers, it is a safe generalization to say that a randomly selected hedge fund is more likly than not to be using sales of liquidity, volatility, or what is effectively the same, following a mean-reverting strategy.

position.[5] A "buy losers, sell winners" strategy also can be shown to be quite similar to the mean-reversion strategy [7]. Whether it is an option-strangle strategy, a mean-reverting strategy, or a reversal strategy in general, conceptually, there is a region of asset price movements within which the strategy makes consistent profits and beyond which the strategy loses big. In other words, the expected value of the positive returns where the strategy spends most of its time compensates for the expected value of losses when the strategy "falls off a cliff." Though the probability of falling off the cliff is small, the consequences are high. Increased competition, leverage, and mark-to-market eventually conspire to increase the expected value of these losses.

Every successful strategy invites imitators. As a mean-reversion strategy shows positive expected return, imitators will enter the area. In a recent paper, Khandani and Lo [21] demonstrate that the daily returns of a simple equity market mean-reverting strategy has fallen continuously over the years, so to "manufacture" the same nominal alpha, investors will lever the strategy into high single or, for the really aggressive hedge funds, into mid-double digits. Creative financial engineering techniques also enable a transport of alpha from one asset class into another asset class, leading to empirically observed increases in the correlation of return profiles of both fundamental assets and hedge fund strategies.

The result of increased leverage and increased correlation of strategies with mark-to-market and risk-management discipline can be devastating. Even though the tails being sold by strangle sellers and mean-reversion players remain far away, increased leverage, when combined with mark-to-market, will force some players to hedge or liquidate

---

[5]Many systematic CTA (Commodity Trading Advisor) or managed futures strategies are the converse of this—they buy when asset prices or faster-moving averages cross above slower-moving averages and sell when the reverse occurs. This is consistent with their long-volatility bias.

their positions either by outright sales of their longs and repurchases of their shorts or by purchase of options or other forms of "insurance." Regardless of the way risk reduction is achieved, their activity is both destabilizing and contrary to the model under which they are expected to operate (sell as prices deviate above average and buy as prices fall below average). The increase in leverage essentially increases the vulnerability of the strategy to noise.

Here is a simple heuristic argument. A deeply out-of-the-money strangle selling strategy sells calls struck at some level $K_c \gg F_0$, where F_0 is the current price of the forward contract, and out-of-the-money puts struck at $K_P \ll F_0$. Both deeply out-of-the-money calls and puts are highly sensitive to implied volatility. For instance, assume a stock with current price of 100 and strike of 100 (at-the-money). The premium on a 1-year option priced with 20 percent volatility is 0.5 percent. If volatility doubles, this premium jumps to nine times (4.5 percent). For the same doubling of volatility, the premium of a 20 percent out-of-the-money option goes up approximately 50 times, and a 50 percent out-of-the-money option goes up 500 times! The conclusion is striking—selling tail risk is extremely vulnerable to volatility spikes and errors in estimates, and when combined with forced unwinds from levered investors acting in their best interests to control their risk, this strategy is a recipe for crisis. Note the recent experience from the structured credit markets—the trade du jour coming into 2007 was to sell default remote supersenior tranches in levered form. As credit markets started to widen, the spreads of these supersenior tranches went up by a factor of 10 or more (the theoretical delta at inception of many of these trades was 0.10, whereas the realized delta was close to 0.5).

The failure of idealized models under tail events suggests that an astute investor would be better served by looking beyond credit models, numbers, and Greeks—particularly at the positioning and embedded leverage of market participants. The probability of implosion that a levered mark-to-market community of investors, all following the same mean-reverting strategies can engender, is typically many magnitudes higher than one would naively expect.

We are also subject to the pseudoproofs that arise from the "cult of the last 20 years of data." Most analysts search for investment ideas that can be validated by some history (which, unfortunately, is available only for the last 20 or so years for most instruments). The life cycle of ideas typically follows this logic:

1. Make a hypothesis.
2. Make a simple quantitative model.
3. Do literature research.
4. Backtest on data.

The backtesting part can easily bias the analytic quality of the results. Since most data have been kept (and is easily accessible) only for the last 20 years, the models are backtested on this set. Unfortunately, this period was dominated by one central banker at the Fed and was accompanied by a secular fall in yields and risk premia as inflation trended down. Any results that are tested on these data will inherit this macroeconomic regime and its inherent bias.

The discussion so far sets the stage for a discussion of the relevance of macro analysis for investment decision making, model building, and risk management.

4

Macro Considerations

"Everything should be made as simple as possible, but not simpler."
—Albert Einstein

"Making the simple complicated is commonplace; making the complicated simple, awesomely simple, that's creativity."
—Charles Mingus

"The aspects of things that are most important to us are hidden because of their simplicity and familiarity."
—Ludwig Wittgenstein

Investing in the bond market is complex. There are a lot of variables, and there are an enormous number of types of securities. A cursory look at the municipal bond market, for example, will show literally hundreds of thousands of individual bonds. Fortunately, the complexity can be simplified by understanding the common risk factors that drive the prices of these bonds. Of course, the idiosyncrasies of each individual security results in relative value and perhaps relative risk, but at the zeroth level, it's the major economic factors that drive returns rather than the idiosyncrasies.

For the holder of a bond the biggest threat is a rapid rise in yields. We have already learned from the Preface that this interest-rate–duration sensitivity can be estimated. When we look deeper, the roots of this sensitivity lie in inflation, both realized and expected. While the performance of many other assets can vary with inflation in often unpredictable ways, the performance of Treasury bonds is persistently negatively correlated with changes in the rate of inflation (see, for example, [8]). Since inflation and deflation are recurrent macrophenomena, the change in inflation rates and their expectation can impact long-term returns of bonds over many years. Thus it is important to forecast inflation accurately to make better investment decisions.

Experience shows that not all relative-value strategies work equally in all macroeconomic environments. When bond yields are rising, municipal bonds and inflation-linked bonds typically outperform other bond asset classes. Corporate credit also usually outperforms in rising-yield environments, especially if the starting level of yields is not too low. Naive statistical analysis of the relative-value opportunities can be misleading if it does not properly include initial conditions. As macroeconomic and fiscal policy changes, the initial conditions and uncertainty in evolution of the environment can lead to very different outcomes.

In the recent crisis, one easily could have gotten blinded by the complexity of mortgage-market instruments and the promise of high yields and been unable to see that the essential macroeconomic risk factor driving the prices of mortgage-backed securities (MBSs) was increasing property values and lax lending standards. Stressing the underlying housing-price forecasts would have demonstrated the embedded risk of many of these securities. However, forecasts of the evolution of housing prices could not have been done purely based on history alone. There are few data on housing in a protracted decline. To forecast the possible scenarios for the housing market required looking at the macroeconomic environment, especially liquidity, flows and standards for lending and their future evolution.

We can bring the concepts from the Preface into operation by implementing the macroeconomic views. Once a macroeconomic view is formed we translate it into precise statements of how much each one of the systematic risk factors is expected to respond to various macro scenarios. Once we quantify the uncertainty and expected return of each of the risk factors over the holding horizon, we can allocate an appropriate portion of the risk budget to that risk factor.

Macroeconomics of Model Building

In this section we will focus on incorporating economic principles into investment analysis (see also [48]). Demand and supply, investor behavior, and preferences from microeconomics and monetary policy, macro aggregates, deficits, trade balances, and so on from macroeconomics can help to make our models more flexible and hence more robust. Economic incentives drive the action of market participants, investors, and even quantitative modelers. Recent work has shown that we can build better models without giving up the basic principles that form the foundations of arbitrage-free pricing. Having economics as the backdrop enables better estimates of the distribution of future outcomes than a simplistic stochastic process of an unobserved factor estimated over a period of decades. Models fail not because the math underlying them is wrong but because by blindly going to the risk-neutral framework we often misprice risk premia and hence misprice risk.

A skeptical reader may ask why all this is necessary. Doesn't risk-neutral valuation make real-world probabilities irrelevant for pricing? Recall that risk-neutral valuation argues theoretically that if you can decompose the movement of any security into continuously tradable replicating portfolios, and if you actually traded the replicating portfolios continuously, you could choose any probability measure you want. This assumption causes problems and breakdown between theory and reality. There is no instantaneity in real markets. Economics, risk aversion, and preferences creep in. Even if you could overcome the technical difficulties, the approach to model building that we have been taught might lack in key nontechnical aspects, and the difference between investors who deliver returns with a good risk profile over multiple cycles and realizations of the real world and those who don't actually might be explainable in terms of how their approach to investment explicitly incorporates the economic environment. Incorporating economics explicitly simply makes better models without throwing away any of the gains from our well-developed theoretical arbitrage-free framework.

Let us begin by discussing the main reason why quantitative models are built, whether they are reasonable, and how we can improve them by using economics. At the end of this discussion, we will show a simple toy model that incorporates economics and arbitrage-free concepts from the very beginning.

Relevance for Investment Returns and Managing Risk

There are basically four honest ways to generate returns:

1. Taking factor risk exposures (macro)
2. Intermediation (brokering)
3. Liquidity and/or risk transfer "(insurance)"
4. Mispricing (arbitraging inefficiency)

Most money-making enterprises are combinations of these modes. To make a model relevant to the particular combination of these profit-making modes, it has to be calibrated to the relevant combination of modes that is expected to yield excess returns for the investor selecting the combination. The economic environment is the backdrop within which modes for profit are evaluated and models calibrated. A good example comes from option-pricing models used on derivatives trading desks. Whether used for taking factor exposures, intermediating, warehousing, or arbitraging, the model-development process works in the following sequence:

1. Assume a distribution for the fundamental variables (for the standard LIBOR market model, forward rates are assumed lognormally distributed), and estimate the parameters using history and common sense as input.
2. Generate probable paths of evolution.
3. Fit remaining free parameters in the model to traded security prices.
4. Price other securities with the model.

The framework as laid out is consistent for relative pricing, but because it has a substantial number of underlying distributional assumptions, it might not be equipped to automatically adapt as the underlying dynamics undergo a structural shift. These shifts have to be incorporated by hand to ensure that the model is well calibrated for what the model is designed to do. A case in point is the failure of many models as Japanese nominal rates dropped to zero over the last 15 years and in the United States in the last couple years. The lognormal framework, of course, would make it impossible for rates to fall below 0 percent. But 0 percent floors indeed have been marketed and traded. A model that works well for long-term investing and is designed to warehouse risks would fail miserably if it were used for high-frequency directional trading or arbitrage, and vice versa. Dealer desks make money through the flow of business; they only need models that can be locally calibrated to today's market because tomorrow the position will be unloaded to another customer. For shorter holding periods, it does not make a big difference if the model is improperly calibrated to the big picture. We have already mentioned how many of these models got into trouble in the recent crisis because they missed the housing factor, which is notoriously hard to forecast. Hedge funds make money through taking residual risks—it does matter that the models they use are properly calibrated to possible episodes of missing liquidity. Mutual funds and insurance companies do not lever much; hence their risk-taking necessarily reflects their ability to hold illiquid positions for longer periods. Hedge funds and mutual funds seemingly operate in the same mode but differ fundamentally in their ability to obtain funds with lower haircuts and for longer commitment periods. This financing difference makes all the difference on how holding-period returns are computed. Between the time of putting a position on and taking it off, the world can change; recalibration shocks should not force an unwind of the position. Dealer desks and hedge fund operations are suited to risk-neutral and physical measures, respectively, because that's the most appropriate measure for their investment objective.

It is critical that the fundamental variables in the model reflect observables or " executables." It might be elegant to build models that can be described in terms of a small set of factors (principal components for interest-rate models), but if a portfolio manager cannot quickly translate the change in the market into simple combinations of market instruments, the models become irrelevant to practical investing.

Stability, Analytical Tractability, and the Ability to Stress Test

Exact solvability has forced many term-structure and credit modelers to restrict their attention to a subclass of models called *affine models*; with a limited set of prices of bonds and swaps as inputs, but not their options as inputs, these models typically do not replicate the underlying dynamics of the yield curve and its volatility very well. For example, the evolution of the covariance of the term structure is largely undescribable in this framework. Good models would have rates and volatilities described simultaneously because practitioners know that the shape of the yield curve also reflects premium owing to uncertainty.

Even if we could surmount the technical limitations of affine models using more sophisticated, albeit numerical, models, there are other assumptions that most analytical models make that are harder to get around. Analytically tractable models are based on assumptions of continuity, but the world is full of structural breaks. Most models lean very heavily on the notion of stability by assuming stable distributions for the dynamics. After a hundred years of stochastic calculus, this is all we really have to work with mathematically because stable distributions and processes are easy to model and solve. But markets and policies undergo rapid structural breaks. No avalanche is allowed in typical models until it happens in the reality the model is describing. Since most term-structure models are based on the principle that long rates are time averages of short rates plus risk premia, there is no way to account for the possibility of structural breaks unless it is done right from the building-block level.

To explore structural breaks further, let's discuss the basic building block for interest-rate models—the short rate. Note that the Taylor rule (widely argued to be the Fed's rate-setting rule during the Greenspan era at least) is specified as

$$i_t = (r^* - \theta_1 \pi^*) + \theta_1(\pi_t) + \theta_2(u^* - u_t) + \pi_t \qquad (4.1)$$

where i_t is the short rate, $r*$ is the equilibrium real rate, π_t is the inflation rate at time t, and u_t is the unemployment rate at time t. π^* and u^* are, respectively, the target inflation and unemployment rates, and θ_1 and θ_2 are coefficients to be estimated. Any other rate in the yield curve can be obtained by integrating the time evolution of this rate and computing the log expectation. Fed behavior in setting monetary policy has seen some major structural breaks (e.g., when transitioning from the pre-Volcker era to the Volcker-Greenspan era)[38] and perhaps more recently with Long Term Capital Management (LTCM) in 1998. If the ultimate provider of money, the central bank, changes its structural framework, it seems reasonable that asset-pricing models should be flexible enough to capture these structural shocks as well. Indeed, there was widespread discussion about the appropriate Taylor rule rate, with some analysts forecasting that the rate should be negative 5 percent. Since nominal rates cannot be that negative, the appropriate macro substitute has been "quantitative easing" of monetary policy, that is, the pumping of significant amount of excess currency into the economy.

To see the footprints in the change in the rule, let us econometrically estimate Eq. (4.1); the estimate of the constant term tells us the relationship between the equilibrium real rate and the target inflation rate.

As Table 4.1 illustrates, there is a large amount of variation in the constants as well as the weights on inflation and growth during the tenure of different Fed chairmen. In the absence of some measure of

Table 4.1 Estimation of the Relationship Between Target Real Rate and Inflation Rate for Different Fed Regimes Using Eq. (4.1).

Period	c^*	θ_1	θ_2	R^2
Burns (1970Q3–1978Q1)	−2.118 (1.835)	0.555 (0.326)	2.737 (0.483)	0.54
Volcker (1979Q3–1987Q2)	1.295 (1.120)	0.561 (0.178)	0.623 (0.280)	0.72
Greenspan (1987Q3–2005Q1)	−0.435 (0.295)	1.107 (0.110)	1.995 (0.128)	0.859
Greenspan (1987Q3–1998Q3)	1.109 (0.188)	0.540 (0.059)	1.940 (0.069)	0.96
Greenspan (1998Q4–2005Q1)	1.379 (0.546)	0.161 (0.339)	2.494 (0.093)	0.96
(1960Q1–2005Q1)	1.279 (0.372)	0.330 (0.090)	0.562 (0.136)	0.58

*The constant c is given by the relationship $c = r^* - \theta_1 \pi^*$. (Source: Author)

the possible variability of this response function, it is impossible for the model to be robust to structural shocks. If one takes the approach of modeling the yield curve directly without reference to the Taylor rule and simply fitting yields to some nonlinear function, we run the risk of running afoul of what fundamentally is the driving dynamics for the short rate. Figure 4.5 illustrates the structural break.

Let's next take a look at models for structured credit. For ease of computation, the current state of the art of credit modeling assumes a copula function to describe the joint behavior of loss; quants know the limitation of the approach, but as of today, there is no common benchmark model to improve on the gross shortcomings of the copula approach. The gaussian copula is to structured credit what the log-normal assumption is to option valuation. The base correlation skew of copula-based models is like the volume skew of options. The key simplification in the copula approach is provided by the assumption of a default correlation parameter that is an input. However, the default correlation that goes into the model is not directly observable. When Northwest and Delta entered bankrupty within minutes of each other in September 2004, we saw default correlation rise, and it was 1! No estimation devoid of ex ante input would have this as an input. When describing the reason for the simultaneous defaults, most ana-lysts would use macroeconomic variables as the cause—underfunded pensions, falling revenues, competition, increased oil prices. It seems hard to include macro inputs as complex as these into one parameter. So analysts settle for fitting traded prices to imply the value of the model parameters. We even trade tranches assuming that they can be pack-aged together in an essentially arbitrage-free way, which is just a wrong assumption unless liquid recovery products can be traded. Table 4.3 shows the actual and realized delta-adjusted return of tranches in the spring of 2005. Not only was the hedge not a hedge in magnitude, for many tranches, the sign was wrong. At the very least, if the cop-ula model for trading default correlation has any value, it should be possible to attribute portions of the default correlation to real economic factors. In other words, if the model is required to possess any depth, what is exogenous has to be made endogenous. We come back to the economics of credit correlation later in this chapter.

Perhaps the most important reason for using simple parametric models is that these models can be solved and the parameters stress-tested to obtain hedge ratios. For trading desks trained under the risk-neutral approach, the local hedge ratios, mark-to-market constraints, and running "flat" books can take a life unto itself. This approach works well when markets are liquid and price discovery is easy. However, locally risk-neutral models fail horribly when securities are illiquid or markets are under stress. The limitations of using risk-neutral pricing become all too obvious. The most perverse outcome is that the hedge ratios take on a life of their own. To hedge, underlying securities are traded. When the market hedge ratios are large enough, the act of dynamic hedging can lead to modification of the prices of the hedging securities in an amplifying feedback. When large enough in magnitude, these models actually can lead to systemic market distortions, such as the numerous mortgage debacles of the last decade and perhaps even the crash of 1987. Anecdotally, the rapid rise of quantitative credit models has coincided with numerous proprietary "capital structure arb" desks and dedicated hedge funds. With a Merton-like modeling framework applied to credit and equity, a new theoretical connection has become all too practical.

But doing away with risk neutrality is not a cure-all. Simple actual-world value-at-risk (VaR) models are notorious for failing when you need them most and for working great when you don't need them. The reasons are many. First, since most VaR models are usually based on historically estimated covariance matrices, they simply cannot see stresses unless the covariance matrix is taken to its mathematically extreme values. To systematically take covariance matrices to logical extreme values, economic priors and portfolio risks under those outcomes have to be built in right from the beginning [44]. For example, a VaR model based on history alone would almost never capture major low-probability episodes such as bull flattening, where yields and the steepness of the curve fall simultaneously. As many mortgage investors recently found out, valuation and risk models did very badly in the 2004–2005 bull-flattening episode. This is analogous to the question of category 5 hurricanes in Canada. They are theoretically possible if you allow for parameters to take values under structural shocks.[1] The risk model has to be simple enough to enable translation of envisioned outcomes into ranges of outcomes for the risk factors.

Freedom from Arbitrage

Models are approximations; in most models, demand and supply considerations are largely ignored. When we are unable to estimate the impact of clientele effects, we resort to the assumption of freedom from arbitrage to make the models work. With this approach, we have seen some major technical breakthroughs in our time. Black-Scholes for options is a good example—and it depends on some simplifying assumptions regarding the underlying distributions. The copula approach is another, increasingly used for credit-correlation products, and it also depends on some simplifying assumptions regarding the form of the copula. However, even armed with the best arbitrage-free quantitative models possible, experts can and do disagree. For example, Table 4.2 shows the option-adjusted spread (OAS) and duration numbers from a survey of the top mortgage-backed securities (MBS) dealers on Wall Street for the same security. A levered derivative structure such as an interest only (IO) would magnify these errors even further. Given the dispersion, it's not a stretch to imagine that there are routine blowups in the mortgage-derivative markets. It is often argued that you can reconstitute the collateral from the IO to principal only (PO), so

---

[1] Hurricane Hazel hit soutwestern Ontario on October 14, 1954.

Table 4.2 FNMA 5.0 precent 30-Year Passthrough Option-Adjusted Spreads and Option-Adjusted Durations as of May 5, 2003.

Dealer	Treasury OAS	LIBOR OAS	OAD (Research)	OAD (Trading Desk)
Lehman	26	3	4.8	4.6
Goldman	81	34	4.6	4.0
Greenwich Capital	36	17	4.0	4.0
CSFB	52	18	6.1	4.4
Salomon	51	16	5.2	4.4
Morgan Stanley	52	29	5.0	4.2
Bank of America	64	25	4.2	4.5
UBS	44	20	4.9	4.7
Countrywide	107	50	5.1	4.1
JP Morgan	54	23	6.1	4.1
Merrill	52	21	5.0	4.1
Bear	65	21	5.3	4.3
Average	57	23	5.0	4.3
Range	81	47	2.1	0.6
Minimum	26	3	4.0	4.0
Maximum	107	50	6.1	4.7

(*Source*: Pimco Survey)

given two of the three, the remaining one should trade at fair value. The problem is that liquidity, risk aversion, and transaction constraints make it largely impossible for investors to reconstitute and arbitrage away the mispricing. Thus, given the model risk, both IOs and POs should trade with a risk premium. The magnitude of this risk premium, of course, cannot be modeled, but we do observe that it increases in periods of economic uncertainty and risk. What also stands out is that the research desks and trading desks don't usually agree—the trading desk effectively adds on a risk correction to the reserach models. Since risk takers are the ones who have the most to lose from bad models,

Table 4.3 Delta-Adjusted Performance of IG4 Tranches.

	5-year		10-year	
	US	Euro	US	Euro
0–3 % (points upfront chg)	4.0 bp	3.9 bp	1.5 bp	−2.5 bp
3–7 %	(84)	(49)	133	28
7–10 %	(38)	(24)	(85)	(19)
10–15 %	(15)	(11)	(37)	(55)
15–30 %	(2)	(1)	(14)	(6)

Note: Delta-hedged positions involve selling protection on the tranche versus buying protection a delta-adjusted notional amount of the underlying index.

(*Source:* Morgan Stanley.)

they supplement the research models with their economic priors via a "haircut" applied to the model numbers. It would be nice if such expectations of changing economic conditions could be systematically incorporated into prepayment models, if for nothing else but for calibrating the model risk premium, and indeed some progress has been made. Theoretically, we also can construct a corporate bond with a credit default swap (CDS) and "risk-free" instrument, but the equivalence only holds true if gross assumptions that have no hope of holding in real markets are made. Traders routinely trade the cash bond versus CDS basis for profits. Even portfolio products such as the CDX indices of default swaps (which are PV01 weighted averages of 125 five-year single-name CDS) have traded portfolio spreads very different from intrinsic values computed from the single names. We saw an example of the breakdown of these basis trades in 2007 as liquidity evaporated from the markets.

For fixed income instruments, we can think of any yield over a benchmark instrument as arising from an embedded option. Even more yield from duration extension is the price for the option to reinvest at a higher rate than that implied in the forward curve. Investors do not all value options efficiently, and even if they did, under different economic conditions they do not have the will or the means to exercise those options in the most optimal fashion. This can lead to what appear to be grossly inefficient markets from the viewpoint of arbitrage-free models unless principles of economics—demand and supply—are imposed endogenously.

Here is a striking example from the interest-rate futures markets. The Treasury futures market is one of the largest and most liquid derivative markets anywhere. When the contract was designed, the open interest in the contract was expected to be comparable with the size of the cheapest-to-deliver securities. So one could use good, arbitrage-free derivative models to value the delivery option and trade the cash versus futures basis. As time passed, the ease of use of futures increased the participation in the futures contract, whereas the size of the Treasury bond market dwindled (for various reasons, including the fact that the Treasury started a buyback program in 1999–2000). The mismatch in the size of the deliverable to the open interest in the contract (approximately $20 BN in the CTD T 4.375 of August 2012 to approximately $160 BN in the December futures contract) made application of arbitrage-free theoretical models largely relevant for rich-cheap valuation.

The Investor's Behavior and Preference Are Irrelevant to the Model

Risk premia in incomplete markets cannot be hedged, and unhedgeable risk premia come with unhedgeable risk. The risk premium is where the structural value is, and successful investors know this. Security prices reflect the prices of risk transfer, and in the real world, investors are not identical, so it is impossible that all securities can be modeled without taking investor risk preferences/behavior into consideration. However, most pricing taught in schools assumes that investors always can be made locally risk neutral; the market is assumed to be complete, and risk aversion is assumed to be irrelevant because one always can transform to the risk-neutral measure. As time and time again we have witnessed, large, unhedgeable moves in the market are routine, and even the best structured relative-value trades expose their absolute risks.[2]

Locally hedgeable portfolios frequently cannot be created—as a matter of fact, locally hedgeable portfolios are the exception rather than the rule. The infamous CDX mezzanine versus equity tranche trade of the summer of 2005 illustrates this clearly. The correlation-based model assumes that tranches can be reconstituted to make up the underlying index and comes up with a theoretical value based on this. However, when the underlying economic environment suffered a shock with a possible automatic default, securities behaved in exactly the opposite way than their theoretical deltas would have us believe they should owing to what could be called "irrational" deleveraging. So, in practice, we are left with the problem of how to deal with risk premia. Risk premia are not constant. Far from it. Theoretically, the risk premium is proportional to the covariance of the investor's utility with the economic state of the world. In other words, assets that lose their value when you are poor suffer a penalty (because when you are poor, you value the marginal dollar more), and assets that gain in value in bad states of the world carry a premium (such as Treasury bonds).

---

[2]The key idea of risk-neutral pricing is that if a locally hedgeable portfolio can be created, then you can replace the risk-premium term with zero (or equivalently, the discount rate with the "risk-free" rate). We can write the risk-neutral probability in terms of the risky probability as arising from shifting the means:

$$\bar{q} = N\left[N^{-1}(q) + (\bar{\mu} - \mu)\sqrt{T}\right] \qquad (4.2)$$

where N represents the cumulative normal distribution, and the physical probability is $\bar{q}$ with risk-neutral probability q.

In practice, most consumers probably do not do the life-cycle consumption-maximization exercise but rather look at the economy they can observe and expect. This is also why asset classes can quickly influence each other and lead to simultaneously lower expected returns across the cross section. Assuming that assets will covary according to historical correlations in all environments is a dangerous assumption— it throws out the understanding that asset performance comes eventually from the need for the asset in a portfolio, not from a stand-alone pure value. This portfolio need for assets changes as the economic environment changes.

The Modeler Should Be Irrelevant to the Model

The variation in the modeler's preferences on what shortcuts to take or what logic to follow in the creation of models, that is, the value of the modeler's human capital, is assumed to be largely irrelevant. It is no secret that in recent years the single largest impact on fixed income markets has been the growth of mortgages as an asset class and the commoditization of prepayment risk. Since the right to prepay is an option for the home owner, the investor in mortgages is short the prepay option. Now assume that you are a large pension fund or agency trying to figure out how much your interest-rate risk can change as prepayments change. The way you go about solving the problem is to build a model to value the prepay option. The prepay option is priced using econometric inputs. In other words, home owners do not prepay efficiently (and this is what presumably makes selling the option worth it to the investor), and the inefficiency of the prepay option exercise is quantified using the behavioral response of the collective home owners in the past. But the behavior in the past depends on a multitude of actual economic conditions (rate levels, credit conditions, demographics, unemployment rates, availability of housing, tax rates and breaks, etc.). The hedge ratios for mortgages thus are related to economic inputs directly, and the model-driven hedging activity, if large enough (as in fall 2002), can impact the prices of related securities and lead to a vicious feedback mechanism such as the need for duration leading to the buying of Treasuries and falling yields leading to higher prepayments and more need for duration. People's behavior changes as a response to the economic environment, so the models have to be able to capture this. Experts can disagree! We stress-tested a number of models on their essential inputs for the same econometric variables and found that the response of the models to the same set of inputs was very different. In other words, two modelers working across the street from each other with the same inputs and the same training in finance come up with very different models.

True Price Should Reflect Value

This assumption is frequently violated. The following quote from none other than Adam Smith jumps to mind:

> The things that have the greatest value in use have frequently little or no value in exchange; and, on the contrary, those which have the greatest value in exchange have frequently little or no value in use. Nothing is more useful than water; but it will purchase scarce any thing: scarce anything can be had in exchange for it. A diamond, on the contrary, has scarce any value in use; but a very great quantity of other goods may frequently be had in exchange for it.

It is relatively easy to create a model to justify the price of a security without reference to the economic environment because in equilibrium, demand and supply match. It is harder to create a model to justify the value of a security. Even for the most liquid securities, there is one price but different values for different investors. The muni puzzle, that is, municipal bonds yielding higher than Treasury yields, even after adjusting for taxes, credit, call option, and liquidity risk, has been present for decades and violates arbitrage principles, that is, that forward implied tax rates should be nonnegative. However, to take advantage of the arbitrage opportunity, you would need to short a muni bond, which is notoriously hard to do. One can, of course, lock in the potential of sure gains over some finite horizon by buying munis and shorting taxables according to some model-based hedge ratio, but the trade then is subject to volatile markets, especially flight to quality to the Treasury shorts. The difference between price and value is captured by using risk-neutral versus risky distributions. In the world of credit, reduced-form models such as Duffie-Singleton are pricing models, whereas the Merton model is a valuation model. Regressions that forecast 10-year bond yields based on macroeconomic variables are valuation models, whereas term-structure models such as Heath, Jarrow, Morton (HJM) and its descendants are pricing models.

Prices of Securities Are Irrelevant for the Evolution of the State of the World

Our friction-free models assume that today's price of a traded security should not impact the state of the world in the future. But it is widely acknowledged now that yields remained very low by any standards and led to a boom in housing and perhaps other long-term asset prices that depend on low funding rates. Eventually, the boom deflated either because of policy or the sand-pile effect. Whatever the mechanism, it is hard to argue with the fact that current prices can impact tomorrow's economic environment, and tomorrow's environment will impact tomorrow's prices, and so on. The price of credit risk before the crisis was lower than in a couple of decades and could be traced to the same common economic sources. Prices of securities do not simply indicate value in transaction; they also have an important signaling effect that cannot be evaluated without putting the prices in the correct economic context. When the Treasury started to tinker with the long bond, the immediate impact was the loss of signaling ability of that part of the yield curve.

Incorporating the economic environment can only add to the accuracy of pricing models. It is fair to say that recent financial research is seeing a resurgence of an approach where it is clear from the outset that economic variables can affect price, value, and risk, and price, value, and risk can affect economic variables. This direction of research is bringing to the forefront of our profession what we already know intuitively: The economic state of the world *does* matter. In classical models of asset pricing, investors are taken to be fully rational automatons who systematically forecast and discount future cash flows to price securities. Recent studies into the dependence of yield curves on sentiment show that this is a very strong and inaccurate assumption.

An example of quantifying sentiment is from the work of Baker and Wurgler [27], who create a sentiment index based on certain equity market indicators. Their idea was to test the hypothesis that high sentiment is likely to be associated with high investor demand for speculative stocks relative to investor demand for stable, mature firms and government bonds. A question for bond investors immediately arises: How are traditional bond market predictors of sentiment, such as curve shape, correlated with sentiment.

Figure 4.1 shows the time history of the sentiment index (1962–2004 year end; authors only create the index annually).

The sentiment index (after taking out systematic macroeconomic effects) is

$$
\begin{aligned}
\text{Sentiment} = {} & (-0.198 \times \text{CEFD}) + (0.225 \times \text{TURN}) \\
& + (0.234 \times \text{NIPO}) + (0.263 \times \text{RIPO}) \quad (4.3) \\
& + (0.21 \times \text{S}) - (0.243 \times \text{PD})
\end{aligned}
$$

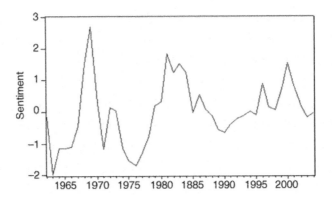

Figure 4.1 Baker-Wurgler sentiment index.

The series are in Figure 4.2.

CEFD = closed-end fund discount (NAV-market value); value weighted average discount of stock funds only

TURN = natural log of the raw share turnover ratio (reported volume per shares listed)

NIPO = number of initial public offerings (IPOs)

RIPO = average first day returns from IPOs

S = share of equity [defined as gross equity issuance/(gross equity + debt issuance)]

PD = percentage difference of the market-to-book ratios of dividend payers versus non–dividend payers.

The main finding is that even after taking out the correlation with systematic market variables [they regress on growth in consumer durables, nondurables, and services and National Bureau of Economic Research (NBER) recessions to find the residuals], this sentiment index properly picks out periods of speculation versus conservatism and can

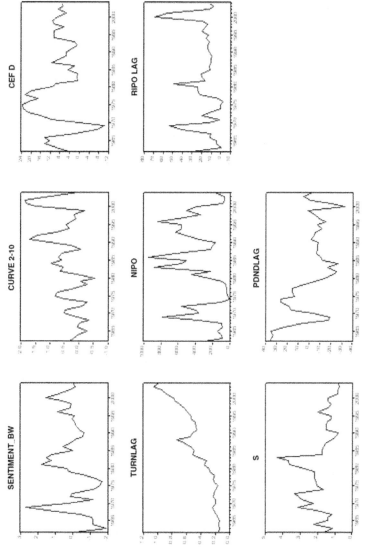

Figure 4.2 Series in Baker-Wurgler sentiment index.

be used to forecast whether bondlike or speculative instruments will deliver excess returns. Applying it to government bond markets, they find that the index has good predictive power for intermediate-term bond returns. In other words, when the sentiment index is low (high), tend to be attractive bondlike (stocklike) securities. In our language, when the sentiment index is low, duration ought to be is a good risk.

The 2–10 part of the yield curve has a mixed record of predicting/following market sentiment. Cataloguing the correlation of the yield curve with this index:

1961–1962 (tronics bubble): No predictive power from yield curve.

1967–1968: Yield curve has little predictive power.

Late 1970s to mid-1980s (biotech bubble): Yield curve steeper with high sentiment.

Late 1990s to 2000 (Internet bubble): Yield curve steepens with high sentiment.

2000–2006: Low sentiment/flattening yield curve.

In Figure 4.3 we see that while the sentiment index followed the 10-year yield level rather closely until early 1990, the relationship since then has broken down (foreign investment in United States/deficit recycling,

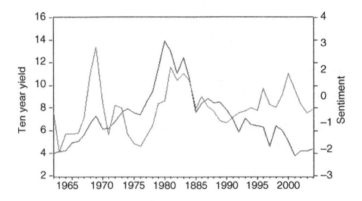

Figure 4.3 Ten-year yields versus Baker-Wurgler sentiment index.

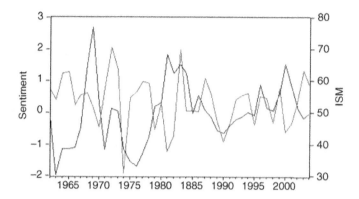

Figure 4.4 ISM versus Baker-Wurgler sentiment index.

etc. to blame?). We also find that the ISM index (more on this later), of purchasing manager's sentiment, has a strong relationship with yield levels.

In Figure 4.4 we show the sentiment index against the ISM index, which is used as a leading indicator for prospective economic growth.

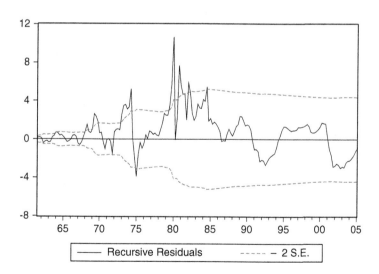

Figure 4.5 Recursive residuals. This demonstrates the possibility of structural breaks in the Taylor rule in the mid-1970s to mid-1980s. (*Source*: Author)

Asset Return Comparisons (Rebalanced to LBAG Duration Monthly, LIBOR Financing)   (07/91 07/05)

Date	LBAG	MBS	TSY	AGCY	CORP	CMBS	TIPS	Muni	EM	HY	ED5	FV	TY	US
MTD	(0.91)	(1.17)	(1.00)	(1.01)	(0.63)	(1.16)	(1.12)	(0.17)	(0.06)	1.59	(1.58)	(1.38)	(1.25)	(0.91)
YTD	1.58	1.09	1.93	1.46	1.60	1.20	1.01	2.17	3.91	2.50	(0.97)	0.31	1.66	3.25
0.25	0.71	0.30	0.59	0.59	1.13	0.49	(0.26)	0.86	3.40	5.06	(0.18)	(0.10)	0.36	1.10
0.5	0.95	0.39	1.29	1.03	0.94	0.66	0.98	1.53	3.39	2.61	(0.51)	0.39	1.26	2.15
1	4.79	4.66	4.54	4.25	5.27	4.58	5.07	4.81	12.82	10.43	0.96	3.14	4.72	6.61
2	4.81	5.21	4.06	4.26	5.20	4.73	5.97	4.31	11.33	11.48	2.14	4.37	5.00	5.42
3	5.02	4.10	3.96	4.28	6.14	5.07	6.10	3.74	14.95	14.85	4.58	4.84	4.82	4.60
5	7.01	7.27	5.90	7.13	7.08	8.16	7.93	4.93	9.55	6.58	10.62	8.21	7.26	5.53
7	6.21	6.23	5.59	6.18	6.11		7.38	4.75	9.60	4.43	8.12	7.27	6.70	5.42
10	6.75	6.92	6.25	6.75	6.69						8.07	7.48	7.22	6.32
14	7.29	7.24	6.89	7.26	7.46						9.15	8.28	7.85	6.78

Information Ratio Comparison (Annualized Excess Return over LBAG / Annualized Standard Deviation of Excess Return, monthly data)

Date	LBAG	MBS	TSY	AGCY	CORP	CMBS	TIPS	Muni	EM	HY	ED5	FV	TY	US
0.5	0.00	(1.82)	1.37	0.62	(0.01)	(1.28)	0.05	0.72	1.55	0.46	(2.37)	(1.01)	0.61	5.60
1	0.00	(0.21)	(0.52)	(1.29)	0.72	(0.29)	0.19	0.01	3.03	1.06	(1.98)	(1.32)	(0.09)	2.87
2	0.00	0.44	(1.56)	(1.31)	0.66	(0.10)	0.60	(0.27)	2.18	1.43	(1.04)	(0.26)	0.21	0.77
3	0.00	(0.30)	(1.55)	(1.36)	1.32	0.05	0.52	(0.62)	2.02	1.64	(0.16)	(0.09)	(0.15)	(0.50)
5	0.00	0.10	(1.35)	0.14	0.05	1.04	0.44	(1.01)	0.34	(0.05)	1.07	0.56	0.17	(1.30)
7	0.00	0.01	(0.65)	(0.03)	(0.07)		0.50	(0.69)	0.22	(0.20)	0.53	0.50	0.31	(0.59)
10	0.00	0.09	(0.62)	0.00	(0.05)						0.42	0.39	0.34	(0.36)
14	0.00	(0.03)	(0.55)	(0.06)	0.17						0.57	0.54	0.42	(0.43)

Excess Return Correlation vs. LBAG

Date	LBAG	MBS	TSY	AGCY	CORP	CMBS	TIPS	Muni	EM	HY	ED5	FV	TY	US
0.5	1.00	0.45	0.18	0.43	(0.35)	0.93	(0.55)	(0.94)	0.03	(0.44)	0.94	0.51	0.54	0.43
1	1.00	0.10	0.07	0.34	(0.22)	0.74	(0.47)	(0.95)	0.08	(0.43)	0.74	0.58	0.52	(0.10)
2	1.00	0.32	(0.30)	0.48	(0.28)	0.73	(0.41)	(0.92)	0.24	(0.45)	0.77	0.75	0.73	(0.48)
3	1.00	0.39	(0.32)	0.28	(0.27)	0.59	(0.18)	(0.93)	(0.02)	(0.46)	0.38	0.56	0.62	(0.21)
5	1.00	0.42	(0.13)	0.36	(0.33)	0.49	(0.24)	(0.87)	(0.20)	(0.38)	0.51	0.55	0.58	(0.17)
7	1.00	0.38	(0.14)	0.27	(0.26)		(0.32)	(0.82)	(0.13)		0.47	0.51	0.52	(0.18)
10	1.00	0.32	(0.11)	0.24	(0.22)						0.44	0.52	0.55	(0.09)
14	1.00	0.20	(0.07)	0.14	(0.12)						0.53	0.57	0.59	(0.13)

Figure 4.6 Asset excess return performance and monthly correlation to overall bond market as represented by the Barclays/Lehman Brothers U.S. Aggregate over 14 years.

(*Source:* Author)

The relatively strong relationship, especially at turning points, is not surprising because we would expect manufacturing sentiment in general to filter into investors' behavior.

To practically create an economically motivated model, we begin by translating economic priors into possible economic scenarios and realization of the factors. Typically, but not always, low inflation and low gross domestic product (GDP) are associated with low interest rates and relatively flat yield curves. When pricing a credit-"risk-free" security, the arbitrage-free price can be compared or supplemented with pricing obtained by the risk premia of these factors on the security. If under shocks of the factors a so-called arbitrage-free package yields nonzero excess returns, it has to hold true that the risk-neutral price is wrong, or there are hidden factors, or there are "risk-free profit" opportunities.

- We can start by defining risk exposures in terms of specific factors, for instance, duration, curve exposure, spread exposures of various kinds, and structural components such as the magnitude of embedded volatility sale, and the static aspects such as roll-down in the curve. For each of these factor exposures, we obtain factor risk premia. For packages that allow factor risk premia to be hedged out, we can price using the arbitrage-free approach. Our model is general enough to have the economic content incorporated right from the beginning. We already discussed this approach to risk measurement in Chapter 1.
- Depending on our outlook of the world and the expected variation in risk premia, certain sources of risk are better than others at different times. Whenever we expect to be able to earn high risk premia in a sector, we overweight that sector/security. For example, the term premium is the premium that is earned by increasing duration. To quantify the term-premium content of the yield curve, we build models that can simultaneously extract the term premium from the whole yield curve.

- To enable relative pricing, we need to be able to create an arbitrage-free model for the discount factor; to do this, we need to have the proper forward rates in the risk-neutral measure as well as the physical measure. To connect the physical measure forward rates to the economic variables, we can build up an economic model for the short rate. The Taylor rule connects the short rate to the deviation of inflation and output from targets. Since the Fed appears to follow the Taylor rule in setting the short nominal rate, this input is crucial if we want to extract the economic content embedded in the yield curve.
- Once economic variables are included, one can investigate the impact of changing demand and supply dynamics. For example, has the valuation of the Treasury curve changed owing to the participation of foreign central banks, and if so, by how much?

To show that such models are viable, we can build well-motivated simple toy models with latent factors without economic variables, estimate the latent variables, and then regress the latent variables on economic variables to see if we can find a relationship.

Let us build a quantitative term-structure model with economic content. Our approach will be to build a well-motivated term-structure model that is based in economics, estimate the parameters in the model using market data (in an arbitrage-free way), and then pick relevant economic variables that are related to the latent variables by regression. Figure 4.7 shows the key economic variables we will use—the inflation rate, real GDP, current-account deficit as a percent of GDP, and the difference in the 10-year and 1-year Treasury rates as a proxy for the term premium.

A general form of a two-factor latent variable model is given by

$$dx = -\mu_x(x - \theta_x)\, dt + \sigma_x\, dw_x$$
$$dy = -\mu_y\, y\, dt + \sigma_y\, dw_y$$
$$dz = k(x + y - z)\, dt$$

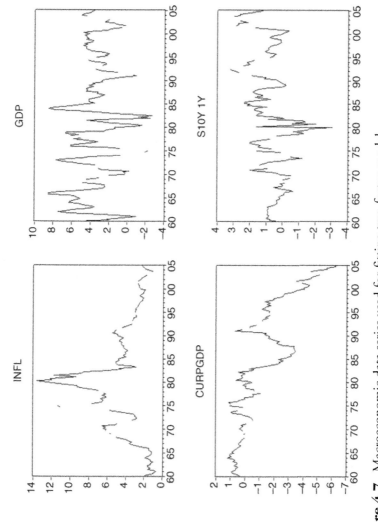

Figure 4.7 Macroeconomic data series used for fitting two-factor model.

(*Source*: Author, Bloomberg)

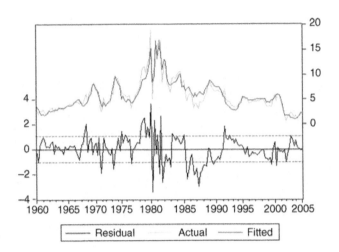

Figure 4.8 Fed funds rate and z. Residual scale has been expanded.
(*Source*: Author, Bloomberg data)

We can think of z as the instantaneous short rate, with fit results in Figure 4.8. We can think of x as related to inflation and θ_x as the long-term target for this variable.

   Since the change in z is related to the diffence from the sum of x and y, it is tempting to identify these variables with the inflation and GDP gaps as in the Taylor rule and the difference equation for z as the Taylor rule. The benefit of this specification is that now we can bring in the machinery for solving for zero-coupon bond prices and yields using

$$P(t, T) = E_t(e^{-\int_t^T z(\alpha)d\alpha}) = e^{-y(T-t)} \qquad (4.4)$$

which can be solved in closed form. Now that we have an analytical model for the discount factors, we can fit the model to the term structure every day. Going back to 1960, we do this exercise and obtain the estimated values of the parameters and variables of interest (see Figure 4.9). Now we can try combinations of economic variables that correlate well with these estimated parameters. By construction, the structural changes in the Taylor rule are transmitted across the yield curve via the latent factors x and y. Figure 4.10 shows that θ_x fits well

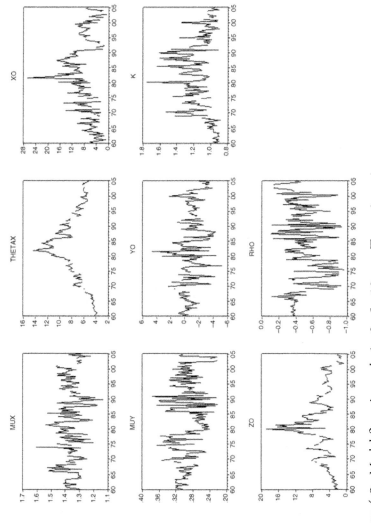

Figure 4.9 Model fits using only 1-, 3-, 5-, 10-year Treasuries as input.
(*Source:* Author, Bloomberg data)

145

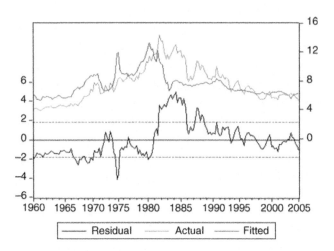

Figure 4.10 Model-implied long-term inflation rate regressed against actual inflation. Regression equation $\theta_x = 4.868 + 0.619 \times$ INFL yields r^2 of 0.46, with inflation t-stats $= 11.9$. Dataset 1960–2005.
(*Source*: Author, Bloomberg)

with the inflation rate (plus some premium), and Figure 4.11 shows the dependence of the factor y on the slope of the yield curve (curve risk premium). Since the inflation risk factor is best expressed in terms of duration risk, and the curve risk premium is best expressed in terms of yield-curve steepening or flattening exposure, now we have a methodology to connect macro variables with risks of securities to these macro factors in an arbitrage-free way (we simply compute the sensitivity with respect to the factors for every credit-"risk-free" bond using the model).

We also can investigate the impact of the U.S. current-account deficit by adding in the current-account deficit as a percent of GDP to the regression for the long-term inflation rate θ_x. As expected and shown in Figure 4.12, we find that the market-implied long-term inflation expectations have been kept much lower than they would have been otherwise; for very long horizons, long-term inflation expectations could be almost 2 percent higher (difference of fitted residuals in the

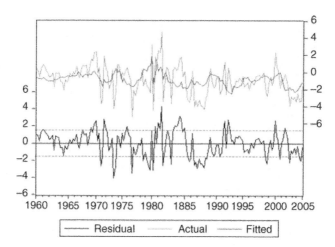

Figure 4.11 Second factor y versus economic and market variables. Regression equation $y_0 = -0.14 - 0.0422 \times \text{GDP} - 0.00579 \times \text{INFL} - 0.667 \times (10Y - 1Y)$. Only the slope factor $10Y - 1Y$ is significant. This indicates that the strongly mean-reverting second factor might be more correlated with risk premia and preferences than with economic cycles. Regressions against market volatility indicators also show a high correlation with the second factor. Dataset 1960–2005.
(*Source*: Author, Bloomberg)

model with and without the current-account deficit as an explanatory variable).

Now that we see that economic variables have good explanatory power for the latent variables, we can build the economic variables into the model right from the beginning; in other words, one could argue that before fitting to the yield curve and security prices, we should constrain the ranges of the parameters and factors using our economic priors. In a sense, when we specify the model to have two sources of uncertainty, plus policy, we are already imposing economics (i.e., we know from experience that yield-curve fluctuations can be described by at most three factors and in most circumstances by two factors). We also know that credit-free fixed income securities are predominantly determined by inflation (and inflation expectations), Fed behavior, and risk premium.

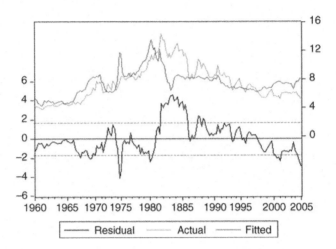

Figure 4.12 Long-term inflation expectations implied by term-structure model regressed against actual inflation rates and current account deficit. Regression equation $\theta_x = 4.13 + 0.687 \times \text{INFL} - 0.387 \times \text{CURPGDP}$, where t-stats on inflation rate equal 13 and on current-account deficit equal 5, so both variables are significant. Regression $r^2 = 0.54$. Data 1960–2005. (*Source*: Author, Bloomberg.)

So a simple, economically well-specified model is better suited to fit the market than a very general model that has little to do with the real world in its specification. An advantage of such a model is also that the effect of the yield curve on the macroeconomy, as well as the effect of the macroeconomy on the yield curve, can be estimated. The model is efficient enough to stress-test with. We have also explored an extension where credit risk, prepayment risk, and tax risk are introduced into the model explicitly from the start with stochastic intensities correlated with macro factors. We can throw all relevant economic variables into the mix right from the beginning. Minimization of fitting errors then picks out the relevant economic variables. Given the simultaneity of the market and economic variables, the impulse-response functions show the impact of each set of variables on subsequent realizations of the others.

Macro Drivers of Correlation Risk in Credit Markets

Correlation drives the risk of credit portfolios just as volatility is the primary driver of options portfolios. This section discusses correlation in the context of credit derivatives markets and focuses on interpretation relevant to investments. The basic issue is stated easily: If we could access the true joint distribution of all the assets in a credit portfolio and simultaneously forecast their evolution, recovery levels, and timing of default, we would theoretically have no problem pricing and managing the risk of any credit derivative product; we would know the full portfolio loss distribution at all times. The complications in practice arise owing to the technical complexity of obtaining these all-important loss distributions, and market practitioners have had to resort to some powerful yet limiting approximations. Thus use of the term *correlation* in the context of credit derivatives requires an understanding of the limitations of statistics and models that have been used to understand the joint behavior of corporate spreads. Even without a model, we have a sense of correlation using statistical measures, that is, by looking at historical data, and for many investment applications, this intuitive understanding is sufficient. However, recent product development has enabled the extraction of implied correlation using correlation-sensitive traded securities. The implied-correlation approach adopts the risk-neutral pricing framework and makes strong assumptions about the liquidity and risk-premium content, as well as the distributional characteristics of assets.

We should note that the expected loss on straight portfolio products or baskets is not sensitive to changes in correlations, so tranches or other correlation-sensitive securities are required to extract any implied correlation content. Statistical measures of correlation can be differentiated further. We can measure the correlation between asset values of the various entities, between the equity prices of the entities, or actual defaults of the entities. Default statistics by nature consist of rare-event counting and thus are not easily quantified. The standard model for default correlations assumes some form of structural model for the underlying entities whose net assets evolve under a stochastic process (typically taken to be jointly lognormal), and a default occurs when the net asset value falls below a default threshold. Calibration of models poses another set of problems, and as of this writing, most practitioners use a mix of structural and reduced-form (hazard-intensity-based) approaches. We can extract implied correlation out of correlation-sensitive securities, such as tranches and default baskets, but there is no guarantee that the correlation so extracted has anything to do with the real world. The problem with using naive implied correlation is that it assumes that the default swap market is complete, that is, all risk frontiers can be exactly hedged. This is a strong and incorrect assumption in reality, because there is no way to arbitrage mispricings in these instruments. May 2005 exposed the weakness of so-called arbitrage trades between tranches whose hedge ratios were determined by blind reliance on model sensitivities.

Correlation is to tranched portfolio credit losses what volatility is to plain-vanilla options, so we should explore the analogy with options models a bit further to build intuition. When we price options, we can choose to use historical or implied volatilities to plug into an option-pricing formula. A number of assumptions are made to obtain the price of options. First, we assume that we know the option payoff. Second, we assume that we know the probability distribution of the underlying variables over which we can average the payoffs. And third, we assume that we know how to discount the probability-weighted payoffs. If we think of the underlying asset as being lognormal, then volatility (the second moment) is sufficient for capturing the uncertainty in the possible outcomes, that is, the shape of the distribution. However, if we estimate these volatilities using historical data or some other ad hoc method and plug it into an option-pricing formula, a trader who has access to the options markets can take advantage of us if our estimate is wrong. Over time, therefore, the value of realized volatility and implied volatility should track each other closely owing to arbitrage. The arbitrageur does not necessarily have to even trade using options. Assuming that he or she can trade frequently, he or she can dynamically create a locally replicating portfolio and trade it against the option we have priced using the incorrect volatility value. Over time, he or she will be able to harvest the relative mispricing if our forecast of realized volatility is wrong. In this sense, the implied volatility indicates a good forecast of future realized volatility. We also can think about what happens when we change the strikes of the options. If we price a put spread where the strikes of the two put options are far from the forward, we can observe the prices of each of the two options and back out the one volatility number that would price the put spread to equal the traded price. In the limit that the put spread becomes a digital (i.e., the spread narrows to zero), the implied volatility is a point estimate of some realized volatility for that level of the underlying. It is still hard to develop intuition for the statistical analogue of this tail volatility.

Think of the skew in the Standard and Poor's 500 Index (S&P500) option prices. The implied volatility of deeply out-of-the-money puts is higher than that of deeply out-of-the-money calls. The common explanations for this phenomenon are "crashophobia" or Black's leverage phenomenon, but these explanations cannot uniquely determine the magnitude of the effects. What we can say with some degree of confidence is that the lognormal distribution of returns assumed for the underlying is inadequate to simultaneously explain the realized volatility of the underlying for all horizons and for all levels. We also can look at calendar spreads of options (i.e., options with the same strikes but different maturities). Again, depending on the shape of the term structure of the volatility, the relative value of the two options can be quite variable. In periods of market crises, short-term volatility rises, and the term structure of volatility usually flattens. The underlying reasons for this can be traced to rise in risk aversion, higher transactions costs for hedging, and the demand for short-term crisis protection. Despite the serious shortcomings of the Black-Scholes model, these features of the implied volatility are consistent with our understanding of what risk means, and hence they are sensible.

Let us see what, if any, is the analogue in the credit-derivatives markets. For simplicity, we will use tranches [collateralized debt obligations (CDOs)] on traded indices such as the CDX and the ITRAXX because they are the most liquid correlation products (we also could use n^{th} to default baskets, but their liquidity and uniformity are far smaller). Tranches on indices can be thought of as put spreads on index losses. There are 125 names in the widely traded CDX Index. There are tranches that cover 0 to 3 percent of losses (equity), 3 to 7 percent of losses (junior mezzanine), 7 to 10 percent of losses (senior mezzanine), 10 to 15 percent of losses (senior), and 15 to 30 percent of losses (supersenior), and by construction, there is the 30 to 100 percent tranche, which is the remainder when all the losses from the index are allocated.

As correlation between the names increases, we expect that there is a higher probability that either more names will default together or they won't. Thus the junior tranches (e.g., the equity tranche that covers losses from 0 to 3 percent) will tighten in spread as correlations increase because there is a relatively higher probability of no defaults (note that we are not making a model-dependent statement yet). On the other hand, as correlation increases, the higher-rated, or senior, tranches will fall in value because they are now exposed to higher tail risk. So we should expect that as systemic risk increases, the impact on the senior tranches would be relatively higher. The dependence of the mezzanine tranches on correlation is not that easy to explain and, among other things, depends on their attachment and detachment levels (lower and upper strikes). There are also tranches on indices with different final maturities. We would intuitively expect that as correlation rises, the shorter-maturity tranches would have different sensitivities to correlation than the longer-maturity tranches. To what degree this holds out will be discussed in a later section.

The Market for Implied Correlation

In this section we will discuss implied correlation from the perspective of the Black-Scholes analogue for correlation products: the gaussian copula model. The gaussian copula model has more than a passing similarity with the simple Black-Scholes model for options and has suffered its shares of attacks. However, just like its older cousin, the Black-Scholes model, the gaussian copula not only has survived but also has thrived. The reasons are multifold: (1) No one who trades correlation products really believes that the gaussian copula model is the last word, but by their usage, they all agree that it is an excellent starting point and relatively easy to conceptualize (no one believes that Black-Scholes for options is the last word either, but the formula, by virtue of its clarity and simplicity, has survived 30 years in great style); (2) exact solutions are easy to obtain for products such as tranches under reasonable assumptions, and when exact solutions are not available, the framework allows for straightforward numerical simulations; and (3) it is easy to communicate the value of the variables and parameters although the meaning of these parameters is not always transparent. However, we should hasten to add that much research has continued to expand the simple copula model to make more realistic assumptions. A thorough review of this exciting field is beyond the scope of this book. Tranche markets are not limited to investment-grade indices. There are also tranches on the high-yield indices that are reasonably liquid as of this writing, as well as tranches on indices of subprime mortgage issuers (ABX and TABX). Discussion of the subprime tranche market would require us to delve into mortgage credit and prepayment models, so in this discussion we will focus mainly on pure credit tranches.

Let us review how correlation enters the pricing of tranches. As discussed earlier, a tranche is a spread on the losses of the underlying index. A tranche is defined by an attachment point (lower strike K_d) and a detachment point (upper strike K_u). If the loss on the underlying index is $L_i(t)$, then the tranche loss is simply

$$L(\text{tranche})(t) = \max[L_i(t) - K_d, 0] - \max[L_i(t) - K_u, 0] \qquad (4.5)$$

If we divide the expectation of this quantity by the tranche notional $K_u - K_d$, we obtain the tranche default probability. Finally, subtracting the resulting quantity from unity gives the tranche survival probability. To price a tranche, we impose the condition that the present value of the expected premium payments (premium payments get reduced proportionately to the reduction in notional on default) should equal the present value of the expected protection received (i.e., when a name defaults, we obtain 1 minus the recovery rate). The tranche survival probability, equal to the expected percentage notional of the tranche surviving at some time t, is the key quantity that is affected by correlations. To obtain the expectations for each maturity requires knowledge of the loss distributions for each maturity, and this is not always a computationally tractable task in real time. In a brute-force model, we can take all the names in the index and generate Monte Carlo paths for defaults. In this approach, we generate default times based on default intensities extracted from a reduced-form model for each name and apply the pricing algorithm given earlier. When there are a lot of assets, specifying each element in the correlation matrix of default times is not only tedious but also computationally intractable. In addition, if we are interested in backing out the correlations from traded products by standing the pricing equation on its head, we are not guaranteed that the result would be unique or sensible. As an alternative, we can assume a simple factor model. Each asset return depends on the market factor and an idiosyncratic factor. A common correlation determines how much the correlation drives asset returns. If we assume that the standardized asset returns are jointly normal with the market, then the decomposition is given by the standard Cholesky decomposition formula for generating correlated random variables from independent ones. We thus can generate random numbers for the realization of the market factors and the individual factors and combine them using the Cholesky formula to obtain the asset return realization. If we compute the cumulative distribution function of these asset returns, we obtain a uniformly distributed set of numbers. Since the probability of default lies between 0 and 1, we can use this uniformly distributed set of numbers as default time probabilities at each firm level after computing the probability of survival embedded in single-name CDS spreads. If the asset return distributions are related in a gaussian copula, then the default-time probabilities are also related with a gaussian copula. Note that at each stage we are working in the risk-neutral framework, so we are throwing out any risk-premium information. Thus it becomes critical that the parameters are retrospectively evaluated through the lens of common sense real-world experience.

Regardless of whether we start with the brute-force simulation of default times or a structural model, the assumption that the underlying components are related via a common market factor makes correlation a critical variable in the pricing of tranches. The market has adopted the gaussian copula model owing to its speed and clarity, and there are two different ways in which correlation based on the gaussian copula is quoted. In the compound-correlation convention, each tranche is quoted using a single tranche-specific correlation number, so different tranches appear with different correlations, and we observe a compound-correlation smile. Using the base-correlation convention, we think of each of the mezzanine and senior tranches as the difference between two equity tranches. We start with the equity tranche specified by its own unique correlation (for equity tranches, the base and compound correlations are the same). For the next-higher tranche, we use the fact that it is the difference between a wider equity tranche and the first equity tranche. We can solve for the correlation (holding the correlation for the first equity tranche fixed) such that the price of the difference of the two equity tranches equals the market price of the next-higher tranche. We can keep repeating this process until all tranches are associated with a unique correlation specific to its detachment point. The correlations so obtained are the base correlations. There is no extra information in the base-correlation approach compared with the compound-correlation approach. The base-correlation approach is preferred for some applications because it guarantees that for any tranche prices there are unique solutions for the implied base correlation. Despite the problem of multiple solutions for mezzanine tranches, compound correlation is still useful in connecting theory to observation.

Do the Market's Estimates of Correlations Make Sense?

Compound correlations implied by tranche prices demonstrate a skew. For instance, on April 16, 2007, the 5-year IG8 Index was trading at a spread of 37. Looking at the implied correlations of various tranches, we would find that generally the junior mezzanine tranches trade at the lowest implied compound correlation. The equity tranche typically has positive correlation sensitivity (i.e., as correlation rises, the equity tranche present value rises in value, whereas all the other tranches lose value). The fact that compound correlation exhibits a smile is not surprising; it is akin to option volatilities exhibiting a smile with strikes as one moves away from the at-the-money level. Admittedly, the simple gaussian copula assumption is too restrictive to explain the full correlation structure of 125 names. But, just as we ask the question for options, we can ask: Is there a logical explanation for this? There are a few possibilities: One possibility is simply a demand and supply mismatch for particular tranches; another explanation is the possibility of modeling error even after accounting for the limitations of the distribution. Similar to the Black-Scholes framework, the gaussian copula has no way to account for jump risk. If there is a risk of jump to default (as in the May 2005 correlation crisis), the equity tranches would be most directly impacted and hence would command a risk premium.

How might demand and supply impact the pricing of tranches and hence the correlation structure? Long-term equity correlations of investment-grade names in the equity market indices are about 20 to 25 percent. Similarly, the average equity return correlation for the underlying components of the IG8 CDX Index is 22 percent. Then an implied correlation of 13.45 percent for the equity tranche implies that the equity tranche is cheap (because as correlation rises, the equity tranche gains in value and its spread tightens). However, as discussed earlier, this could be due to the inability of the model to price jump risk. For the mezzanine tranches, as correlation rises, its value falls, so a reversion to historical correlation levels would make the tranche widen in spread.

However, what is interesting is that the junior mezzanine tranche is so much tighter than historical correlations would imply. We can get a hint of why this might be so by again resorting to our options analogy. As of April 16, 2007, the index spread is 37 basis points, and with spread duration of approximately 4.5 years, the present value of the index expected loss is approximately 1.67 percent, so the equity tranche with 0 to 3 percent losses is in the money, whereas the junior mezzanine tranche is just out of the money. In an environment of credit-spread tightening, low volatility, and low systemic risk perceptions, selling the junior mezzanine tranche is akin to selling out-of-the money options to collect an "insurance" premium. Before the May 2005 correlation debacle, hedging equity tranches with mezzanine tranches was a popular trade implemented by hedge funds. The unwind of those positions, and the consequent breakdown of the relationships at steep losses for some investors who have a preference for such relative-value trades could have further been responsible for the correlation mismatch we observe in the equity and junior mezzanine tranches. As we move to the senior tranches, we observe that their compound correlation begins to converge to long-term equity correlations. We also know anecdotally that in periods of market stress, equity correlations rise because there is a general flight to quality. Therefore, in periods of crisis, we would expect equity correlations to rise, and assuming that senior tranches track this, we would expect their value to fall with correlation rising. In other words, purchasing hedges on senior tranches would benefit from systemic shocks in a more dependable way.

Note that insurance companies are typically sellers of synthetic "insurance" via supersenior tranches, and this is not very different from selling reinsurance on hurricanes or catastrophes. Even with its severe limitations, we can use the compound correlation as a diagnostic tool. Suppose that equity and mezzanine spreads were to widen drastically—widening equity spreads mean tightening compound correlation and widening mezzanine tranche spreads mean rising compound correlation. Then the compound-correlation curve would flip or invert. This could be the situation observed in reality if levels of risk aversion rise in the credit-derivatives markets.

We also can discuss the sensibility of base correlations. First, as we move up the subordination structure, we find that base correlations rise (the correlation skew). This makes sense in the context of the pricing of mezzanine tranches. Note that the junior mezzanine can be thought of as the difference between the 0 to 7 percent equity and the 0 to 3 percent equity. Once the correlation for the 0 to 3 percent is determined by the price of the equity, the richness of the 3 to 7 percent tranche can be possible only if the 0 to 7 percent is richer. But this is an equity tranche, which is long correlation risk, so its implied base correlation has to be higher.

Continuing this for the higher tranches, it makes sense that the base correlations reflect the demand and supply mismatch, as illustrated by the demand for the mezzanine tranches. Second, let's assume that we move in the index-maturity dimension. For the IG8 series, we have the 5-, the 7-, and the 10-year indices, and on each one of these we have all the standard tranches discussed earlier. As we move to longer maturities, the implied base correlations fall for all tranches. This also makes sense because as we go out in the maturity, the same equity tranches are more in the money (expected index losses are higher), and hence they are expected to trade cheaper. As the base correlation for the 0 to 3 percent equity tranche falls, so does the base correlation for all the higher tranches.

We also can move in the vintage dimension (assuming that the components are essentially the same). As we move to older indices, we would see that the base correlations rise for the same tranches. Thus, for instance, if the base correlation for the ITRAXX7 5-year (ref. index 24 basis points) 0 to 3 percent is 16.4 percent, for the ITRAXX6 5-year (ref. 21 basis points) 0 to 3 percent it is 17.5 percent.

Invoking demand and supply considerations to explain correlation skews and smiles might be less than convincing to some. An astute arbitrageur would ask why investors do not create combinations of the tranches to take advantage of the correlation skews/smiles. First, there is clear market segmentation: Hedge funds and banks are typically equity tranche investors, whereas insurance companies are investors in (sell protection) the senior structures. Crossover buyers, pensions, and retail and single-tranche CDO hedgers dominate the mezzanine structures. So there is not much mobility of investors between the tranches, and different investors show preference for different parts of the capital structure (rating-agency ratings also assist in habitat formation). Another explanation relies on our often-used analogy with options. We know that the implied volatility of deeply out-of-the-money puts in the equity market is much higher than the implied volatility of options close to at the money. But this does not automatically suggest that arbitrageurs should sell a lot of out-of-the-money options and hedge them with at-the-money options. The failure of such a strategy would almost be guaranteed if realized outcomes on the underlying deviated from a continuous lognormal behavior or if there were less than perfect liquidity in the hedge instruments. However, there is considerable evidence that tranches have become a lot more efficient as carriers of correlated credit risk.

Another approach is a top-down approach, and it removes the need for specifying a copula and is discussed in Chapter 5. Three types of default events, corresponding to firm-specific and industry- and economy-wide default events, drive spreads. Attempting to fit the movements of the indices and the tranches with a single-factor model fails, confirming the fact that default correlations matter. Fitting the model to traded tranche prices on the investment grade (IG) indices shows that the average time for firm-specific default is approximately a year, for industry-wide defaults is 40 years, and for economy-wide risk is approximately 750 years. For the industry- and economy-wide factors, they find that 10 and 35 percent of the index firms would default, which is in the zone of sensibility. This way of looking at correlation risk highlights the economics behind default risk embedded in credit-portfolio products.

Risk Management with Macro Views: Forecasting Betas

From a risk-management perspective, the mixing of different types of securities in a portfolio leads to additional complications. For instance, how do we capture the risk of treasury inflation protected securities (TIPS) in a portfolio that has nominal Treasuries. To practically achieve the task of putting risks on the same footing, investors use the concept of a *beta*, that is, a normalization factor to put all risks on the same footing. As a case study, in this section we show how we can try to estimate this beta using theoretical and empirical arguments for inflation-linked securities. To be precise,

- Are TIPS likely to exhibit significantly different betas from long-term betas with respect to nominal yields in certain periods of GDP growth and inflation?
- In such periods, what is the best beta factor that we should apply to TIPS' real duration to get TIPS' nominal duration?

Suppose that we expect higher than normal real growth and lower than normal inflation. We should expect that the correlation of real yields (that signify higher real growth) with inflation (plus risk premia) would turn out negative; then, do TIPS betas have to be adjusted downward from long-term levels? It is not enough to forecast the sign; for risk-management purposes, we also need to quantify the magnitude of the downward (or upward) adjustment.

As a review, let's summarize what we expect in different environments of inflation and real growth changes:

1. *High inflation, high growth.* High real yield changes and higher nominal yield changes, positive correlation of real yields and inflation expectations, TIPS tend to outperform nominals.
2. *High inflation, falling growth.* Small real rate changes, high inflation changes, negative correlation of real yields and inflation expectations, TIPS tend to outperform nominals greatly.
3. *Low inflation, high growth.* Large real yields changes, moderate inflation changes, negative to zero correlation of real yields and inflation expectations, TIPS tend to underperform.
4. *Low inflation, low growth.* Small real yield changes, small inflation changes, positive correlation of real yields and inflation expectations, TIPS probably underperform.

Economic growth is related to the average level of real yields. Perceptions of a growing real economy creates real investment opportunities and demand for capital, which results in higher real rates. Nominal to real spreads are related to inflation.

To quantify the effect of such periods on TIPS' durations, first we turn to history to obtain some analytical starting points. One lab is the U.K. inflation-linked market in the 1992–94 period, which is similar to our assumed U.S. scenario. Between September 1992 and August 1994, the Bank of England (BOE) eased lending rates from 10 to 5.25 percent. Inflation remained low at 2 percent, with robust GDP growth of 3 percent annualized.

- The period to September 1990 had relatively tight monetary policy, high base lending rates, and high and volatile inflation. In September 1990, base lending rates stood at 15 percent, with Risk Probability Index (RPI) at 11 percent and no GDP growth over the previous year.
- October 1990 to August 1994 saw lowering of base lending rates by almost 10 percentage points and inflation falling from 11 to 2 percent.
  - October 1990 to August 1992: Easing from 15 to 10 percent. Exchange rate mechanism (ERM) event (sterling locked into ERM with high real rates at a time of recession that finally led to the sterling falling out of the ERM). Inflation fell to 3.8 percent from 11 percent, and real GDP contracted at rate of 1.05 percent.
  - September 1992 to August 1994: Further easing from 10 to 5.25 percent. Inflation fell to 2.07 percent from 3.8 percent, and real GDP grew at 3.13 percent.
- September 1994 to April 1995: Moderate tightening. Rates go from 5.25 to 6.75 percent, and inflation goes from 4.49 to 7.14 percent.

- Over the 1992 to 1994 period: The ratio of the range of real yields to nominal yields (as well as standard deviation of weekly changes) averaged about 0.47; that is, real yields were half as volatile as nominal yields.

Under the Fisher hypothesis, real yields and the nominal–real yield spread should be independent. Leaning on the U.K. experience of September 1992 to August 1994, analysis shows that the correlation between real yield and yield spread was significant and −0.21. In the two other periods where correlations were significant and negative (January 1985 to July 1985 correlation −0.60 and March 1987 to May 1988 correlation −0.248), the BOE was in an aggressive monetary easing mode. So, assuming that risk premium is not correlated with real yields, aggressive monetary easing, at least in the U.K. inflation-linked market case, historically has led to a lowering of expected future inflation.

The converse relationship is not statistically significant; that is, when monetary policy was being tightened aggressively (June 1988 to October 1989), the correlations were slightly negative but not statistically significant. Also, for moderate changes in monetary policy, as in September 1994 to November 1996, correlations between real yields and yield spreads were close to zero.

Beta-Adjusted Durations

Let us define

$$
\begin{aligned}
n &\equiv \text{nominal yield} \\
r &\equiv \text{real yield} \\
i &\equiv \text{expected inflation} \\
\mu &\equiv \text{effective risk premium}
\end{aligned}
\tag{4.6}
$$

Then the returns on the nominal and real securities are related by

$$(1 + n) = (1 + r)(1 + i)(1 + \mu) \tag{4.7}$$

which, to leading order, is the well-known relationship

$$n = r + i + \mu. \tag{4.8}$$

Expected inflation is a *monetary* phenomenon, depending on the credibility of the central bank. Risk premia and convexity are primarily driven by the market's best guess of the future volatility of inflation.

The effective risk premium μ is equal to the product of expected value of the inflation index ratio at a future date and inflation convexity that depends purely on the volatility of future inflation. For periods of ordinary inflation (30 to 40 basis-point volatility annualized), the convexity term adds roughly a basis point or so to the effective risk premium. For higher inflation volatility, the contribution scales like the square of inflation volatility. For our current analysis, we can assume that inflation will not be too volatile, so we can replace the effective risk-premium term with the simple risk-premium term. Further, we will define the sum of inflation expectations and risk premium to be the nominal–real yield spread s, that is,

$$s = i + \mu \tag{4.9}$$

By taking partial derivatives of the price with respect to nominal and real yields, we can write the nominal duration of a TIP in terms of the real-nominal correlation $\rho_{n,r}$, volatility of real yields σ_r, and volatility of nominal yields σ_n as

$$D_n = D_r \rho_{n,r} \frac{\sigma_r}{\sigma_n} = D_r \beta_{r,n} \tag{4.10}$$

where the beta between real and nominal yields is defined to be

$$\beta_{n,r} = \rho_{n,r} \frac{\sigma_r}{\sigma_n} \tag{4.11}$$

We also can show that the correlation $\rho_{n,r}$ between nominal and real yield (changes) can be written in terms of the more intuitive correlation between real yields and the nominal–real yield spread (changes) $\rho_{r,s}$:

$$\rho_{n,r} = \frac{\sigma_r}{\sigma_n}\left(1 + \rho_{r,s}\frac{\sigma_s}{\sigma_r}\right) \tag{4.12}$$

in terms of the nominal–real spread s defined earlier. Thus, in determining the effective betas, we need quantification of correlation of real yields to the nominal–real yield spread, as well as the volatility of the real yields, nominal yields, and nominal–real yield spread.

It also will be useful to have the ratio of volatilities of nominal yields to the nominal–real yield spread, that is,

$$\frac{\sigma_n}{\sigma_s} = \frac{\sigma_r}{\sigma_n}\left(2\rho_{r,s} + \frac{\sigma_r}{\sigma_s} + \frac{\sigma_s}{\sigma_r}\right) \tag{4.13}$$

Long-Term Betas Under normal conditions, we can estimate correlations and volatilities by looking at historical data from the United Kingdom and the United States. But, remembering the Fisher hypothesis, $\rho_{r,s} = 0$, and the fact that real yields are half as volatile as nominal yields, we get

$$\rho_{r,s} \approx 0 \tag{4.14}$$

$$\frac{\sigma_s}{\sigma_r} \approx 2 \tag{4.15}$$

$$\frac{\sigma_r}{\sigma_n} \approx \frac{1}{2} \tag{4.16}$$

so that

$$\rho_{r,n} \approx \frac{1}{2}(1 + 0) = 0.5 \tag{4.17}$$

and thus

$$D_n = D_r(0.25) \tag{4.18}$$

that is, the long-term beta is close to 0.25. A good rule of thumb is that the effective long-term beta is equal to the square of the ratio of real yield volatility to nominal yield volatility (assuming the Fisher hypothesis of zero long-term correlation between real yields and nominal–real yield spreads holds).

On the other hand, if we enter the quadrant of short-term growth and low/falling inflation over the next 6 to 12 months, we might expect a situation analogous to the United Kingdom in September 1992 to August 1994. Use the United Kingdom September 1992 to August 1994 correlation estimate between real yields and nominal–real yield spread of −0.20. Further, with a credible Fed expected to remain proactive in quashing incipient inflation, we expect the volatility of inflation to remain low, roughly of the same order of magnitude as real yield volatility.

The key result to remember is that the effective betas depend not only on the correlations in the "bad quadrant" but also on the ratio of the volatilities of real yields, nominal yields, and nominal–real yield spreads. Table 4.4 summarizes the possibilities.

To read this table, pick a correlation between real yields and nominal–real yield spreads from the first column, ratios of expected nominal to real yield volatilities from the second column, and ratio of

Table 4.4 Betas for Different Correlations of Real Yields and Inflation Expectations and Volatility Ratios of Nominal Yields, Real Yields, and Inflation Expectations.

$\rho_{r,s}$	$\frac{\sigma_n}{\sigma_r}$	$\frac{\sigma_r}{\sigma_s}$	$\frac{\sigma_n}{\sigma_s}$	$\rho_{r,n}$	$\beta_{r,n}$
−0.20	2	2	1.05	0.45	0.225
−0.20	2	1	0.80	0.4	0.2
−0.20	1	1	1.60	0.80	0.80
−0.50	2	1	0.50	0.25	0.125
0	2	2	1.25	0.50	0.25
0	1	1	2	1	1
0	2	0.5	1.25	0.50	0.25

(*Source:* Author's calculations)

real yield to spread volatility from the third column. Then the fourth column gives the effective implied nominal yield volatility to inflation expectation volatility, the fifth column gives the correlation of real to nominal yield changes, and the last column gives the real versus nominal yield beta.

TIPS sometimes trade with negative beta; that is, even as real yields fall, nominal yields rise. To discuss this in our formalism is easy. Referring to Eqs. (4.11) and (4.12), we can see that for $\beta_{n,r}$ to be negative, we need $\rho_{n,r}$ to be negative because the volatility ratio cannot be negative. But, for $\rho_{n,r}$ to be negative, we need the correlation of real yields and inflation expectations to be negative ($\rho_{r,s} < 0$), and the product of $\rho_{r,s}$ and σ_s/σ_r to be greater than 1. For example, if $\rho_{r,s} = -1$ and $\sigma_s/\sigma_r = 2$, then $\beta_{r,n} = -0.25$. The key point is this—to obtain betas between real yields and nominal yields to be more negative than 0.25, the ratio of inflation expectation volatility and real yield volatility has to rise substantially more than the long-term ratio. For the beta between real yields and nominal yields to be -0.50, the inflation expectation uncertainty has to be almost three times the uncertainty or volatility in real yields. Near turning points in the economy, this condition can be obtained easily but should be short-lived.

New Macro: Modeling When the Government Is a Participant

A financial engineer will tell you that he or she can price any asset if you give him or her the basic trio of P's: payoff, probability, and present value. A relative-value trader will add to this list the prevailing price of related securities. Using the pricing of closely related securities, the relative-value trader or arbitrageur first calibrates a risk-neutral model and then uses it to price the security at hand. On the other hand, a long-term investor interested in the absolute value of securities will add to this list of P's his or her preferences via a utility function. Based on how much the performance of the security adds to the utility of the investor's portfolio determines the price he or she is willing to pay. Events of last year have forced us to add to this plethora of P's another one that modelers have largely ignored but cannot continue to do so any longer: participants, both public (the government) and private. We explore pricing and risk management of portfolios in an environment where public participants are having an increasingly potent impact on valuations and market functioning. The string of recent announcements of various public-sector initiatives render this exercise far from simply being academic.

Let us review how pricing works with the three basic P's. Let's take the example of a simple corporate bond that pays off par if there is no default and zero if there is a default (i.e., no recovery value). In this example, we have only one probability: the probability of default. The probability of no default is just one minus the probability of default. To obtain the current fair price, we discount the probability-weighted future random price. In other words, the price is obtained simply by averaging all random outcomes by taking the expectation of present value × probability × payoff. To summarize, for the defaultable bond,

$$\text{Current price} = \text{present value} \times \text{probability of not defaulting} \times \text{ par}$$
$$(4.19)$$

Now let's explore how participants can impact the right-hand side of this equation. First, they can guarantee no default. Second, they can tilt odds so that there is less symmetry in the outcomes, that is, by making the probability of not defaulting higher. Finally, they can attempt to change the discount factor. The net effect is that a public participant with an infinite amount of capital theoretically can make prices of securities whatever it wants them to be. It is hard to argue with any degree of conviction whether participant actions of the magnitude we have seen so far is good or bad in the long run. However, we still can look back at recent events and enhance our pricing framework. To put the discussion in the context of what we have recently observed, we first note that the government's guarantee of loans from banks (e.g., through FDIC guarantee) can be construed to be an attempt to alter payoffs because it substantially reduces the likelihood that the lender would get anything less than the par amount. Opening up credit lines and accepting collateral in exchange for Fed loans presumably reduces the probability of liquidity-driven default risk (e.g., under the new-term repo facilities). Outright purchases of Treasuries, especially in the long end, as well as purchases of agency mortgages, may be translated as an effort to raise asset prices by reducing the discount factor. When the Fed announced on March 18, 2009, that it would purchase up to $300 billion of long Treasuries, it resulted in an intraday jump in the long bond futures contract of 4.82 percent on the news. From a risk-management perspective, this is massive because the annualized volatility of the bond futures contract in the options market is currently only 25 percent, which is extremely high by historical standards. Under the assumption of a lognormal price distribution, this annual implied volatility translates to only 1.5 percent daily volatility; that is, the best estimates of market participants was only a third of what was delivered on that day. This suggests that market pricing going forward should pay more heed to fatter-tailed events.

The government also has stepped in to provide leverage to investors via nonrecourse loans against consumer ABS (via the Term Asset-Backed Loan Facility (TALF)). A hypothetical example might make the impact on pricing clearer. Under the TALF program, each type of underlying collateral will have a Fed-designated haircut, that is, the amount of money that the investor has to put up. Assuming that the haircut is 7 percent, an investor can obtain 93 percent of nonrecourse funding from the Fed. The total buying power is now 100 percent. Assume further that the rate on the loan is LIBOR + 100. Then the borrowing cost per $100 invested is $93 $\times$ (L + 100). Suppose that the asset returns L + 200;

then the gross return to the portfolio is $100 \times (L + 200)$. The return on equity to a levered TALF investment equals the net portfolio return (= gross return − borrowing cost) divided by the investor equity; that is, $[\$100 \times (L + 200)] - [\$93 \times (L + 100)]/\$7 = L + 1529$. This asymmetric payoff has resulted in many recently issued TALF-eligible securities outperforming their non-TALF-eligible counterparts by a huge margin. Since the loan for each security is separate from the loans and asset values of all other securities, a portfolio of levered TALF holdings is a portfolio of puts (see "Master Loan and Security Agreement" at the N.Y. Fed Web site: www.newyorkfed.org/markets/TALF_MLSA.pdf). It is easy to understand the asymmetric impact of this on security prices because a portfolio of put options is much more valuable than a put on the portfolio [53].

In a similar vein to our bond futures example, note that when the announcement of May 20, 2009, that commercial mortgaged-backed securities (CMBS) would become eligible for TALF became public, the prices of these securities immediately jumped up. CMBX AAA indices (which constitute TALF-eligible bonds) jumped up by 5.9 percent between May 19 and May 20, 2009. Initially, other CMBS securities also showed similar price gains, but those which were not eligible for public funding immediately started to lose their gains. There is further evidence that targeted liquidity provision is leading to disperse outcomes. The impact of the massive amount of liquidity injected by the central bank has resulted in compression of the LIBOR–overnight indexed swap (OIS) rate. This spread is a good measure of the short-term default risk in the banking sector. Since LIBOR is also used as a reference for quotation of risky product spreads, making this spread narrow is tantamount to obtaining a lower risk premium for risky products that are indexed off this rate.

At this stage of the discussion, private participants and their preferences have to be considered. Private participants prefer more profits to less, and all else being equal, they prefer profits that come sooner to profits that come later. Public participants may well have a different objective function; that is, they may prefer longer-term prosperity over shorter-term profits. For instance, they might want to stabilize housing markets at any cost because this stabilizes so many other economically important variables. This creates a delicate equilibrium in which security prices are the result of a balancing act between the two different sets of preferences.

There is another subtle aspect to this pricing calculus that so far we have ignored. We have assumed that the averaging over scenarios (or the calculation of expectation) remains unchanged. But this assumption also needs to be challenged. If the distribution of security returns can be modified willy-nilly or is unknown, then the expectation cannot be computed reliably; in this case, the price cannot be determined with any degree of accuracy regardless of complete knowledge of the discount factor and the payoff. This type of uncertainty is the most perverse and, all else being equal, tends to depress prices toward lower values. This lower bound of security prices then is the most pessimistic outcome under any distribution. The fatter the tail of the distribution, the more likely is the possibility that the market discounts the price to be closer to the tail. Without public participants, securities naturally would fall toward this lower bound. The only possible cure is for the public participant to select certain asset classes and securities that have a substantial possibility of adversely impacting the social good and bid up their prices. In doing so, the public participant short circuits the basic pricing calculus and changes the arithmetic from one based on probability to one based on its selection criteria.

Finally, we know that prices of securities have multiple purposes. One of the primary purposes is the information content of the price. As a matter of fact, our financial engineer can extract the information content embedded in the price by the process of calibration of the prices to the basic trio of P's we mentioned at the start of this section. Once the price becomes subject to the impact of a participant, the calibration process fails. Since calibration of future price evolution is based on the availability of reliable (and under risk-neutral pricing, tradable) information on prices of all maturities, this failure to calibrate introduces a path dependence on valuation even for assets that are basically path independent under the classic three P's pricing framework.

What about risk management of portfolios in such an environment? The market risk to a security is the sensitivity to shocks to the trio of P's above. For many complex securities, the payoff depends on the path (another P) taken by the security. For instance, for mortgage-backed securities (MBS), the balance in a mortgage depends on the path of prior prepayments and defaults; shocking the parameters that define the probability distribution of prepayments and defaults changes the price of the mortgage security. Now include into the risk model the participant who can change any of the basic trio of P's, and we have a new risk factor, that is, the magnitude and frequency of its actions. Unfortunately, this risk factor lies beyond the reach of traditional risk-management models. The existence of a wide variety of traded instruments in the market has been to facilitate the ability of participants to transfer risk among each other and to "hedge" out the unwanted risks. To hedge against the risk resulting from the actions of a public participant, we would either need securities that adjust immediately to their actions or a blanket guarantee that the public participant would mitigate any risk arising from its own actions. To my mind, such securities (with perhaps the exception of sovereign bonds) are not easily available. The impactful actions of participants thus can make formerly complete markets into incomplete markets. However, I am sure the investment community will rush in to fill this gap as derivatives markets recover.

An interesting example for risk measurement is found when computing interest-rate durations of floaters. Floaters are simply fixed income instruments that pay some contractual spread (known as *discount margin*) above a floating-rate index such as the 3-month LIBOR. As long as the bond is trading close to par, we know that the interest-rate duration on this floater is close to the reset period. Now, if the issuing corporation suffers a decline in its credit quality, the contractual margin will not be sufficient to compensate investors for increased default risk. This translates into a lower price for the floater or, stated another way, a market spread that is much larger than the discount margin. One can think of the discounted floater as a long position in a par floater and a short position in an annuity that pays the difference between the margin and the market spread. As the market spread becomes much larger than the margin, its impact on the risks of the floater grow. The outcome is that a long-term, discount floater can have a large negative interest-rate duration; that is, as LIBOR rates rise, the price of the floater rises rather than falling. Another way to see this result is that as the credit deteriorates, the front-end cash flows are more likely to be received, whereas the bond principal might not be received owing to defaults. Thus, as the LIBOR rises, the front-end coupons increase in value. But putting the government in the mix easily can change this most fundamental of risks. First, with an infinite amount of capital, the spreads can be driven down to make the bond trade like a par bond, trivially making interest-rate duration positive. Second, the government can make an implicit change to the payoff on the bond by reducing the face value of the bond (e.g., under burden sharing) and mitigate the likelihood of further defaults. This bond again has negligible nonnegative interest-rate duration. Our example shows that when participants are able to have such substantial impact on capital markets, not only do prices become hard to assess, but risk measurement also can become a very difficult task. The quantitative metrics we have relied on to make investment decisions become very blunt tools and can give widely conflicting results.

What can one do to manage the valuation and risks of portfolios in this environment of greater public-sector involvement in a range of markets? First and foremost, absolute valuation of securities should balance excessive focus on relative valuation because there is considerable uncertainty as to which security can be targeted for a new paradigm price. Second, security prices are likely to reflect, even more than they have before today, the macroeconomic conditions that are likely to prevail. Third, diversification based on traditional measures of risk and return and comovement relationships can break down as a new common factor becomes critical in determining outcomes. Identifying the key factors that will be relevant for risk management should take precedence over forecasting returns, volatilities, and correlations. Finally, in a world where public and private preferences, which have different horizons of measurement, come into conflict, markets should be expected to be more turbulent, and the concept of built-in "tail-risk" hedges is critical because we should expect to see more frequent jumps. Of course, this story will evolve over the next few years but the phenomenon of increasing influence from potent participants requires an approach where portfolios are constructed from first principles and ranked according to their robustness to anticipants' actions. In a world where historical normal-period experience, even with decades of data, has little relevance to valuation, it should be no surprise to risk managers that risk-management statistics and concepts are also candidates for challenge. While there is no one cure-all, fortunately, the push toward simplicity in investment portfolios that the new environment requires should be a welcome development.

5

Replication

Fixed income derivatives can be classified into linear instruments such as swaps and futures and nonlinear instruments such as options. In this chapter we will discuss the use of derivatives for replication, as well as the risks that arise from embedded leverage. We discussed earlier how derivatives can provide "structural" alpha owing to various features such as the delivery option in futures contracts. Investors with access to robust risk-measurement tools thus can take advantage of derivatives to get exposure to the broad market factors while harvesting the structural alpha.

Leverage with Futures Contracts

Consider a long position in 100 million of the 10-year note futures contracts. The contract size for this security is $100,000 per contract. At a hypothetical price of 105, this translates to a value of $105,000 per contract. To enter into a long position on the contract requires that an investor put up a much smaller amount as margin. For a speculator, the current initial margin is $2,430 per contract, and the maintenance margin is $1,800 (the margin that once the position has been initiated needs to be maintained). In terms of the effective leverage, we can divide the market value by the margin to obtain an almost 20 to 1 leverage on the futures contract. The margin can change based on the expected volatility of the underlying instruments.[1] Most exchanges, for instance, have a mechanism to forecast the probability of a tail event and require investors to maintain sufficient margin against negative mark-to-market events.

Replication

Investment returns are basically the sum of returns from betas (or systematic factors), alphas (nonsystematic), and timing. There are deep liquid markets that allow for betas to be replicated efficiently. For instance, the beta of the Standard and Poor's 500 Index (S&P500) can be replicated using S&P500 futures contracts. The key idea of alpha-beta separation is to use part of the cash to obtain beta effciently and to use the rest to generate better risk-adjusted return through alpha strategies. Typically, equity, commodity, and even currency beta has been easy to obtain, but fixed income beta has been harder. This is due in part to the more heterogeneous nature of fixed income securities and in part to increased transactions costs.

---

[1] To estimate this, assume that the volatility of the contract is 8 percent per year. This volatility either can be estimated from the options markets or can be extracted by looking at historical data and computing the standard deviation and annualizing it (realized volatility). Assuming a normal distribution, we can compute the probability of a left-tail 5 percent outcome by computing the 5 percent quantile of the distribution. This can be represented mathematically as the outcome

$$\frac{1}{\sigma\sqrt{2\pi}} \int_{-\infty}^{a} \phi(x)dx = p(0.05) \tag{5.1}$$

where $\phi(x)$ is the normal density, $\sigma = 0.08$ is the volatility, and $a = 0.05$ is the 5 percent cutoff. Conceptually, we can replace the distribution with another, "fatter-tailed" one to obtain the proper margin amount to set aside.

The biggest advantage of derivatives is that they allow the user to replicate the performance of the underlying systematic risk factors in an efficient manner. We can, for instance, take a broad bond-market index such as the Barclays/Lehman U.S. Aggregate and show that its long-term performance can be tracked with a high degree of accuracy with only a handful of derivatives. This is a significant observation because the index consists of thousands of securities from all bond-market sectors. The key to understanding this risk is that the underlying factors that drive the performance of the index are only a few. At the highest level, duration risk, curve risk, spread risks (from the corporate and mortgage areas), and convexity are the dominant risks [6]. For an index such as the Barclays/Lehman U.S. Aggregate, roughly 50 to 60 percent of the index volatility arises from yield-curve risk such as duration and curve, 10 to 20 percent from spread movements, and 15 to 20 percent from credit during normal times. In periods of crisis, this dependence can change significantly, so it is important to remember that a coarse replication strategy can exhibit significant tracking error. When we expand the approach to bigger indices such as the Global Aggregate, we need to generalize the risk factors to all the different regions. Since the fraction of risks driven by the smaller regions and countries is small, the risk tracking can be handled by including only the factors from the United States, Euroland, the United Kingdom, and Japan. Similar approaches might be taken for other asset-class indices, such as corporate credit, mortgages, high yield, and so on. The interested reader should read the articles on the topic in [22].

To systematically approach the replication exercise, we need to discuss the choice of algorithm, the use of instruments, the trade-off between frequency of replication and the horizon, and how much leverage to build in.

There are basically three ways to think about systematically creating a replication algorithm. First, if we have a pure cash instrument–based replication, we can simply think of slicing the index that we are trying to replicate into buckets. The most easily available buckets are the sector and duration (or maturity) buckets. Then we can set a threshold that each bucket would contribute a minimum amount (both in number and in market value) of securities to the overall replication. Additional constraints are critical as well. For instance, we do not want to sacrifice much yield or structural alpha (convexity) in the replication. The second approach is to use a risk model of some sort to select securities that minimize the tracking error between the index and the portfolio. The risk model effectively computes the volatility and correlation of each security and, based on the index weights and the proposed portfolio weights, computes the tracking error. The last method reduces the risks of the index to some small set of factors. Then one can look for easy-to-transact securities that replicate the risks of the index. Frequently, this is achieved using derivatives.

The closer one wants to track the index, the more cash instruments are needed. Indeed, Figures 5.1 and 5.2 show that increasing the number of bonds reduces the tracking error for a replicating portfolio very quickly for the Barclays/Lehman Global Aggregate. However, the cost is that with a large index, the transactions can get unwieldy. Since every month new instruments are introduced into the index, a full cash replication requires not only purchase of the new instruments but also transactions to rebalance the old composition. At the other end of the spectrum, we can use liquid derivatives. Whereas derivatives can match factor risks such as the ones mentioned earlier, they have their own idiosyncracies that might result in high tracking error. However, if one is willing to evaluate the cost of the tracking error in terms of the potential excess return gains from investing the unencumbered cash elsewhere, this tracking error might not turn out to be significant at all. For investors with longer horizons, allowing a little bit of excess tracking error, say, from using futures contracts for replication, might translate into substantial excess alpha that effectively pays for part of the replication costs.

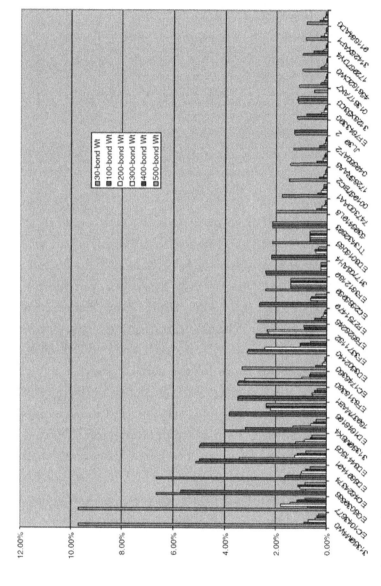

Figure 5.1 Replication of the Barclays/Lehman Global Aggregate Index using cash bonds only. The bars denote the concentration using different number of bonds for replication. (*Source: Author.*)

Bonds in portfolio	Ex-ante Tracking Error Volatility
30	75
100	62
200	53
300	31
400	18
500	18

Figure 5.2 Reduction of tracking error as the number of cash bonds is increased for replicating the Barclays/Lehman Global Aggregate Index. (*Source*: Author.)

Not all derivative markets trade with the same liquidity. In the United States, the 2-, 5-, 10-, and 30-year futures contracts are the most liquid. In Europe, we have a similar liquidity across the yield curve, but in the United Kingdom, typically only the 10-year gilt futures contract trades with comparable liquidity. Similarly, in Japan, the 10-year Japanese Government Bond (JGB) futures contract is really the only liquid point. We can move away from exchange-traded futures contracts and use interest-rate swaps for replication. However, as we have seen, the swap curve can be quite volatile relative to the government curve. Recent credit-market crises indeed drove short-term swap spreads to very high levels, whereas demand for duration- and liability-driven investing drove long-term swaps in the United States and the United Kingdom into deeply negative territory. This increased volatility in swaps makes their usage for replication less desirable. One other comparative advantage of futures contracts is that owing to the embedded option value. We know, however, that this structural value is a consequence of the delivery option, whose value can rise if the yield curve is volatile. However, investors who are not forced to rebalance their portfolios daily to the duration and yield-curve noise can hold these options and harvest the premium, which reduces some of the negative drag from replication transactions.

As an example, by matching factors, we obtained an ex ante tracking error of only 25 basis points per year versus the BCAG in September 2007:

- Futures: 16.4 percent 5-year futures, 27.4 percent 10-year futures, 0.9 percent long bond futures
- Swaps: 3.2 percent 30-year swaps
- Mortgage TBAs: 32.7 percent of Fannie Mae 5 percent TBA
- Credit: 19.3 percent CDX IG9 5-year maturity

This portfolio assumes nothing about the relative value in each of these asset classes. Some "on the run" derivatives trade richer than others simply because they are relatively more liquid. By paying careful attention to their relative value one can improve the performance of the replication substantially.

Figure 5.3 shows the historical performance of a simple derivatives-based replicating portfolio for the Barclays/Lehman Aggregate Index. Note that we use the factor-matching algorithm to figure out the best basket that matches the exposures of the index and then hold the basket fixed for the rest of the month. As we can see, the tracking error of the approach is very low until the crisis of 2007. Since the CDX indices used in the replication are very coarse at tracking the idiosyncratic part of the credit risk, as the financial markets melted down, the replicating portfolio did not lose as much as the index (because the index did worse owing both to more idiosyncratic financials risk and to the increased illiquidity premium of the cash-bond sector). On the other hand, as the credit market has rebounded, the index has perfomed better on the upside and regained some of the underperformance.

Practically speaking, we also want to make sure that the replication portfolio does not change by a large amount month to month. This is critical to ensure that the transactions costs do not become overwhelmingly large. Figure 5.4 shows that whereas there were some

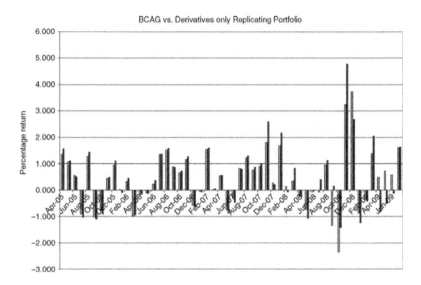

Figure 5.3 Replication of the Barclays/Lehman Capital U.S. Aggregate Index (formerly the Lehman Brothers Aggregate Index) using derivatives. Light bars show the index return, and dark bars show the replicating portfolio returns. (*Source*: Author.)

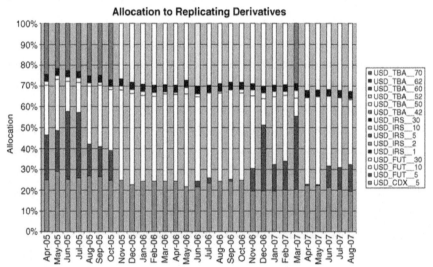

Figure 5.4 Stability of replication of the Barclays/Lehman Capital U.S. Aggregate Index (formerly the Lehman Brothers Aggregate Index) using derivatives. (*Source*: Author.)

switches month to month on particular TBA coupons and swaps, the allocations broadly to the underlying set of derivatives remained fairly stable.

The biggest risk of derivatives is that they provide leverage, hence the ability to magnify the errors in their usage. Of course, there are other risks, such as counterparty risk, especially for over-the-counter (OTC) derivatives that have to be managed. Many investors who had replication trades with now-defunct Wall Street firms in 2007 and 2008 found that not only did they suffer a mark-to-market impact when these firms defaulted (because the bond market generally rallied during the crisis), but they also lost their exposures and had to scramble to find replacements.

When we get to indices that have a larger amount of idiosyncratic risk such as credit or high-yield indices, the replication using derivatives becomes even coarser. As an example, see that in Figures 5.5 and 5.6 we

ML Master II
Method: Least Squares
Date: 09/23/09   Time: 09:58
Sample (adjusted): 2005M07 2009M06
Included observations: 48 after adjustments

	Coefficient	Std. Error	t-Statistic	Prob.
C	0.46	0.31	1.48	0.15
SPX	0.24	0.19	1.27	0.21
NASDAQ	0.05	0.16	0.33	0.74
VIX	(0.32)	0.09	(3.66)	0.00
HYLIQ	(0.02)	0.01	(3.05)	0.00
DUR	1.43	1.26	1.13	0.26
CURVE	2.81	1.73	1.62	0.11
R-squared	0.78	Mean dependent va		0.29
Adjusted R-squared	0.75	S.D. dependent var		4.08
S.E. of regression	2.04	Akaike info criterion		4.40
Sum squared resid	170.34	Schwarz criterion		4.67
Log likelihood	(98.51)	Hannan-Quinn criter		4.50
F-statistic	24.54	Durbin-Watson stat		2.10
Prob(F-statistic)	0			

Figure 5.5   Replicating the Merrill Lynch HY Master Index with derivatives. (*Source*: Author.)

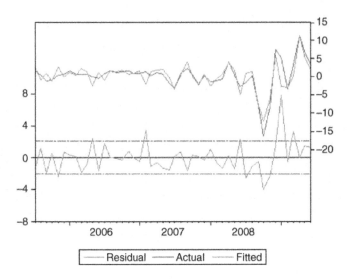

Figure 5.6 Tracking of the Merrill Lynch HY Master Index with systematic risk factors. (*Source*: Author.)

can replicate the broad high-yield (HY) cash market's systematic risks by taking positions in volatility and systemic HY risk (as measured by the HY 35-100 tranche). This realization, that the risks of broad market indices are replicable by a small set of securities, is extremely powerful in separating the beta of a strategy from the alpha.

Fixed Income ETFs

Exchange-traded funds (ETFs) are baskets of assets. While the dominant market is one of equity ETFs (i.e., the underlying instruments are stocks), the fixed income ETF market is showing rapid growth. As of the end of 2009, the total ETF assets globally are approximately $1 trillion, with fixed income assets at $157 billion. This 15 percent fixed income fraction is large given that a decade ago fixed income ETFs were almost 0 percent of the total ETF assets under management. Compare this with the mutual fund industry, where according to the Investment Company Institute, there were almost 66,000 mutual funds, with a total of $20 trillion under management (with $7 trillion in equities, $3.9 trillion in fixed income, and $5.8 trillion in money markets. The rest were in balanced or alternative-fund assets).

ETFs depend on a unique "creation" process, whereby authorized participants (APs) take the cash from the end user, purchase securities, and deposit them into the ETF. In exchange, the ETF provider issues the ETF shares. The reverse "redemption" process requires that the APs return the shares in exchange for an in-kind transfer of the basket of securities.

The ETF markets bring fixed income into the equity world. Since ETFs trade on exchanges like stocks, the baskets can be bought and sold with relative ease. In doing so, they provide the holder with particular exposures to the broad markets or to sectors. This allows ease of implementation of risk-factor-based asset allocation. There are some other major benefits:

- ETFs are transparent, and investors can see the holdings.
- ETFs provide liquidity because they are traded on exchanges. For many fixed income ETFs, the ETF is more liquid than the underlying holdings. Also, the ETF provides daily liquidity because new ETF shares may be created or redeemed for either the component bonds or for cash.
- ETFs provide immediate diversification benefits because there are usually more than a few bonds in the ETF. This reduces the idiosyncratic risks that investors would have if they assembled individual bonds. However, there is a trade-off. If some bonds are trading rich and the ETF holds them, they would have long-term underperformance. So a flexible replication of the desired indices incurring minor excess tracking error to the index is the more optimal strategy.
- ETFs are typically quite cost-effective relative to funds. This is so because the construction of an ETF is a mechanical process,

and the extra fees that most funds command is due to the alpha they promise to add (passive ETFs do not have any alpha).

- Many ETFs also allow for the lending of the holdings via repos or, more accurately, "securities lending." This can significantly reduce the carry cost, especially when particular bonds are in high demand.
- ETFs may offer significant tax benefits. Since the shares that are exchanged for the securities are in-kind, the ETF holder does not pay capital gains taxes when he or she redeems the shares.

ETFs are required to post a frequent intraday net asset value (INAV), which fluctuates with the market value of the securities. Since many fixed income securities do not trade during the day, the pricing at best can be a good approximation to the actual price. However, the activity of ETF arbitrageurs or market makers pushes the traded price of the ETF basket close to its net asset value (NAV). When the NAV is higher than the traded price, the ETF is trading at a discount, and an arbitrageur theoretically can purchase the ETF shares and short the underlying basket. On the other hand, when the ETF is trading higher than the NAV, the arbitrageur can borrow the ETF shares to short and buy the underlying securities. This arbitrage mechanism, however, can fail when there is persistent demand or supply of ETF shares or when the access to purchase or shorting of the basket securities is hard to do.

The industry has pursued the replication of indices in two different ways. In the full-replication methodology, the ETF provider matches the index exactly. The obvious benefit is the elimination of tracking error to the index. However, this type of replication can create long-term frictions as rich securities in the index are purchased along with the cheaper ones. On the other extreme is a risk-based replication, which attempts to match the risks of the index but does not hold expensive bonds. The increased tracking error is the price of reduced replication costs. The intermediate approach, which matches "cells" by picking representative bonds from each category and maturity while also matching the risk-factor exposures, provides a compromise between the two approaches.

6

Stress Testing and Tail Risk Management

The option-based approach to asset valuation requires that any risk-management framework be able to capture the impact of inherent non-linearities in real-world situations. If we think of a portfolio as consisting of various long and short option positions, then stress testing the portfolio to various market outcomes is a reasonable starting point to quantify the risks that can substantially impair a portfolio. As we have discussed earlier, this approach also releases the investor from the clutches of excessive dependence on locally calibrated models that are likley to fail in illiquid, real-world situations. This chapter will systematically discuss the elements of stress testing and tail risk management. This is especially relevant for levered strategies that depend on derivatives or embedded options.

Portfolio risk measurement begins with the identification of a set of fundamental market variables that drives the prices of the securities that constitute the portfolio. The values taken by fundamental market variables are determined by demand and supply, perceptions of

security-specific return, and risk, liquidity, and the overall level of risk
aversion of investors.

Stress Testing

Stress testing is the measurement of the sensitivity of an aggregate portfolio to certain predefined scenarios of the market variables. Reasonable
shock magnitudes and the probability of occurrence can be determined
either by doing a distributional analysis of the past history of the
market factors or by overlaying the forecast of economic conditions
on the forecast factor realizations. End users of the scenario analysis
determine whether the factor shocks should be defined by reference to
orthogonal factors or with respect to correlated factors. They are also
usually responsible for estimating the relative likelihood of different
stress events happening, that is, for the estimation or forecast of the risk
factor distribution, because stress tests intrinsically carry no probability
information. In principle, knowledge of all the moments of the full
distribution of factors, including the factor covariances, is required to
determine the total risk of the portfolio, either with correlated factors
that are intuitive to the end user or with orthogonal factors that are
usually nonintuitive but economical. In practice, however, the risk of
sufficiently well-diversified portfolios can be replicated just by retaining
the leading moments of the full portfolio distribution. Finally, the time
horizon relevant to the stress test has to be identified.

Identification of Market Variables

To ensure that the chosen stress shock algorithm is dynamic and leads to
real-time risk management, the first step is to identify the variables that
are the drivers of security prices. For instance, the price of a Treasury
bond is determined by the level of all rates along the yield curve. One can
choose these market rates to be par yields, spot yields, or forward yields

of the Treasury curve, or if one chooses, a different rate benchmark can be used. The LIBOR swap curve is frequently used as the benchmark. If one uses the swap curve as the benchmark, then the risk of a Treasury bond needs to be measured with reference to two variables—the swap yield curve and the swap spread between the Treasury curve and the swap curve at each forward point. Choosing a good benchmark simply makes interpretation of the output of the stress-testing system more useful and efficient.

As the portfolio becomes more complex, holding, for instance, corporate bonds, mortgage-backed securities (MBS), inflation-linked bonds, tax-exempt bonds, and equity-linked structures, the market variable set has to be appropriately generalized to include credit spreads, implied volatility, prepayments, implied inflation rates, equity prices and implied volatility, and so on. Representative traded securities can be selected whose linear combinations give measurements of each of these factor exposures. This is an extension of the classic option-pricing approach of creating a dynamic portfolio of idealized systematic risks, each of which can be replicated by holding positions in a certain complete set of benchmark securities locally. This point is absolutely key to any stress-testing analysis—unless all possible dominant stress factors are included in the risk management and representative securities that are "carriers" of those securities are found, the approach will not capture portfolio risk.

Translating Market Variables into Systematic Risk Factors

To translate market variables into risk factors, a model is required. The model can be very simple or very complex, and the degree of complexity really depends on the needs of the end user. For instance, for a Treasury bond, the sensitivity of the price of the bond to parallel shifts in the yield can be computed in closed form by a formula for duration or duration plus convexity. On the other hand, the sensitivity of the bond also can be computed to all orders simply by shifting the underlying yield curve in parallel by a predetermined amount. The impact of actual shifts of the yield curve depend on how the dynamic evolution of the yield curve itself is specified and calibrated. There are again numerous choices for yield-curve construction—one can use a simple single-factor model calibrated to points on the yield curve or more complex multifactor models that are calibrated to the benchmark yield curve, volatilities, and correlations of instruments and allow for more sophisticated yield-curve dynamics. There are two key points to remember. First, if there are not enough securities with liquid traded prices, then a complex model can fail in the calibration step, and it actually can be worse as a tool than a simple approximation. Second, going to a complex model drastically increases the number of computations that need to be done and is really justified only if the portfolio consists of complex securities with embedded options that cannot be priced using simple approximations. Thus, whereas the stress testing of a portfolio that is heavy in MBS will benefit from a complex model for yield curves, prepayments, and volatilities, a portfolio that consists simply of noncallable Treasury bonds will not benefit appreciably.

Proceeding analogously, once models for the classes of securities are available, to obtain the stress risk, one simply moves the underlying factors in a self-consistent (arbitrage-free) way, reads the change in prices, and computes the risk-factor exposures. For a complex fixed income portfolio, the risk factors that span the portfolio might consist of impact owing to level shifts (in many different countries if the portfolio holds global bonds), curve steepening or flattening shocks, shocks to spreads via changes of option-adjusted spreads, and so on. At any given point in time, the risk manager will look at this zoo of factor exposures and decide which ones are of concern and which ones are not of concern given what he or she believes the possible impact of market movements will be. Then the partial sensitivity of the portfolio to a given factor shock is simply the product of the factor shock and the expected magnitude of the factor shock.

The factor shocks are like the equity beta concept that anyone who has studied the Capital Asset Pricing Model (CAPM) knows. The expected return of the portfolio is proportional to the beta loading to each different factor. This is the primary reason behind doing scenario analysis—unless one knows the source of returns owing to factor shocks, one does not know whether the performance is due to luck or investor skill. More return generally comes with more risk, unless there are arbitrage opportunities (more on this below).

Nonsystematic Risk

Two different portfolios or, for that matter, any number of investors may be ranked for their skill by first benchmarking them to the same index and then by limiting them in terms of the maximum relative exposures they can take for each systematic factor shock. Given a set of such portfolios, the residual dispersion in performance is, by definition, due to nonsystematic factor exposures. The immediate question, then, is, How does one do scenario analysis for nonsystematic, or security-specific, risk? For example, in the world of fixed income arbitrage, a common trade is to short the on-the-run bond (the most current issue) and buy the off-the-run bond (an older issue). The difference in yields between the two issues is commonly thought to be a free gain, and most stress-testing systems will capture no risk owing to the spread trade (especially if the two bonds are close in maturity and coupon). But this ignores possibly one of the biggest systematic risks of all—liquidity risk. The reason behind the spread between on-the-run and off-the-run bonds is the differential performance of the two securities in periods of crisis. In a very real sense, during periods of crisis, holders of the new issue find it easier to raise cash against the security as collateral in the repo market. In periods of crisis, such as 1998, the value of the liquidity premium got to be enormous, almost a 15 standard deviation event! This example points to two principles. First, the underlying distributions of security pairs frequently may be non gaussian, and the apparent normal behavior is due to the fact that the liquidity risk factor is being ignored owing to its rare large impact. Second, and more important, it points to the completeness problem in its naked glory; that is, if any factor is ignored, the risk system can be fooled into thinking that there is no risk while there is an enormous amount of risk (especially when the assumption of no risk leads to leveraging the opportunity). It is good to remember that what seems to be a nonsystematic, or security-specific, factor will in time get arbitraged away and will become a systematic risk factor that needs to be stress-shocked.

Two questions also arise immediately: (1) How does one measure the liquidity risk factor? and (2) How does one shock the liquidity risk factor? Clearly, one cannot just use the history of the new bond versus old bond spread to measure the distribution of the liquidity factor because it is very fat tailed, and there might not be enough data for calibration. However, the lack of probability information does not mean that one cannot shock the liquidity risk factor to measure its impact on the portfolio. A simple approach is to assume that as liquidity gets spotty, the cost of funding rises by a large amount (i.e., the repo-reverse differential blows out), and to measure the impact of this assumption on the portfolio. Another approach is to think of liquidity shock as equivalent to taking correlations to extreme values during stressed regimes. We discuss liquidity risk measurement in considerable detail below.

Choosing the Shock Magnitudes

The magnitude of each factor shock has to serve three important purposes. First, the shock magnitude has to be large enough to capture a large portion of the factor risk. For example, a 1 basis point shock will not really serve the scenario analysis well for MBS because it does not capture much of the negative convexity, especially when the embedded optionality is more complex. A larger shock magnitude has to be chosen. Second, the shock magnitude has to be realistic in the context of historical and anticipated future outcomes. For instance, shocking interest rates by 500 basis points certainly would capture the negative convexity of an MBS but probably would be useless as a tool to illuminate risk management on a daily basis and thus useless for risk-taking as well. Arbitrage bounds on possible outcomes correspond to the final and most important constraint on stress testing. In many realistic cases, it simply may be mathematically inconsistent to simultaneously shock a number of correlated shock factors by independent large amounts. There are numerous practitioners who advertise stress shocks across various correlated factors that are large and are designed to make investors psychologically comfortable, but unfortunately, many of those stress shocks cannot occur simultaneously. To take an extreme example, assume that there are two independent stress shocks of the currently low-yielding Japanese yield curve; the first one is a parallel shift up or down by 50 basis points, and the second one is a steepening or flattening of 50 basis points. Now, given the low yields in Japan as of this writing, you cannot reasonably have a 50 basis point steepening and a 50 basis point downward parallel shock simultaneously because that would drive some yields below zero. On the other hand, you can have a shock of the level upward of 50 basis points with a 50 basis point flattening. The point is that the correlation matrix of stress shocks is highly constrained, and it is simply not possible to imagine any and all scenario shocks as equally likely. In a recent paper we discussed the constraints on the correlation matrix using a simple geometric rule [44]. Of course, the analysis also can be turned on its head. Given a portfolio with factor exposures and a covariance matrix of the factors (and higher moments if a tail analysis is of interest), one can solve for the combination of factor shocks that would lead to maximal loss or to a given threshold loss.

Historical versus Forward-Looking

Of course, if one were to use historical periods to estimate the shock magnitudes and shock correlations of particular crisis days, one is assured that there would be no mathematical inconsistencies. However, history-based stress testing assumes that the future will repeat particular days or combination of days from the past. Obviously, this rarely holds true in real markets. Every crisis is different in its microscopic details. Future probabilities, especially in stressed situations, are not similar to past probabilities. Stress tests are tools to gauge potential vulnerability to exceptional but plausible events. The risk manager who is really interested in ensuring portfolio safety for the *future* instead of the past needs to forecast what elements of the portfolio stand to negatively impact the portfolio and stress test them simultaneously and consistently. This is necessarily subjective but very flexible because the risk manager has the ability to visualize outcomes that have never been realized and create them consistently. Weighting the likely outcomes higher than the unlikely ones, the risk manager then has the ability to apply the relevant controls to the portfolio according to the risks that make sense.

Details of this approach are presented in Bhansali and Wise [44]. First, the risk manager identifies which factor exposures have the most loading, that is, which factors can impact the portfolio the most independently and in conjunction. Then the risk manager chooses magnitudes for the factor shocks and the level of correlation between the factor shocks, that is, how likely is it that the shocks happen simultaneously. Of course, changing the correlations for some factor shocks cannot be done while freely changing many other factor correlations (otherwise, the correlation matrix can become mathematically inconsistent) at the same time. However, since the risk manager usually has different degrees of confidence in certain correlation forecasts, the approach gives the risk manager the ability to weigh how the correlation matrix adjusts itself to be mathematically consistent while at the same time creating a shocked environment that is complete.

Choice of Time Horizon

The choice of stress-test time horizon becomes very important for portfolios that run a mismatch between assets and liabilities. For leveraged portfolios, the impact of stress tests has special relevance for the time interval for which securities are lent out or borrowed not only because an adverse market movement can result in margin calls and forced liquidation but also because defaults of counterparties can lead to significant loss of mark-to-market. Most stress-test algorithms assume that the scenarios are realized over an instantaneous period. While this is simple to implement, it has the significant shortcoming that for portfolios that derive significant income from options or "carry" trades, the overall risk of the portfolio is overstated. In principle, we find that it is better to shock the arbitrage-free market realization for a forward horizon date, where the horizon date is chosen to be the average time to which the portfolio is expected to perform.

Measuring Systemic and Liquidity Risk

Financial crises are frequently associated with deleveraging and a loss of liquidity. In the language of options that we have used in this book, investors have a procyclical tendency to sell the liquidity option; that is, they replace more liquid securities with less liquid securities in exchange for a small option premium. In fixed income, this liquidity premium is expressed as an excess yield over the most liquid asset, the overnight repo rate.

We can discuss the measurement of liquidity risk using three different approaches. The first approach is statistical; that is, we can look at the behavior of various asset sectors and extract the common liquidity factor in their returns using a factor analysis or principal-component analysis (PCA). The second approach is a market-implied measure where we extract the liquidity risk from traded prices of securities such as tranches. Finally, we also can do a forward-looking estimate of liquidity by polling various participants. The poll effectively gives the specialist the freedom to assign liquidity measures to assets with all the information they have in hand, such as bid-offer spreads, the ability to move size, and the ability to finance positions easily.

To extract the common factor-based liquidity metric, we can begin by collecting option-adjusted spread data on various asset classes, such as agencies, financials, industrial corporates, high yield, mortgages, and so on. Index providers have created indices for each of these sectors and store performance data. The approach is straightforward: Compute the covariance matrix of the option-adjusted spreads, and do a PCA decomposition. The dominant common factor is the liquidity factor. Once this factor is extracted, we can regress the actual returns of asset classes on this factor to get liquidity betas for various assets. The shortcoming of the PCA-based liquidity measure is that it does not distinguish between liquidity and risk premium (because we are looking at real-world historical data). Also, if we are unlucky enough to use periods in the analysis that are "special," the econometric estimates will have no way of telling whether the estimates are expected to be stable for the future. Usually they are not.

As an example, using data from 1990 to 2007, we calculate the liquidity beta of BAA corporates to be 0.15, of Freddie Mac MBS to be 0.17, and of Ba U.S. High Yield Index to be 1.28.

The dramatic meltdown in the subprime market during 2007 and 2008 raised many red flags among market participants about their potential exposure to broader systemic credit shocks. These heightened concerns resulted in dramatic declines in market liquidity, restricted access to credit, flights to quality, sharply increased market volatility, and larger risk premia in many financial markets.

In this section we use the prices of indexed credit derivatives to extract market expectations about the nature and magnitude of the credit risks facing financial markets. Since their inception in 2002, indexed credit derivatives markets have exploded in size and participation. Broad indices are now traded for U.S. (CDX) and European (ITRAXX) credit markets with usually very deep liquidity and to a lesser degree for Japanese and U.K. credit markets. As of the end of 2009, the U.S. investment-grade index was in its thirteenth generation, and its European counterpart was in its eighth generation. What has been even more striking than the success of the indices, however, is the launch and success of tranches on the indices. Tranches can best be thought of as call spreads on the credit losses of a portfolio. Investors can use tranches to control their exposure to particular loss thresholds. To extract the information from these credit derivatives, we first develop a simple linearized version of the collateralized debt obligation model of Longstaff and Rajan [16]. They propose a three-jump model that is calibrated to the traded spreads of tranches and indices directly. Their model allows for the possibility that credit spreads might be a composite of several different types of credit risk. Specifically, they find that the credit loss distribution embedded in index tranche prices includes a component for the risk of idiosyncratic or firm-specific defaults, a component for the risk of broader sector-wide or industry-wide defaults, and a component for the risk of a massive economy-wide default scenario. We then fit the linearized version of the model to the market prices of the credit indices and tranches.

The results have many important implications. Using current data for both U.S. investment-grade and high-yield indexes as well as for longer tenors, we likewise find that the market anticipates three different types of credit risks: idiosyncratic credit events, broader sector-wide credit events, and economy-wide credit events. What is particularly striking, however, is that the nature of systemic credit risk appears to have changed dramatically over time. In particular, systemic credit risk was only a small percentage of total credit risk during the autodowngrade credit crisis of May 2005. In the recent subprime crisis, however, systemic credit risk ballooned and approximated the size of the idiosyncratic component of credit spreads.

Following the work in Lo and MacKinlay [7] and Bhansali, Gingrich, and Longstaff [46], let L denote the proportion of portfolio losses realized on a credit portfolio. We write the proportion of portfolio losses as

$$L = \gamma_1 N_1 + \gamma_2 N_2 + \gamma_3 N_3 \tag{6.1}$$

where $L_0 = 0$, the γ_i (where $i = 1, 2, 3$) parameters denote jump sizes, and N_i are independent Poisson counters that correspond to the number of jumps. Note that this allows for $L > 1$, but in practice, we never realize such large values of L.[1] In terms of constant intensities λ_i over a period T, we can write the probability of j jumps for the ith Poisson process P_{ij} as

$$P_{ij} = \frac{e^{-\lambda_i T}(\lambda_i T)^j}{j!} \tag{6.2}$$

The risk-neutral pricing equation for the index (e.g., the CDX) of maturity T implies that the coupon C for the index can be solved for by setting the value of the premium leg

$$C \int_0^T D(t)\{1 - E[L(t)]\}dt \tag{6.3}$$

equal to the value of the protection leg

$$\int_0^T D(t)\, E(dL) \tag{6.4}$$

---

[1] The benefit of the computational speed from linearizing the model far outweighs this technical difficulty of loss of accuracy.

Here, $D(t)$ denotes the riskless discount factor for time t (for pricing the CDX, we use the swap curve), and the expected loss appears in the integral.[2]

After some straightforward algebra, we can show that the index coupon value is given by

$$C = \frac{\gamma_1 \lambda_1 + \gamma_2 \lambda_2 + \gamma_3 \lambda_3}{1 - (\gamma_1 \lambda_1 + \gamma_2 \lambda_2 + \gamma_3 \lambda_3)A} \tag{6.5}$$

where

$$A = \frac{\int_0^T D(t)\, t\, dt}{\int_0^T D(t)\, dt} \tag{6.6}$$

In implementing the model, it is convenient to rearrange Eq. (6.5) as

$$\lambda_1 = \frac{\frac{C}{1+AC} - \gamma_2 \lambda_2 - \gamma_3 \lambda_3}{\gamma_1} \tag{6.7}$$

Thus, given values of λ_2 and λ_3, Eq. (6.7) now may be used to determine λ_1 as an explicit function of the market index spread C. This approach allows the model to fit the market index spread exactly. We use the index spreads and spreads on standard tranches to obtain the values of λ_2 and λ_3 and the jump parameters γ_1, γ_2, and γ_3.

To calibrate the model, we use the spreads for the CDX investment-grade and high-yield indices of various maturities and vintages. Since the CDX indices roll every 6 months and come in various maturities, with the most liquid point being the 5-year index followed by the 10- and 7-year indices, the investment-grade index derivatives markets are representative of the broad investment-grade U.S. credit market. The index derivatives suite also allows for market participants to implement beta and hedge views on the credit market directly as we discussed in

---

[2] We assume that interest rates are uncorrelated with loss realizations.

the last chapter on replication, without taking the duration or liquidity risk that comes from using cash-bond instruments. We can also use data for the ITRAXX index, which tracks the credit risk of European investment-grade credit markets.

In addition to the index data, we use data on the market spreads for standardized tranches on these indices. The U.S. CDX investment-grade tranches are broken down in terms of losses that attach and detach at the 0, 3, 7, 10, 15, 30, and 100 percent points. The index, by construction, is a 0 to 100 percent tranche. Note that the standard 0 to 3 percent investment-grade equity tranche trades on a points-up-front basis with a fixed coupon of 500 basis points, whereas the other tranches used to trade based on a spread that changes with market conditions (in recent vintages, these tranches are also quoted in points upfront plus a spread). The U.S. CDX high-yield tranches attach and detach at the 0, 10, 15, 25, 35, and 100 percent points. The 0 to 10 percent and 10 to 15 percent tranches trade on a points-up-front basis with zero fixed coupon, whereas the other tranches traded based on a market spread. Similarly, the European investment-grade ITRAXX index has tranches with points at 0, 3, 6, 9, 12, 22, and 100 percent. The 0 to 30 percent ITRAXX tranche likewise trades on a points-up-front basis with a 500 basis point fixed coupon.

To see how we obtain the value of the parameters, first assume that the jump sizes γ_i are given. For a tranche with attachment point a and detachment point b, we can write the loss on the tranche $L_{a,b}(t)$ in terms of the loss function $L(t)$ on the underlying portfolio:

$$L_{a,b} = \frac{\max(0, L - a) - \max(0, L - b)}{b - a} \tag{6.8}$$

This function illustrates that the losses on the tranche can be viewed as the payoffs for a call spread. Specifically, the losses on the tranche equal the payoff of a call on L with strike a minus the payoff of a call with strike b, where the spread is scaled by $1/(b - a)$. As before, the tranche spread $C_{a,b}$ is determined by setting the value of the premium leg

$$C_{a,b} \int_0^T D(t)\{1 - E[L_{a,b}(t)]\}dt \qquad (6.9)$$

equal to the value of the protection leg

$$\int_0^T D(t)\, E(dL_{a,b})\, dt \qquad (6.10)$$

To proceed further, we implement this pricing equation numerically. Specifically, we evaluate the expectations in Eqs. (6.9) and (6.10) by computing the tranche loss function $L_{a,b}(t)$ for values of N_i ranging from zero to some suitably large value and then weighting by the corresponding Poisson probabilities P_{ij} from Eq. (6.2). This then allows us to solve for the model tranche spreads. In fitting the model numerically, we allow for up to 50 jumps for the first Poisson process, up to 10 jumps for the second Poisson process, and up to 3 jumps for the third Poisson process. To identify λ_1, we fit the model exactly to the market-index spread C using Eq. (6.7). To identify λ_2 and λ_3, we minimize the root-mean-square percentage pricing error between the model and the observed market tranche price for every day in the estimation period. Finally, we iterate over different values of the jump parameters γ_1, γ_2, and γ_3 until we achieve the global minimum root-mean-square percentage pricing error.

Once we have the λ and γ values, we can identify three different types of spreads that make up the full index spread in the risk-neutral setting:

$$\text{Idiosyncratic} \equiv S_1 = \frac{\gamma_1\lambda_1}{1 - (\gamma_1\lambda_1 + \gamma_2\lambda_2 + \gamma_3\lambda_3)A} \qquad (6.11)$$

$$\text{Sector-wide} \equiv S_2 = \frac{\gamma_2\lambda_2}{1 - (\gamma_1\lambda_1 + \gamma_2\lambda_2 + \gamma_3\lambda_3)A} \qquad (6.12)$$

$$\text{Economy-wide} \equiv S_3 = \frac{\gamma_3\lambda_3}{1 - (\gamma_1\lambda_1 + \gamma_2\lambda_2 + \gamma_3\lambda_3)A} \qquad (6.13)$$

Now $C = S_1 + S_2 + S_3$, so the sum of the three types of spreads equals the total spread of the index. Intuitively, our simple linear model is a way to decompose the index spread into its idiosyncratic, sectoral, and economy-wide components. Note that all computations are done in a risk-neutral setting, so we have no way of distinguishing how much of the spread might be due to risk-premium terms.

Finally, to compute the sensitivity of a tranche with attachment a and detachment b to the spread S_i (where $i = 1, 2, 3$) as defined here, we numerically compute the change of a tranche price to a shift in the underlying spread.

To implement the methodology just described in practice, we first fit the model to the index values and tranche spreads using current-market data for the the CDX investment-grade (IG), ITRAXX IG, and CDX high-yield (HY) indicies.

There are considerable similarities in the results across indicies. The size of the first jump γ_1 is in the range of 0.9 percent to about 1.5 percent for all the investment-grade indices and roughly 2.3 percent for the high-yield indices. Thus a realization of the first Poisson process clearly can be given the interpretation of the idiosyncratic default of one or two of the firms in the index.

In contrast, the size of the second jump γ_2 ranges from about 6 percent to 10 percent across the different indicies. Since the firms in the CDX and ITRAXX indices are roughly evenly distributed over, say, 10 to 12 broad industries or sectors, this second jump size is consistent with the realization of a credit event in which an entire industry or sector of the market goes into default.

Finally, the size of the third jump γ_3 ranges from about 50 percent to 75 percent. Thus, for all indices, a jump in the third Poisson process translates into a credit event in which the majority of firms in the index default together, implying a catastrophic systemic credit event affecting all sectors of the economy. Clearly, the realization of such an event would be so severe that even the most senior index tranches would experience significant losses. These results parallel those reported in Longstaff and Rajan [16] and extend the analysis using more recent data for a broader set of indicies and maturities.

In addition to the information about the nature and size of potential types of credit events, the model also allows us to infer the three components of the spread: S_1, S_2, and S_3. Around the start of August 2007, all three components of the indices begin to increase substantially. Interestingly, however, the individual components did not all increase by the same percentage. For the investment-grade indicies, the idiosyncratic component S_1 of the spread was roughly 50 to 75 percent higher during the second part of 2007 than its value during the first part of 2007. In contrast, the systemic component S_3 of the spread more than tripled after August 2007. In fact, the systemic spread's value at the end of 2007 was nearly 10 times its value in March 2007. The sector-wide component S_2 of the spread also increased during 2007, but by less than 10 basis points.

In Bhansali, Gingrich, and Longstaff [46] we show that a parallel situation holds for the CDX HY Index. Overall, the values of the idiosyncratic and sector-wide components of the HY spread were only modestly higher during the latter part of 2007. The major difference occurred for the systemic component, which rose dramatically from a level of about 25 basis points during the first part of 2007 to a range of about 100 to 150 basis points during the latter part of 2007.

These results provide valuable information about the market's credit concerns. By decomposing the credit indices into three components, we see that much of the increase in credit spreads during 2007 was driven by concerns about the risk of systemic or macroeconomic credit problems. This is clearly a much different risk than, say, heightened concerns about the creditworthiness of individual firms or even an entire industry.

To provide a longer-term perspective, Figure 6.3 plots the value of the three components of the spread based on fitting the model to the on-the-run CDX IG 5-year index over the entire March 2005 to December 2007 period. In doing this, we are essentially treating the index as a continuous series. While the idiosyncratic risk component currently approximates its 2005 value, what is notable is that the systemic risk component is currently much larger in magnitude than in 2005. Systemic risk is also a larger proportion of the total risk of the index in late 2007 as compared with 2005.

This is logical because in early 2005 the widening of the index was due to downgrades in the automotive sector. On the other hand, the 2007 spread widening can be traced to distress in the financial sector and a market-wide lack of liquidity, which arguably affected the entire economy. Of course, the widening of the senior and supersenior tranches (such as the CDX IG 15 to 30 percent tranche) meant that more risk premium had come back into this part of the capital structure. There have been numerous headlines that suggest that the widening of the senior and supersenior tranches was due to the mark-to-market losses taken by specialized vehicles that had leverage exposure to these tranches. Note that this mark-to-market loss indeed had caused a weakened balance sheet for brokers and money-center banks that effectively had financing exposures to many of these vehicles. Systemic risk is usually measured in terms of widening of the LIBOR swap spread and the CDS spreads of banks and financials. It thus is no surprise that the same period in which the supersenior tranches had widened drastically in spread was accompanied by a sharp widening of swap spreads, financial-sector spreads, an increase in volatility, and a general reduction in liquidity.

As expected, the equity tranche had the largest exposure to the idiosyncratic risk factor, whereas the senior and supersenior tranches had higher exposure to the systemic factor. Thus the tranches had very different sensitivities, and their risk had a multidimensional nature. This has important risk-management implications for these structured credit products. To illustrate, imagine that the CDX IG 5-year index increases by a basis point. The standard copula model would imply that the price of the 0 to 3 percent equity tranche should change by 42.7 cents per $100 notional. In our "macro" model, however, the change in the value of the equity tranche depends on the underlying source of the change in the CDX index. For example, if the change were entirely due to an increase in the idiosyncratic risk of the firms in the index, the valuation effect would be 90.5 cents instead. If the change were entirely due to an increase in the systemic component, the valuation effect would be only 2.2 cents. In the former case, the copula model would underestimate the valuation effect by more than 50 percent; in the latter case, the copula model would overestimate the valuation effect by a factor of more than 10. The bottom line is that if index credit risk is really driven by three distinct factors, the use of a single-factor risk-management measure is simply not adequate.

As an example of the use of these risk factors, assume that we thought that systemic risk would decline from its current elevated levels. Thus, if we wanted to go long (sell protection on) the economy-wide part of the index but remain unexposed to the idiosyncratic and sector-wide components while using 5-year CDX IG tranches, we could go short credit (buy protection) on the 3 to 7 percent and 7 to 10 percent tranches with notionals of $11.7 million and $1.3 million, respectively, and go long credit (sell protection) on the 0 to 3 percent, 15 to 30 percent, and 30 to 100 percent tranches with notionals of $2.1 million, $305 million, and $2,282 million, respectively. With this portfolio, a 1 basis point decline in the economy-wide spread would result in a profit of $1 million, whereas moves in the other spreads would result in negligible profit and loss.

Measuring Risks from Convexity Positions

We know that fixed income markets provide the ability to trade convexity risk for time decay. As a matter of fact, this is a more general result, in that the option gamma is proportional in absolute value to the theta of the option. Since closed-form gamma estimates typically are not available for fixed income instruments, we estimate the gamma by shocking the yield curve up and down and numerically computing the bull and bear durations (bull duration is the sensitivity or interest rate "delta" to a parallel shift down in yields, and bear duration is the same for a parallel shift up in yields).

We showed in Eq. (3.12) that a simple statistic to compute the time decay in a portfolio owing to convexity is

$$\text{Time decay} = \theta \approx -\frac{1}{2}\sigma^2 \left(\frac{D^2}{100} + \Delta_- - \Delta_+ \right) \qquad (6.14)$$

The excess yield (even structural) in a fixed income portfolio is best understood in terms of short option positions. If we miss the nonlinear contribution from these implicit short option positions, then typical risk measures such as tracking error and value at risk (VaR) will underestimate the total risk of the portfolio. In this section we sketch how nonlinear tracking error and volatility risks may be computed.

Now note that the tracking error is defined as

$$\text{T.E.}^2 = \text{var} \left(\frac{dP}{P} \right) \qquad (6.15)$$

By expanding out the right-hand side,

$$\text{T.E.}^2 = \text{var} \left(\frac{1}{P}\frac{\partial P}{\partial y}dy + \frac{1}{2}\frac{1}{P}\frac{\partial^2 P}{\partial y^2}dy^2 \right) \qquad (6.16)$$

$$= \text{var} \left(\frac{1}{P}\frac{\partial P}{\partial y}dy \right) + \text{var} \left(\frac{1}{2}\frac{1}{P}\frac{\partial^2 P}{\partial y^2}dy^2 \right) \qquad (6.17)$$

Note that the covariance terms vanish, leaving us with

$$\text{T.E.} = \sqrt{\text{T.E.}^2_{\text{linear}} + \left(\frac{2\theta^2}{P^2} \right)} \qquad (6.18)$$

where T.E.$_{\text{linear}}$ is simply the old, unadjusted tracking error that does not capture nonlinear effects, and we divide the θ by 100 to convert to the right units before squaring. Note that we also can write this in terms of a theta-adjusted delta equation, that is, adjust the durations by the percentage change in durations owing to negative convexity, as measured by bull/bear delta.

If we assume that the portfolio is sufficiently diverse, then the tracking error can be translated directly to measures for VaR (e.g., at the 1 percent level, the VaR equals 2.77 times the tracking error).

As an example of the formula, let us assume that the portfolio has no exposures except a duration overweight or underweight of 1 year, $D = 1$. Then, with no negative convexity, we would have a tracking error of 100 basis points versus its index if the volatility is 100 basis points per year ($\sigma = 100$ basis points). Now, let us introduce negative convexity—for example, take bull duration minus bear duration to equal 0.4255. Then

$$
\begin{aligned}
t &= 1 \\
P &= 1 \\
C &= (0.4255) + (1)^2/100 \\
\theta &= -\frac{1}{2}(100)^2 PCt \\
\text{T.E.} &= \sqrt{(100)^2 + \frac{2 \times \theta^2}{10{,}000}} = 104.6
\end{aligned}
\tag{6.19}
$$

So the negative convexity increases the tracking error by about 5 basis points year in this case.

Of course, here we have assumed that the only source of negative convexity is measurable in terms of the bull and bear deltas (i.e., all negative convexity has impact only on the duration). In general, if negative convexity results in an impact on other durations (spreads, etc.), we would have cross-convexity adjustments as well. The general formula is in "Non-Linear Value at Risk" [28]:

$$\text{T.E.}_{\text{nonlinear}} = \sqrt{\delta^T \Sigma \delta + \frac{1}{2}\text{Tr}[(\Sigma\Gamma)^2]} \qquad (6.20)$$

In this equation,

$$\Gamma = \frac{\partial^2 P}{\partial f \, \partial f'} \qquad (6.21)$$

is the matrix of the second derivative of portfolio derivatives with respect to the risk factors. The risk factors are denoted by f, the covariance matrix by Σ, and δ is the traditional "duration" with respect to the factors. The symbol Tr represents the trace of the matrix.

Tail Risk Management

The events that unfolded in 2007 and 2008 show the importance of controlling portfolio exposures to fat tail events. The obvious benefit of having appropriate amounts of disaster "insurance" is survival. There is a secondary benefit, that those with tail hedges are able to take advantage of reduced liquidity that accompanies tail events and set themselves up for attractive prospective returns. Thus tail "insurance" is an *offensive strategy* for the long term, even though it may appear to be a cost for defense in the short term. Indeed, simple simulations show that if an investor had systematically purchased tail hedges over the last 90 years, and on the occurrence of a crisis liquidated the hedges to buy the equity market with the extra cash, and again purchased new out-of-the-money puts, the portfolio would have significantly outperformed the raw buy-and-hold portfolio. There is plenty of anecdotal evidence to support the observation that deeply out-of-the-money hedges are valued cheaper than it should be in the real world.

The desire to outperform peers and indices over the last decade forced herds of portfolio managers into reducing or voiding "insurance" in their portfolios for improbable yet possible events, which resulted in a spiraling asset debacle whose ultimate end has yet to be realized. The emergence of structured products that were inefficient packaged sales of "insurance" was a natural consequence of the demand for high returns in a low-return world. The very real quandary a portfolio manager now faces is one that requires estimation of the optimal amount of "insurance" to have in portfolios against tail events, which by their very nature are hard to quantify with traditional models (which pay little heed to rare events). Most investment processes rely on harvesting risk premia from systematic factors whose variations are measured and exposures scaled based on history, and by design, this statistical averaging process underweights the impact of tail events.

The purpose of this section is threefold: First, I want to provide a characterization of tail events that is quantifiable. Second, I want to provide algorithms to quantify the probability and severity of these events. And finally, I want to propose a selection framework for tail hedges that may consist of securities, options, and strategies.

Tail Risk as Macro Risk

Tail risk at the portfolio level for typical investment portfolios is almost always *systemic* risk. Systemic risk is one that brings under pressure the ability to fund levered holdings. In these episodes, everyone desires liquidity, and no one is willing to provide it. In Richard Bookstaber's [36] language, the tight coupling of financial markets requires that liquidity be available to the system at all times at some price; otherwise, the system starts to break down. Financing and liquidity are *macro* risks, so their proper valuation requires macro models; proper hedge construction requires a macro view and uses macro tools and markets. Khandani and Lo [21] have observed that new strategies in the market, especially those provided by hedge funds, are characterized by new betas (systematic selling of liquidity), which can be withdrawn very quickly. Many of these strategies are highly correlated; hence a shock to one type of strategy causes ripples in other strategies. Further, the nature of the relationships is not static; hence a financial-market dislocation in a strategy that is running many different uncorrelated strategies can rapidly influence other strategies. Thus a tail-risk hedge portfolio that provides "insurance" against tail events should carry a"beta" to systemic and macro risks. A statistical analysis of the returns of broad asset classes over long-term history shows the presence of a handful of latent factors (or principal components) that explain the variation of most traditional investable assets. What is striking from analyses such as these is that the presence of regimes follows a similar systematic behavior and loads most heavily on monetary policy. In other words, with suitable leads and lags, the quadrants of early and late recessions and early and late expansions in the developed markets (the United States in particular) can be mapped to early and late periods of Fed easing and tightening. In a finance-driven economy such as the United States, it is no wonder that the tails that develop in these periods can be hedged with macro instruments that respond to central bank activity—deleveraging risk to a large degree is a monetary-policy risk. Thus tail events become macro events.

This observation has far-reaching consequences. The main consequence is that tail risk becomes a macro risk, and to forecast and control against it, one needs to step outside the world of historical estimates and calibration and forecast structural changes (certainly not easy!) and imagine improbable, high-severity scenarios. The immense benefit of thinking of tail risk in terms of a macro risk is that the construction of hedges simplifies; at any given point in time, macro markets are the deepest markets (by macro markets, I mean broad bond, stock, FOREX, credit, or commodity markets and combinations of them) despite pockets of illiquidity (e.g., credit could seize up with FOREX barely touched), and typically there is some sort of "insurance" that remains attractively priced for long enough because of the sheer mass of capital reallocation needed to align all of them. When systemic crises happen, correlations also rise in their absolute value. This provides a so-called "free lunch" in that a completely disconnected macro asset class of normal times becomes a good hedge against the tails in distressed times. In other words, if the cost of credit hedging is too high, a hedge from the FOREX or equity options markets actually might be more efficient as a credit hedge, over a long enough holding horizon, despite the apparent basis risk of normal times.

Valuation of Tail-Risk Hedges

Proper evaluation of the *cost* of "insuring" against tail risk is the second most important factor to evaluate. Credit-market hedges were extremely cheap in 2007 because of the incessant selling of credit "insurance" through structured products and the demand driven by excess liquidity. Today, these same hedges by some measures are at best fairly priced. Thus, hedging credit with credit-market instruments might no longer be an attractive solution. The estimation of option prices and sensitivities in general is based on the academic foundations of continuous trading and risk-neutral investors. These ideal conditions are rarely met in turbulent markets, so using what are now traditional models of option pricing are flawed because of their oversimplifying assumptions. A viable alternative approach is to run scenarios that investors are averse to and evaluate the expected value of portfolios under those scenarios with and without "insurance" assets. The difference in these two portfolio values is indicative of the fair price for the insurance from the investor's perspective, not the market price of the "insurance." We all know that catastrophe "insurance" can trade too cheaply in the natural "insurance" markets—the best time to buy "insurance" is when it is not needed. It is obviously possible for this also to happen in the world of finance, especially in a world of innovative financial engineering that ports risks from one type of market to another type of market.

There is more than one method to implement tail hedges—but our framework adopts a natural unity that would seem obvious to someone who is involved in "insurance." The simplest way to "insure" portfolios is to buy high-quality "insurance" securities. For instance, credit-market crises almost always occur with deleveraging and a grab for liquidity that usually results in Treasuries rallying in price terms, especially those at the shortest maturities. So short-term cash and Treasuries are a natural asset-based hedge for tail risk. But these securities can become overpriced for other technical reasons. The second way is to buy contingent claims or "option-like" securities. A couple of years ago, out-of-the-money tranches on CDX and ITRAXX indices were literally being given away because of the demand for CDOS, levered superseniors, and other default remote-structured transactions. These option-like payoffs were priced below their theoretical expected value under a systemic risk outcome. The third alternative is to invest in strategies that are negatively correlated with tail risks. Among the traditional established strategies, Figure 6.1 demonstrates that only the systematic,

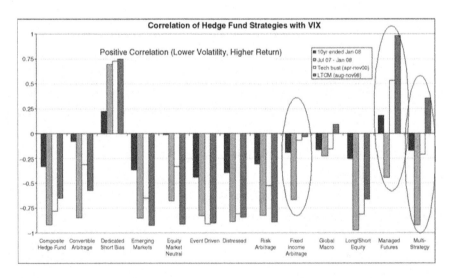

Figure 6.1 Monthly correlation of typical hedge-fund strategies versus the VIX Index for different periods.
(*Source*: Author, HFRI, Bloomberg.)

trend-following managed futures strategy provides positive correlation with tail-risk indicators such as the VIX while also being largely uncorrelated with the stock market. Copious amounts of research have been done to demonstrate that trend-following strategies empirically behave like a long position in look-back straddles and hence are naturally long tail risk [52]. The fourth approach is to move the portfolio off the optimal frontier; that is, accept less return for the same amount of risk, which explicitly recognizes that the simplest mean-variance optimal frontier falsely assumes that risk can be measured by volatility (second moment) alone and that the investor has perfect forecasting ability (almost never true). One example of this is to reduce the exposure to spread products, such as corporate bonds, or low-quality mortgages, which have higher yield because of embedded default and illiquidity options. When it becomes evident that technicals have made risk premia compress to rich enough levels, these assets promise high probability of low to negative future returns. As shorts, these assets actually might become candidates for tail-risk control.

I am not advocating dynamic portfolio "insurance," in which one plans to adjust exposures to changing market conditions. The problem with these types of zero-cost tail solutions is that they assume liquidity will be present in crises, and usually liquidity all but evaporates during systemic shocks. In the approach we are describing, the portfolio is subjected to possible but rare supershocks, and "insurance" may purchased using one of the four techniques discussed earlier. Thus there is certainly an upfront or running cost to the tail hedge. The role of the tail-risk portfolio manager is to reduce the cost of these hedges over the hedge horizon. This might not be as hard to achieve as it sounds. Frequently, with a long enough horizon, hedges can be almost bought for "free." For instance, recently, long-dated options on FOREX such as the dollar-yen exchange rate had zero carry cost over a 1-year horizon (owing to the roll-up of forward rates from the interest-rate differential between dollar rates and yen rates). If in periods of stress one of the outcomes is deleveraging and flight to low-yielding currencies such as the yen, the directionality of the FOREX movement and the associated increase in volatility make the real-world expected value of the package much higher than the theoretical, risk-neutral value. Thus it is the possibility of asymmetric payoffs in particular states of the world that makes the hedges worth more to investor than their standalone theoretical value.

To ascertain the value of a particular tail hedge, it is essential that the scenario analysis be performed with many variations of the inputs for the parameters. The inputs are more important than the level of refinement of the models. In the simple language of Black-Scholes options, this boils down to running the performance of option positions under various maturity, rate, volatility, and spot-rate environments—using the option model simply as a crude nonlinear transformation machine between inputs and outputs. Special attention has to be made to consistently take the volatilities and correlations to extreme values because the underlying assumption of joint lognormality undervalues the tails of the distribution [44]. It is also possible to approach the problem by specifying other distributions with naturally fat tails, such as the Levy distribution, but in practice, I find that moving away from simple distributions creates more problems with intuition than is compensated for by more accurate empirics. In any case, today's computational power makes it easy to substitute for theoretical closed-form solvable models with empirical distributions that can be evaluated numerically, especially on the tails.

The extension of Black-Scholes to credit is the gaussian copula model. While used and abused, this model, which is a simple and efficient way to value options on portfolio losses, still has the ability to provide good intuition about the performance of tranches in periods of stress. Figure 6.2 displays the performance of a 7 to 100 percent tranche on the IG8 Index for instantaneous shocks and 1-year delayed shocks. The first scenario table is the percentage impact on a long protection tranche position for an instantaneous shock. The second scenario table is the percentage impact on a tranche position

PriceDate	3/26/2008
index	IG8
tenor	10
funded	0
attPoint	7.00%
detPoint	100.00%
Coupon(bp)	76.7

Delay for shocks (years) : 0

Spread Boost (bp)	(Attachment %) 63.38	95.08	31.69
	(Detachment %) 0.00	0	0
-25	-1.36	-0.39	-2.49
-10	-0.55	0.45	-1.68
0	0	1	-1.13
10	0.55	1.56	-0.57
25	1.39	2.39	0.29
50	2.77	3.76	1.74
100	5.54	6.46	4.66
200	10.84	11.58	10.25

Delay for shocks (years) : 1

Spread Boost (bp)	(Attachment %) 63.38	95.08	31.69
	(Detachment %) 0.00	0	0
-25	-1.99	-1.07	-3.08
-10	-1.28	-0.34	-2.38
0	-0.8	0.16	-1.91
10	-0.32	0.65	-1.42
25	0.41	1.38	-0.67
50	1.65	2.6	0.61
100	4.1	5.01	3.2
200	8.89	9.64	8.26

Figure 6.2 Tranche shock scenario analysis for a 7 to 100 percent senior tranche on the 10-year IG8 investment-grade index for various shocks to the underlying spread level and base correlations.
(*Source*: Author, PIMCO)

for a shock at a 1-year horizon. Tranche returns can be different as the implied base correlation moves around. As correlations rise, the senior tranches pick up additional return owing to a higher probability of many names defaulting simultaneously, a hallmark of systemic risk. The 1-year horizon shock accurately captures the cost as the tranche (which is an option on losses) shortens in maturity and rolls down the credit curve (which typically is upward-sloping).

Using credit derivatives as a reference, we also discussed in the last section yet another way to measure systemic risks. In Figure 6.3, the idiosyncratic component is the darker solid line, the sectoral risk is the dotted line, and the economy-wide risk is the light solid line. The economy-wide or systemic risk reached highly elevated levels during the height of the crisis and ebbed as liquidity was injected by central banks. Since the economy-wide risk is carried by senior and supersenior tranches, it provides a microscope for the valuation of liquidity and

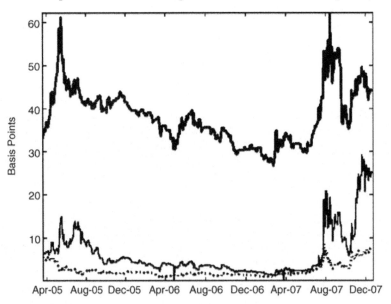

Figure 6.3 Allocation of CDX 5-year index to idiosyncratic, sector-wide, and systemic risk factors.
(*Source*: Bhansali, Gingrich & Longstaff [46])

systemic risk in the market. If we proxy systemic risk by the fraction of spread allocated to the systemic factor (or roughly speaking, the fraction of expected losses accounted for by default remote supersenior tranches), we can construct a high-frequency measure for a systemic risk factor. Regression of other, optically unrelated markets, such as municipals, asset-backeds, and other spread products, on this factor shows significant betas to systemic risk. In other words, many asset classes carry large amounts of systemic illiquidity risk. For example, we find (with significant *t*-statistics) for the period from June 2006 to end of March 2008, and without adjusting for duration, that for every 10 basis points widening of the systemic component, the Barclays-Lehman ABS Floating Rate Index would return negative 53 basis points, the ML U.S. High Yield Index would return negative 58 basis points, Barclays-Lehman Municipal Bond Index would return negative 51 basis points, the Barclays-Lehman CMBS Index would return negative 63 basis points, and the Barclays-Lehman Securitized Index would return negative 38 basis points. All these asset classes carry liquidity-risk (different from credit risk), and stressing our liquidity risk measure shows how they can be expected to perform in periods of stress. No wonder that as of this writing municipal bonds, which have one of the largest betas to this risk factor without much direct credit risk (especially general-obligation bonds of natural AAA-rated states), are trading at higher yield levels than even Treasuries despite the fact that they are federally tax-exempt!

The construction of a tail portfolio hedge thus depends on the answer to three main questions. First, what is the scenario behavior of the portfolio? Second, what is the scenario behavior of the hedges, net of cost? And third, what is the probability of the scenario occurring? To find the best combination thus requires knowledge of the underlying portfolio that is being hedged under various shocks. The best combination of hedges is the one that optimally performs in reducing the negative return to the portfolio in the stress scenario and also manages the risk at horizon to the dangerous factors in the stress scenario. The second part is critical because it enables the portfolio to survive to play in the multiperiod game—you want your risks to adjust down in periods of stress so that you are the one with the liquidity, while everyone else is clamoring for it. This might appear to suggest that tail hedges always have to be custom designed. Fortunately, the fact that correlations between risk factors increases in periods of stress mitigates this need for all but the most exotic portfolios. For most investment portfolios, the underlying exposures to market factors such as the Barclays-Lehman Aggregate or S&P500 is all that is needed to optimize tail hedges.

The critical reader might wonder why is it that cheap tail hedges can be found in almost all market environments. There are many candidate reasons. For example, speculative demand of particular types and classes of assets may drive the price of these assets very high. In periods of low returns, as observed until the middle of 2007, "yield hogs" increased options sales as a source of carry. The belief of mean-reversion participants is that out-of-the-money options will never be exercised. This is generally true, except that as the leverage in the marketplace increases owing to everyone simultaneously executing levered option sales, the notional size has to increase to generate the same carry. At some point this type of system becomes unstable to small noise, and this creates a domino effect of either forced liquidation or hedgers all trying to hedge at the same time.

A cost-calculation example will make this obvious. In June of 2007, buying protection in the form of a 7 to 100 percent tranche on the IG8 10-year index cost 15.63 basis points per year. For a spread duration of 7.45 on the underlying index, the cost per unit of spread duration equaled 2 basis points. Since the tranche also rolls down to a shorter maturity, the annual roll-down cost of 2.67 basis points added to the previous number gives a total of 4.67 basis points of cost per unit of spread duration. To buy protection on a $1 billion notional, total lifetime cost is about $12 million (annual cost times PV01 of 7.45). The same tranche in February of 2008 was trading at 91 basis points per year. The new running cost per year of spread duration = 10.1 basis points; roll-down = 2.2 basis points for a total of 12.3 basis points per year. The new total lifetime cost is about $67 million. The delta of the tranche before the crisis last year was approximately 0.53, which when multiplied by the spread duration of the 10-year index of 7.45 gives an approximate sensitivity of 3.95 percent per 100 basis points of index widening. In February 2008, the delta rose to 0.77 (because the index widened and was closer to at-the-money), giving almost 5.66 percent of spread risk. Evaluating the market and risk change, one can see immediately why supersenior levered notes (which essentially sold protection using these structures in the form of securities) are in severe distress today. First, the mark-to-market loss is huge (5 times) because it equals the net present value of premium change. Second, the mark-to-market is more variable (because the delta has increased); and third, the collateral that has to be posted to make up for the mark-to-market fluctuations is much more expensive (lower Treasury bill rates and higher LIBOR rates). The fact that all these happened simultaneously is typical of systemic tail events.

Another reason why hedges are available for long-term investors willing to commit capital to them is because of natural habitat formation of option-market participants and the limitation of models used by short-horizon participants such as option market makers. Most traditional option-trading models are appropriate for short-term trading, that is, for about the time it takes for a dealer desk to unload the package to another customer. Implicit in this framework is the assumption that deltas, gammas, vegas, and other Greeks can be computed and executed. When the standard analysis is extended to longer-dated options, the unavailability of reference instruments, the failure of risk-neutral pricing, continuous trading, and the limitations imposed by counterparty risk controls make the likelihood of mispricing higher.

The probability question for tail events is also not answered satisfactorily by looking at traded option prices. The reason is that the pricing of tail options in particular carries a significant amount of risk-premium compensation to the seller (lottery-ticket risk), which alters the probability distribution. Simulation that is based on past observations is also not a totally satisfactory approach because each crisis is different in severity and magnitude. The practical approach to coming up with probabilities can take a number of parallel approaches. One approach is to sample from historical events with replacement and to magnify the rare-event likelihood by some scale factor (this effectively reshapes the tails). Simultaneously, changes in a tail-risk indicator such as the VIX can be measured to indicate the likelihood of being in a crisis versus a normal environment in which correlations and volatilities from a distressed regime are used. Regardless of how these probabilities are estimated, it should be emphasized that since tail hedges are usually cheap in the context of long-lived portfolios, the probability calculation is relatively less important than knowing that potential hedges exist at the right price that can make the difference between survival and almost certain ruin.

Once the macro portfolio tail hedges are put in place, much active management is still needed. As the cost of "insurance" across markets and maturities changes, a "dashboard" that shows the cost of hedges for different horizons for different markets provides direction on rebalancing the tail-hedge portfolio. There are frequent opportunities to add pseudoalpha (value that reduces the cost of the hedge), especially during times of rolls for indices or owing to short-term imbalances in pricing. The portfolio manager faces the choice of whether to keep the hedges static (let them age) or keep them current in the most on-the-run versions by evaluating the trade off between basis risk and liquidity/transactions costs. There is also the key issue of monetization. When the rare event does happen, will one be in a position to convert the hedges into cash efficiently? In our experience, the fact that tail risks are accompanied by deleveraging has skewed the transaction efficiency to the part that is long the hedges; that is, when there is demand surge, the seller of "reinsurance" is the price setter for liquidity. Since hedges are usually implemented through derivatives, another key issue is one of financing—for out-of-the-money equity options and FOREX options, the payment is usually made upfront. On the other hand, for credit derivatives, the payment is as you go. The structure of the current crisis has revealed that counterparty risk is important—for instance, many participants found that "insurance" written by monoline insurers was not as solid as they had thought.

I have discussed the need to think of tail risks in portfolio construction as systemic risks. Since systemic risks are macro risks, a proper tail-risk hedging program takes into account the relative pricing of broad macro markets and strategies and evaluates the best alternatives from combinations of these alternatives to immunize the portfolio against improbable but not impossible shocks. Lest it appear that tail-risk hedging is only about crisis events, note that the current low yields on long-term Treasuries may indicate that while credit "insurance" is fully priced, tail inflation risk is still cheap; that is, the tails to watch out for might arise from an uncontrollable rise in inflation that erodes the value of the dollar and of the fixed coupons from long-term bonds. Indeed, stochastic simulations show that in a world where the central bank is simultaneously pursuing inflation targeting and asymmetric policy against deflation, yield curves will be flatter as long as the economy is robust and significantly steeper when the central bank is forced to ease aggressively [45]. While only the unfolding of time will show the truth or falsity of this prognostication, one thing is certain—the hedge for this type of tail risk will not be a micro hedge.

The Behavior of Volatility

Data on implied volatility show its schizophrenic nature. They are strongly mean reverting to localized average levels. The localized averages jump to longer-term average levels sharply after they make new highs or lows. The best predictor for future volatility in the short term

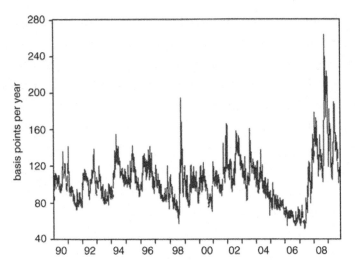

Figure 6.4   History of interest-rate volatility as measured by the
BOA/Merrill-Lynch MOVE Index.
(*Source*: Author, Bloomberg.)

is the level of current volatility relative to long-term history (this is
the backbone of the GARCH-based approach to volatility forecasting).
Since 1990, interest-rate volatility as measured by the BOA/Merrill-
Lynch MOVE Index averaged approximately 100 basis points per year
(see Figures 6.4 and 6.5).[3] The standard deviation is approximately 25
basis points per year. Volatilities have spent 15 percent of time below and
20 percent above this 1 standard deviation band. Low levels of volatility
usually do not last. The 1998 low preceded the long-term credit market
(LTCM) meltdown. The triggers have been hard to forecast, but they
are usually accompanied by the unwind of excess leverage and inver-
sions of yield curves, which make it hard to obtain leverage (since short
rates exceed long rates) and set the stage for this sort of unwind.

---

[3] The BOA/Merrill-Lynch MOVE Index is an index of short-dated (1 month) Treasury
   options, weighted 20 percent on the 2-, 5- and 30-year points and 40 percent on the
   10-year point. Using other proxies for long-dated interest-rate volatility gives similar
   qualititative results, though arguably the levels are not so extreme.

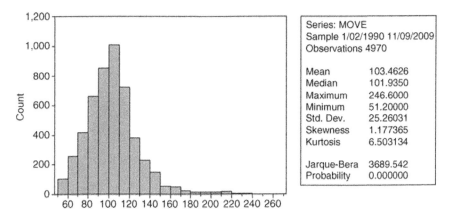

Figure 6.5 Distribution of interest-rate volatility as measured by the BOA/Merrill-Lynch MOVE Index.
(*Source*: Bloomberg.)

Volatilities are also strongly autoregressive, and selling of volatility can feed on itself. Periods of low volatility are followed by more periods of further low volatility until implied volatility levels get so low that the only way to long-term averages is to jump; the jumps usually happen as highly levered short volatility positions are unwound. Low implied volatilities mean that more notional options have to be sold to maintain the same amount of carry income; that is, there is more negative gamma to hedge. Large negative gamma hedging can push asset prices far from equilibrium and set up a cascade of unwinds when it unravels, leading to volatility clusters. A simple autoregressive model with two lags shows the average since 1990 for the MOVE at 103 basis points per year as well as a 0.99 coefficient of persistence, that is, a high degree of autoregression.

The same behavior exists for other asset classes. Figure 6.6 shows the VIX Index of equity volatility, and Figure 6.7 shows the distribution. Again, volatility jumps up more and grinds down. Simple econometric estimates also show a high degree of persistence (almost 90 percent) from day to day. The correlation between short-term interest-rate volatility,

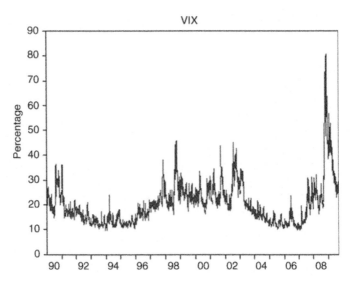

Figure 6.6 History of equity volatility as measured by the VIX Index.
(*Source*: Bloomberg.)

as measured by the MOVE, and equity volatility, as measured by the VIX, is almost 0.65. Vector autoregressions that try to estimate the interrelationships between implied volatilities in various asset classes show that while the dominant driving factor for volatility is the asset's

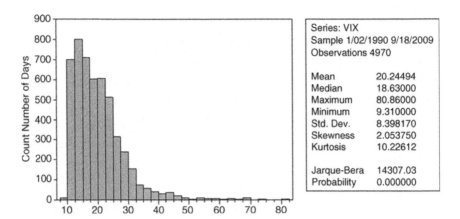

Figure 6.7 Distribution of equity volatility as measured by the VIX Index.
(*Source*: Bloomberg.)

own volatility, equity volatility changes lead both changes in rate and currency volatility, at least historically.

The fact that volatility jumps rather than grinds up has significant impact on portfolio construction. Since many options traders delta hedge their options positions with the underlying, a sudden change in the volatility can affect the hedge ratios and the movement of the underlying. Investors can take advantage of instruments such as volatility forwards and variance swaps to hedge against volatilities risk. Also, different maturities and strikes of options do not behave in the same manner. By studying the volatility "cube" whose dimensions are time to expiration, strike, and the various points of the yield curve, we can obtain better points to take structural volatility risk.

The existence of discontinuous movements in asset prices creates tail risks because it becomes impossible to rebalance portfolios against jumps. To evaluate jump risk, we naturally want to measure what portion of total volatility is from jumps. We know that selling options as a structural strategy works well when the likelihood of jumps is low and not so well when jumps are more likely. Recent work on high-frequency market statistics may be used to get a handle on the jump risk of asset prices (see [43]). The returns of asset prices can be decomposed in terms of

$$\text{Return} = \text{drift} + \text{brownian motion component} \quad (6.22)$$
$$+ \text{jump component}$$

The variance of the return is simply the sum of the brownian variance and the sum over all the jumps:

$$\text{Variance of return} = \text{variance from brownian motion} \quad (6.23)$$
$$+ \text{variance from jumps}$$

Suppose we use daily data for the left-hand-side variance. Then the right-hand side is obtained by summing the variances from many high-frequency (e.g. 5-minute) intervals during the day. To identify how much of the variance is obtained owing to brownian motion, we can use a new result that relates the nonjump component to the limit of the so-called bipower variation [33]: Variance from brownian motion component = bipower variation. In the limit, the intervals go to zero. To replicate this limit, we use high-frequency data. For example, in this section we used approximately 14,000 five-minute intervals.

Bipower variation (BV) is defined as

$$BV = \text{sum over all time intervals (absolute value of return at interval } t \\ \times \text{ absolute value of return at interval } t - 1)$$

We frequently want to know if implied volatility is fairly priced. Typically, implieds are higher than realized, and the implied/realized ratio is greater than 1 (because option sellers require a premium over the actuarially fair value from realized volatility). In my view, the more fruitful comparison is to look at the ratio (implied − realized)/ nonjump component. Basically, if the nonjump component is small, then implieds carry a higher jump premium. If the embedded jump premium is high and mean reverting, then selling implieds is more attractive than when the jump premium is small. On the other hand, if the nonjump component is large, the jump component, by definition, is smaller and likely to increase and cause more damage to short option positions than the time decay can make up for. This, for example, would be the case when we are looking at currencies that are pegged (such as the RMB). Even though the implied (2.5 percent) is greater than the realized (0.5 percent), the nonjump component is negligible, and a much larger implied/realized premium should be required to sell options on the RMB. Is the jump component persistent or mean reverting? Does the jump component depend on the level of volatilities? For data for 10-year futures (see Figure 6.8), we find that the jump component is indeed strongly mean reverting and, hence, amenable to structal option sales (compare this with our discussion in chapter 3 on portfolio structure where lower-frequency time series analysis reveals that futures showed

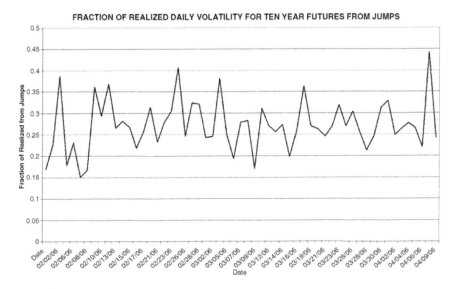

Figure 6.8 Fraction of volatility in 10-year futures attributable to jumps.
(*Source*: Author, Bloomberg.)

little mean reversion), although it is not clear what type of macro events cause the jump component to rise. In other words, the selling of options exposes an investor to jump risk, and much of the premium really is compensation for this jump risk.

Since jumps are relatively rare, we are interested in the estimation of the likelihood and impact of rare events. The standard approach to valuation can yield wrong answers if distributions are estimated using history, and if history shows few extreme events, the tails are under-estimated using typical distributions such as the normal distribution. One can choose to replace it with fatter-tailed distributions, such as the Weibull or the beta, but the problem with this is that assuming one of these distributions imposes a particular tail behavior, which might not be appropriate or transparent.

A separate set of methods does not assume a parametric distribution, but rather uses the actual sample data to generate the realization of asset returns. This approach in its simplest form is called the *bootstrap*.

Basically, the bad events are sampled with replacements from actual history and scaled up by a factor. Since markets are serially autocorrelated, we can also include "blocks" of data in a block-bootstrap to maintain some of the autocorrelation. While providing an idea of the inherent uncertainty in the data set, this approach is not able to capture a changed regime, which is so critical to ex ante portfolio positioning.

7

Bonds in a Portfolio Setting

The reason investors include bonds in their portfolios is because bonds provide diversification to other exposures. A typical investor's portfolio consists of equities, bonds real estate, and even their jobs and intellectual capital. Understanding the contribution to risk and return that arises from bond exposures in a portfolio context is critical for the use of fixed income (or any other asset classes) for best long-term performance. This becomes even more critical when one thinks of excess return as compensation for nonlinear risks (or options). A robust portfolio then is a combination of attractive long and short option positions, or more accurately the inherent risk factors of these options positions.

Simple principles for asset allocation are surprisingly hard to find and certainly not always easy to implement. In Chapter 4 we discussed the importance of putting economic considerations back into quantitative financial models. Among the main reasons for doing so are (1) that including economics from the very beginning in model construction makes models more believable and intuitive, (2) that the assumptions that drive the quantitative output can be challenged and stressed with real-world considerations, and (3) that unreasonable outputs are made more obvious and can be challenged. The focus of that chapter was on models for security valuation, and we did not address the equally important question of portfolio construction.

Most investors face both questions—how to model and pick attractive securities for inclusion in their portfolios and how to combine these securities in the proper way to match the risk and return characteristics that they desire. The purpose of this chapter is to emphasize the relevance of economic intuition for asset allocation using the simple yet elegant language of risk factors that we introduced in Chapter 1. In my view, the proper process for asset allocation must start with the question, "What should be our allocation to various sources of risk?" In contrast, a purely asset-weight-based approach can obscure the prospects for a portfolio because risk factors are what drive long-term performance. Practitioners and plan sponsors know that the fate of an investment portfolio over time is driven primarily by asset-allocation decisions, and security selection only improves on this primary decision ("beta dominates alpha"). Unfortunately, it is easy to get paralyzed by the stupendous amount of academic research on the topic. I will keep the current discussion practical and lucid, highlighting the important techniques I think a practitioner should know when approaching asset allocation from a risk-management perspective using the tools from the risk-factor approach.

Asset Allocation

Given the copious amounts of quantitative research being done in the area, asset-allocation exercises suffer from many maladies of approaching the investment problem from a purely quantitative angle—it is tempting to equate asset allocation with optimization, ignoring the most important issues, such as asset/risk-factor selection, return forecasting, risk forecasting, comovement analysis, and sanity checking. While optimization indeed forms the financial engineering backbone of asset allocation, it is only one step in converting inputs to outputs. Bad or incomplete inputs frequently result in bad and incomplete outputs. It is well known that Markowitz mean-variance optimization suffers from too much reliance on the ability of the portfolio manager to forecast excess returns and hence becomes an engine for "error maximization." A number of consequences follow: (1) Mean-variance-optimal portfolios are highly concentrated and pick out extreme positions; (2) optimal portfolios are unstable to small changes in the return estimates; and (3) there is no way to incorporate investor views and confidence levels in forecasts. In the now classic work by Black and Litterman [12, 13, 15], a new methodology was proposed that addresses these issues and has become part of the arsenal of quantitative portfolio management. Resampled efficient frontiers is another approach where the average efficient frontier is obtained by averaging over the set of frontiers computed with forecast errors [40]. The important point is that for robust asset allocation it is crucial to have forecast errors in the asset-allocation exercise right from the beginning. The exercise of incorporating forecast errors into forecasts requires the *process* of return forecasting to be both simple (using a small set of factors to explain the majority of the prospective variation), consistent (the return and risk equations should have a common principle), and iterative (it should be easy to go back to the starting point and start over with new inputs), as we will discuss in this section. To address these, and many of the other allocation decisions, any asset-allocation framework (I emphasize the word *framework* over the word *model* because asset allocation is really more of a set of systematic approaches rather than any one particular model) needs to deal with a number of key issues:

- Which assets are included?
- How are returns forecasted?
- How is uncertainty forecasted?
- How are asset comovements forecasted?
- How is the optimal portfolio constructed?

- What is the impact of constraints?
- Is the portfolio sensible?

I use the term *forecast* to emphasize that asset allocation is a forward-looking exercise. Too frequently practitioners use historical data for the estimates of returns, uncertainty, and comovements and ignore structural changes that substantially impact risk, returns, and correlations of the investments. I also have been careful in using the terms *uncertainty* instead of *volatility* and *comovements* instead of *correlation* to highlight that care has to be taken when using simple, linear proxies such as standard deviation as measures of volatility and correlation as measures of comovement. In the following sections I will address each of these issues one at a time. However, with my belief that all powerful insights are simple, I ask the reader to refer to Eq. 7.9 later in this section, which, though trivial, anchors the risk-factor approach to asset allocation that forms the central point of this approach. Although (almost) trivial, this equation has so much content for the practical process of asset allocation that I will use it repeatedly to address most of the important topics that come up when discussing allocation for investment portfolios. Note that this discussion has come back full circle from the Preface. I identified risk factors as an approach to measure risk, and now I will use these factors to construct robust portfolios.

Asset Selection and Risk Factors

Everyone has heard the story of the man who lost his keys in a dark alley. When asked why he was searching for the keys under the lamp, his response was, "Because that's where the light is." Asset allocation suffers from a similar problem. Assets that are most likely to result in high returns are the ones that are usually the hardest to invest in. An article in the *Financial Times* (November 13, 2007) recognized that the Baltic Dry Shipping Index had brought in the highest return

(140 percent), beating traditional commodities (Lead was the best-performing traditional commodity a 114 percent) by a wide margin. While most commodities are investable, the shipping index is hard (if not impossible) for ordinary investors to invest in and hence would not find a representation in most asset-allocation portfolios. What fraction of the world's assets, most broadly defined, are not investable? What assets can be proxied through the use of derivatives or side bets? Certain assets, such as real estate, have become more investable through the operations of entities such as real estate investment trusts (REITs), which have figured out how to package primary assets and pass the exposure to investors. But there are numerous assets that have not graduated to such a level. Just the fact that cash flows can be packaged into securities is also no assurance that the package qualifies to be called an *asset*— Recent experience with structured credit tranches based on multiple layers of repackaging illustrates the dangers of this approach.

For an asset-allocation framework, a good working definition is to select any asset class for inclusion whose long-term returns depend on factors that are not replicable by other factors. Simply using past correlations to decide which assets to include and which to exclude is not a robust technique; the very observation of negative correlation increases the diversification benefit of an asset and may create artificial demand and reduction in ex ante value to the portfolio. Greer [41] has defined an *asset class* as a set of assets that bear some fundamental economic similarities to each other and that have characteristics that make them distinct from other assets that are not part of that class. He distinguishes asset superclasses based on whether they are capital assets (i.e., whose value can be computed by appropriate cash-flow discounting), consumable/transformable assets (e.g., grains), and store-of-value assets (e.g., fine art). Another definition of an asset class is as a grouping of investments the exposure to which (positive or negative) has the potential to raise the utility of a portfolio, whose risk-return characteristics cannot be replicated by some combination of other assets, which are relatively homogeneous, and which can be accessed in reasonable size. Thinking in these terms makes great sense because the asset-allocation decision is based on providing true economic diversification, and here has been a tendency recently toward asset-class pollution—a tendency to divide the world of investments into more alleged asset classes than are warranted or useful. The underlying factors that drive the economic returns are what need to be identified from the beginning to make sure that the asset-allocation mix remains robust over cycles.

The Factor Approach to Asset Allocation

Most asset-allocation decisions traditionally have been made in asset space. The outcome of the asset-allocation exercise in this approach is a set of weights for assets that can be bought or sold. We will focus this section on the necessity of transforming from the percent asset-weight/asset-return (denoted by w, r) approach to the factor-exposure/factor-return approach (denoted by β, F):

$$w_j, r_j \leftrightarrow \beta_i, F_i \tag{7.1}$$

Note that the number of factors is not equal to (and usually is less than) the number of individual returns.

Assuming our investable set to consist of N assets, if the weight of the ith asset is w_j and its return is r_j $(j = 1, \ldots, N)$, then the portfolio return at time t is

$$r_P(t) = \sum_{j}^{N} w_j(t)r_j(t) + \epsilon_P(t) \tag{7.2}$$

Once the asset returns are forecast, the expected returns of the portfolio are determined. Also, and as is well known, the risk of the portfolio can be obtained by taking the covariance matrix and multiplying by the asset-weight vectors on the left- and right-hand sides.

The idea behind the factor approach is to decompose the returns of assets into a smaller set of variables. Decomposition of the risks of the yield curve to level, slope, and curvature movements is a classic application of the factor approach that reduces the dimensionality of the forecasting problem for fixed income securities. Once stable factors are isolated, the task of the allocator is to decide how to use his or her forecasts for the factors in scaling bets. In doing so, the asset allocator is automatically separating "beta" from "alpha." Beyond simplification from the reduced dimensionality of the problem, another advantage of the factor approach is that if the behavior of factors can be mapped to economic variables, then the allocator can make a clean forecast of the risk and returns to the factors based on views of the economic variables. In practice, broad asset classes are seen to follow half a dozen or so factors in their long-term systematic returns. With over 200,000 liquid bonds and millions of individual equities, the ability to make broad asset-allocation decisions is substantially simplified by using the factor approach, as is evident in the continued dominance of the level, slope, and curvature paradigm in fixed income. In equities, the decomposition of equity returns into risk factors such as value, growth, momentum, and regional and industry factors similarly finds use in quantitative equity investing.

We will now connect traditional asset-based allocation to factor-based allocation by a sequence of simple manipulations (see Lo [26]). At the end of this exercise, we will be left with Eq. (7.9), which is basically a restatement of the classic factor approach that (still) has a tremendous amount of practical content. It is really the only equation needed to make sensible decisions when faced with incorporating forward-looking views into the asset-allocation process.

If we assume that the returns at time t of the jth security can be explained by n factor returns $F_i(t)$ $(i = 1, \ldots, n)$, then using the definition that $\beta_{i,j}$ is the beta of the jth security on the ith factor, we can write

$$r_j(t) = \sum_{i=1}^{n} \beta_{i,j}(t)F_i(t) + \alpha_j(t) + \epsilon_j(t) \tag{7.3}$$

Then, using Eq. (7.2), we can write the portfolio return

$$r_P(t) = \sum_{j=1}^{N}\sum_{i=1}^{n} w_j(t)\beta_{i,j}(t)r_i(t) + \sum_{j=1}^{N} w_j(t)\alpha_j(t) + \sum_{j=1}^{N} \epsilon_j(t) \tag{7.4}$$

Using the following definitions for the portfolio betas to the factors and alphas

$$\beta_{Pi}(t) \equiv \sum_{j=1}^{N} w_j(t)\beta_{ij}(t) \tag{7.5}$$

$$\alpha_P(t) \equiv \sum_{j=1}^{N} w_j(t)\alpha_j(t) \tag{7.6}$$

we obtain

$$r_P(t) = \alpha_P(t) + \sum_{i=1}^{n} \beta_{Pi}(t)F_i(t) + \epsilon_P(t) \tag{7.7}$$

Note the somewhat trivial but important result that the portfolio betas equal weighted averages of the security-level betas. This is relevant when we discuss leverage below.

We can take expectations on both sides and expand using the definition of covariance (see Lo [26]):

$$E[r_P(t)] = \underbrace{\alpha_P(t)}_{\text{Pure alpha}} + \underbrace{\sum_{i=1}^{n} \text{cov}[\beta_{Pi}(t), F_i(t)]}_{\text{Factor timing}} + \underbrace{\sum_{i=1}^{n} E[\beta_{Pi}(t)]E[F_i(t)]}_{\text{Risk premium}}$$

$$\tag{7.8}$$

We can get more intuition about this by writing the active term using the correlation between the factor exposures and the factors and the volatility of the factors and the dynamic weights:

$$E[r_P(t)] = \underbrace{\alpha_P(t)}_{\text{Pure alpha}}$$
$$+ \underbrace{\sum_{i=1}^{n} \text{corr}[\beta_{Pi}(t), F_i(t)]\sigma_{\beta_{Pi}(t)}\sigma_{F_i(t)}}_{\text{Factor timing}} \quad (7.9)$$
$$+ \underbrace{\sum_{i=1}^{n} E[\beta_{Pi}(t)]E[F_i(t)]}_{\text{Risk premium}}$$

This equation is the key asset-allocation equation in the factor approach, and it is worth some pause and discussion. From the decomposition, we see that any asset-allocation approach has three contributions. Harvesting risk premia, also known as *structural return*, is represented by the last term, which effectively sets and locks the exposures to the factors. This term lives in the "secular" domain; that is, it requires long-term forecasting. Dynamic exposure selection and scaling are represented by the second term, and this term lives in the "cyclical" domain. The return owing to dynamic exposure selection is magnified by both the volatility of the factors and the changes in exposures and by the ability of the manager to overweight and underweight at the right time (the correlation between factor betas and factor returns represents this). Finally, any security-selection prowess is reflected in the first term ("pure alpha"). While some security-specific alpha characteristics can survive for long periods, most vanish quickly as they are arbitraged away, so the alpha terms are the target of shorter-term forecasts and specialty investors. If we combine the cyclical and the pure-alpha terms into one, we can see how factor timing can be interpreted as alpha if beta is defined to be static risk-premium harvesting. Since we have not constrained the weights $w_j(t)$ to be strictly positive, both long and short positions are allowed, and the only thing that matters in the end is how the combination of the long and shorts affects the portfolio-level factor exposures. Note this form of writing (see definition of the portfolio alpha and beta earlier) makes it explicit that if assets are combined for their alpha contribution, then they automatically have a beta contribution as well, unless, of course, the betas are identically zero (almost never) or cancel out (by construction).

The factor approach makes it clear that to add value, a manager has to (1) forecast risk premia for long horizons and keep relatively static exposures to these sources of risk premia, (2) forecast returns for intermediate or cyclical horizons and actively increase and decrease weights when particular asset classes have higher expected returns, and (3) add alpha by security selection.

Looking at the return-generating process in this light brings to the fore all the main issues we face with asset allocation. There are three ways to add value: to identify long-horizon risk premia and expose portfolios to assets that provide them (in a more or less static manner), to identify intermediate-horizon factor performance and using skill (the correlation term) increase and decrease weights to those factors in a timely manner, and to identify securities with short-term pure-alpha potential. To perform this exercise in practice, we need three different types of forecasting models: a long-term risk-premium model, an intermediate-term cyclic model, and a short-term demand-supply mismatch or liquidity-premium model. This building-block approach yields interesting and generally robust results.

We actually can simplify even further when we look at liquid capital assets. The traditional 60 percent stocks and 40 percent bonds allocation has has been a robust neutral long-term portfolio because it is based on quite robust principles for long-term investors (see further discussion, however, in the next section on its exposure to equity-factor tail risks). Capital asset class returns can be classified broadly as stocklike or bondlike. The actions of central banks and monetary policy in general create a third factor exposure. To support this, we will provide some statistical evidence (which we should immediately handicap somewhat as being backward-looking and hence not a great way to forecast the future). I collected total returns on a broad set of assets and extracted factors using principal-components decomposition as displayed in figures 7.2 to 7.6. What we find is that three or four factors explain over 60 percent of the variation in returns of a large set of asset classes. Further, the loadings of broad asset classes on these factors are consistent with intuition.

The careful reader will at this stage feel uncomfortable: The factor approach I have laid out makes general sense, but I have not said much about what the factors are. This is where much of the "art" of asset allocation lives. The factors can be purely macroeconomic, such as gross domestic product (GDP) or consumer price index (CPI) forecasts, or they might be more fundamental, such as earnings; dividends; cash flow; momentum (for equities); level, curve, spread durations; convexity risk (for fixed income); backwardation/contango; momentum; inventory situation (for commodities); and carry and volatility (for currencies). Finally, they might simply be statistical and obtained from the much-abused principal-components analysis (PCA). To be fair, each one of these methods by itself is not a complete description of reality and should be used as a cross-check against forecasts from each of the other methods. Where there are egregious mistakes, the combination of methods will lead to creating a more complete mosaic. As an example, a purely statistical method such as PCA applied to the bond markets in the period from 2004 to 2008 would pick up some commonality but miss identifying it as the housing risk factor, which, for a forward-looking investor, was the most important macroeconomic/fundamental factor, which could convince the investor to void his or her portfolio of securities with positive exposure to it. Similarly, the performance of a broad spectrum of markets and the increased correlation between assets that were thought to be independent or diversifying are currently being driven by a factor that has laid dormant for a few years—liquidity. To extract this factor would require more than a purely statistical analysis because the loading of assets (such as mortgages) can be very different in both magnitude and sign in periods of normalcy and in periods of stress. For a statistical approach to reveal the presence of a factor with confidence, the factor must be strong, long, and well represented across the assets.[1] In normal periods, the volatility of the liquidity factor is very small, and statistical analysis will not find it. On the other hand, in periods of stress and crisis, this same factor becomes very volatile, dominates the returns of assets, and swamps any statistical analysis, crowding out other economic factors. Given the lack of a commonsense structure, a purely statistical analysis also will pick up coincidences in the sample data as suggesting spurious relationships. Where statistical factor analysis is most useful is in picking up the factors that a fundamental analysis has somehow overlooked.

Factor-based asset allocation obviously has its limitations. The first limitation is that it does not work very well when the asset allocation consists mostly of value added from idiosyncratic risks—because systematizing the returns from such strategies is hard. Second, and related, is the problem that the factor approach requires the clean separation of alpha and beta. Third, to actually model the factors and their risks and interrelationships demands persistence and the ability to forecast the factors using proxies from market variables. Finally, the factor approach is great for modeling, forecasting, risk management, and comparison across managers and styles, but it requires actual assets to implement. Thus, eventually, the task of mapping factors into assets and assets into factors requires foresight, analytics, and systems, and this, in turn, requires a deeper understanding of the causes of asset-price movements. In my view, the investment is well worth it because it also expands the

---

[1] Assuming returns are observed over T periods, n out of N assets carrying exposure to the factor f, and the factor being present for τ periods, the condition is $\frac{\tau}{T} \frac{n}{N} \frac{\sigma_f^2}{\sigma_s^2} > 1$. Here σ_f is the factor volatility and σ_s is the specific volatility of the assets.

understanding and hence the positioning against fat tail events, to which we will return shortly.

Return Forecasting

Return forecasting is perhaps the most important step in an asset-allocation framework. There are three distinct reasons for this: First, the sensitivity of asset-allocation results (the weights) is an order of magnitude as sensitive to return forecast errors as it is to volatility and correlation forecast errors. Second, during the return forecasting step, the allocator is first faced with the decision as to the horizon and objective function. Finally, return forecasting brings the problem of investability to the forefront. It really does not make sense to think about returns that are not in the investable universe. Traded securities do not provide any "free" way of forecasting market embedded returns because, in aggregate, the market is in balance, and the risk aversion of investors is balanced out.

The most important disclaimer on any investment product is typically, "Past performance is no guarantee of future performance"; however, most asset-allocation decisions are made using past estimates of returns for future forecasts of returns. While flawed, this is not entirely incorrect—markets may not repeat, but they do rhyme, and over long periods of time, historically there has been persistence of outperformance for particular asset classes. However, returns are also a function of overall risk-aversion levels in the market and the tolerance of investors, so realistically, the cycles of returns are just as important; the expected excess returns to any asset class are products of the volatility (or risk) of the asset class, the risk aversion of the marketplace as a whole, and the correlation of the asset class to the broad "market" (the stock market being a good proxy). Since each of these three elements varies with time, it makes sense that the expected returns vary with time. Estimation of historic returns is straightforward: Download the price data, compute the returns from the prices, and make the *strong* assumption that the returns can be extrapolated into the future. This is clearly dangerous because it extrapolates recent history into the future by assuming that the sample history is representative and most likely to repeat.

For our discussion, we will take three periods to be representative: the secular period, covering forecasts of 5 to 10 years or longer; the cyclic period, covering approximately 1 to 5 years; and the short term, between a few months and a year. Different tools are appropriate for forecasting returns over these different horizons.

Secular Forecasts   Long-term asset-class or factor returns are assumed to be a sum of returns from income, price appreciation, and adjustments for inflation, defaults, and other transactions costs. Just as important as the forecast of the returns is the forecast of the standard errors in the forecasts because the standard errors will determine just how much of an asset class or factor risk to hold. We will come back to the importance of forecast errors and robustness in a later section. Table 7.1 shows a sample approach to building long-term real forecasts for broad asset classes. These are sample forward-looking estimates that use history as a guide for sanity checking but don't rely on history as the only input for return forecasts. When creating secular forecasts for certain factors, it becomes critically important to evaluate whether the structural advantage is really more than accounted for as compensation for fat tail risk. Since short-term history is not a great guide, tail-risk hedging strategies naturally have to be considered at this stage. More on this in the next section.

Cyclical Forecasts   One of the hallmarks of modern economies is their cyclical behavior over a period lasting, on average, 3 to 5 years. Roughly speaking, most developed economies can be divided into four separate phases: early recession followed by a late recession followed by an early expansion followed by a late expansion. While arbitrary, this breakdown assists in identifying two important features of returns to

Table 7.1 Sample Secular Nominal and Real Return Inputs.

	Income	Price Change	Inflation	Defaults/ Fees	Real Return	Estimation Errors
U.S. large cap	2.0	4.0	−2.5	0.0	3.5	1.5
Long bonds	4.5	0.0	−2.5	0.0	2.0	0.5
TIPS	2.5	2.5	−2.5	0.0	2.5	0.1
High yield	8.0	0.0	−2.5	−4.0	1.5	3.0
EM	7.0	0.0	−2.5	−1.5	3.0	1.5
Commodity	−5.0	2.5	−2.5	0.0	−5.0	2.0
Real estate	4.0	1.0	−2.5	−2.5	0.0	5.0
Hedge funds	1.0	5.0	−2.5	−3.0	0.5	3.0

Note: All numbers are in percentages. Return assumptions and computations are for illustrative purposes only and are not a prediction or a projection of returns. Return assumptions are estimates of what investments may earn over the long term. Actual returns may be higher or lower than those shown and may vary substantially over shorter time periods.

(*Source:* Author)

different assets: First, asset returns are quite variable in these periods. Typically, early recessions (see Table 7.2) are periods of best performance for most asset classes; this can possibly be traced to the fact that the market quickly realizes that the central bank and fiscal authorities will have to act to counter the recession. The fact that monetary policy acts by reducing interest rates quickly feeds into a boost in asset prices. Second, the correlation between asset performance is very different in each of these periods. Diversification benefits are different in different periods owing to changing correlations. This is also a signature of exposure of assets to underlying common factors.

Why do asset classes perform differentially in different quadrants of the economy? The main reason is perhaps attributable to the change in risk aversion. While notoriously difficult to identify, we saw previously that periods of high sentiment mean periods of low risk aversion and hence low ex post returns to asset classes where risk can be taken most

Table 7.2 Sample Secular Nominal and Real Return Inputs.

Asset Class Excess Returns

Asset Class	Early Expansion	Late Expansion	Early Recession	Late Recession
Low-duration bonds	1.5	0.3	1.1	1.8
Long-term bonds (U.S.)	1.7	−0.2	−8.6	7.5
High yield	8.6	4.0	4.6	3.8
Global FI	5.3	−0.1	−6.2	4.7
TIPS	3.3	0.3	3.5	7.0
U.S. equities	10.5	7.9	−5.3	4.0
International equities	12.9	17.2	−8.5	−1.7
Commodities	3.9	6.9	11.7	−3.2

Note: All numbers are in percentages. Return assumptions are for illustrative purposes only and are not a prediction or a projection of returns. Return assumptions are estimates of what investments may earn over the long term. Actual returns may be higher or lower than those shown and may vary substantially over shorter time periods.

(*Source:* PIMCO, Ibbotson Associates, Research Affiliates.)

easily (e.g., small stocks, initial public offerings etc.). Similarly, when risk aversion is high, expected ex post returns are high. To measure the waxing and waning of risk aversion, we can take some market indicators or economic indicators. Typically, the yen and Swiss franc are positively correlated with risk aversion (high risk aversion leads to these currencies outperforming), as are the shape of the yield curve (higher slope = higher risk aversion) and high implied volatility (e.g., high value of VIX Index = high risk aversion).

However, knowing that asset returns can be different in different periods of risk aversion is only half the exercise. We cannot look at historical data on cycles and hope to use them very confidently for forward-looking analysis. The reason is simple—it is hard to forecast when cycles will start and end. One simple indicator that has worked reasonably well in picking up cyclical turns is the Institute for Supply Management–Purchasing Manager Index (ISM-PMI) as shown in Figure 7.1, which is a forward-looking forecast of the economy.[2]

An idea, original to McCulley [34] is to use the ISM-PMI indicator as an asset-allocation timing tool. Using the ISM-PMI turning points as indicators to go long 100 percent bonds at peaks and 100 percent stocks at troughs with perfect foresight beats a naive 60/40 equity-bond

---

[2]The ISM-PMI is a forward-looking index because it is based on survey data. Respondents are allowed to respond only with better, worse, or same as prior as answers regarding conditions about the industry compared with the previous month. The ISM-PMI is the result of a monthly survey of over 400 companies in 20 industries throughout the 50 states (so the index is a diffusion index based on survey of 40,000 members who are in the purchasing and supply management business). The survey queries respondents on a number of monthly indicators, including orders, production, employment, inventories, delivery times, prices paid, export orders, and import orders. Respondents are asked to characterize each indicator as higher, lower, or unchanged for the month (or faster/slower in the case of delivery times). They are not asked for specific numbers—only a thumbs up or down. Based on these responses, the ISM-PMI calculates diffusion indexes for each of the components. These diffusion indexes are calculated by adding half the percentage of respondents answering "unchanged" to the percentage answering "higher" (or "slower" for deliveries). These diffusion indexes do not yield estimates of specific magnitudes of strength or weakness, but the more respondents who are indicating trends in the same direction, the better the chance that the magnitude of that move is larger. A diffusion index of 50 percent is the theoretical breakeven mark—with readings above indicating strength and readings below indicating weakness. The ISM-PMI provides only the raw data—the Department of Commerce produces the seasonal factors that are used to provide more meaningful, seasonally adjusted indexes. The total index is not the result of a separate question regarding general business conditions. Instead, the index is calculated using the weighted sum of five of the subindexes. The weightings are production level (25 percent), new orders (30 percent), supplier deliveries (15 percent), inventories (10 percent), and employment level (20 percent). A score of 50 indicates an equal number of respondents reporting better conditions and worse conditions.

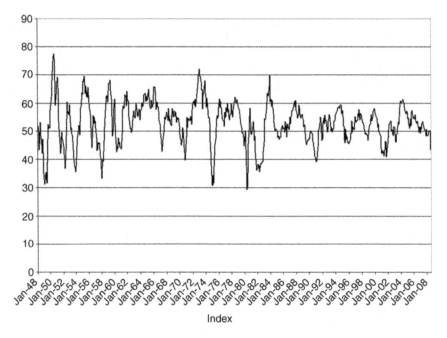

Figure 7.1   ISM-PMI. The vertical axis is the survey result and can range from a minimum of 0 to a maximum of 100. The units for the vertical axis are in percentage terms with details for the computation of diffusion indices, as described in the text. (*Source:* Institute of Supply Managers, Bloomberg.)

portfolio by 3.25 percent with volatility of 5.5 percent to give a macro timing tool with a Sharpe ratio of approximately 0.6. The reason that this indicator seems to work is that ISM-PMI is a survey indicator, and it best reflects the opinions of purchasing managers of large corporations. Since these purchasing managers' forecasts have to be accurate on average (they determine how to allocate their manufacturing resources), the indicator, on average, is a reliable forecast and is an excellent forecast near local turning points and extremes. While manufacturing is not the predominant driver of the U.S. economy it once was, it is still the area where signs of impending recession or expansion appear first. The index is also superior in my view to the Index of Leading Indicators published by the Conference Board because the ISM-PMI is based on

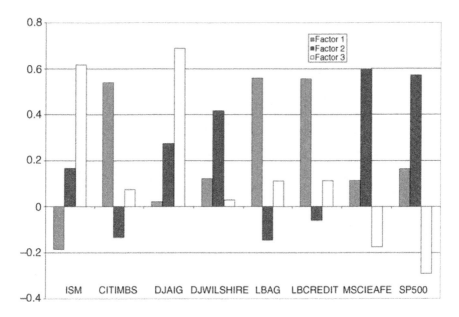

Figure 7.2 The three main principal components (eigenvalues greater than 1) of returns to the ISM-PMI. LBAG, S&P500, DJ Wilshire, Citi Mortgage Index, Lehman Credit Index, DJAIG, MSCI EAFE. The first eigenvalue accounts for 37 percent of variance. Including the second factor increases cumulative variance explained to 62 percent, and including the third one increases the cumulative variance to 75 percent. All data is monthly from 1991 to January 2007. The vertical axis represents the coefficients of the principal components (or loadings) and is in normalized units of variance and shown for comparison purposes only. The vertical scale has no absolute significance. (*Source:* Author)

surveys and forecasts, whereas the Index of Leading Indicators is based on observation of 10 macro and market variables. Figure 7.2 shows the principal component decomposition of the ISM-PMI against some of the main asset classes—it is not surprising to find that the leading factor, which explains almost 35 percent of the variance, is the one where a downward shock in the ISM-PMI results in asset class outperformance for all asset classes. This is related to the importance of the Fed in the

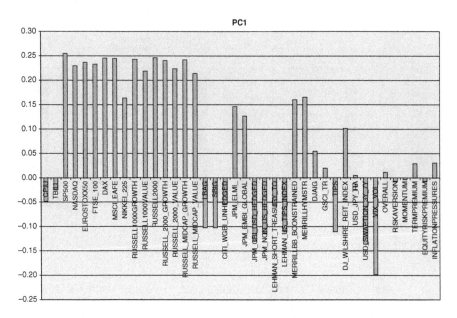

Figure 7.3 The first principal component of asset returns from 1999 through 2007 (monthly data). The vertical axis represents the coefficients of the principal components (or loadings) and is in normalized units of variance and shown for comparison purposes only. The vertical scale has no absolute significance. (*Source:* Author)

U.S. economy. Any fall in expectations for a highly levered economy such as the U.S. economy results in anticipation of rate cuts, which has (at least in the past) had a positive leading-order impact on asset classes.

Return Forecasting with Views and Confidence

The inability of classic mean-variance optimization to account for forecast errors is the cause of many of its problems. The problem arises because there is nothing in the mean-variance approach to peg the return or variance forecasts to; that is, the user directly enters the return and risk forecasts and finds the optimal weights based on a return-maximization/variance-minimization objective function. The Black-Litterman approach makes the process to obtain the returns more systematic and also integrates forecast errors into the exercise right

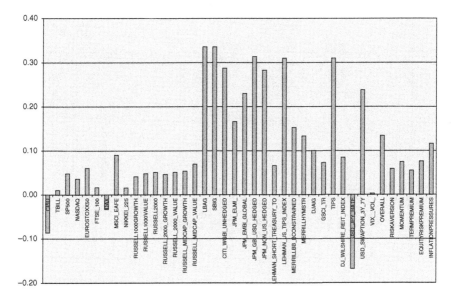

Figure 7.4 The second principal component of asset returns from 1999 through 2007 (monthly data). The vertical axis represents the coefficients of the principal components (or loadings) and is in normalized units of variance and shown for comparison purposes only. The vertical scale has no absolute significance. (*Source:* Author)

from the beginning. By doing so, it allows investors to systematically deviate from the neutral or market portfolio. The strength of the Black-Litterman approach comes from two of its attractive features: (1) If the investor has no view or no confidence in a view, then the portfolio is the market portfolio because asset returns are the same as those embedded in market prices, and (2) if the investor has complete confidence in a view, then the asset returns are the view returns, and the portfolio is the optimal portfolio with these view returns. Too frequently practitioners abandon the Black-Litterman approach because of the words *CAPM equilibrium* that went along with the original papers on this methodology. The Bayesian approach that gives Black-Litterman its power is distinct from the assumptions of the capital assets pricing model (CAPM), which is one of many ways of obtaining central return

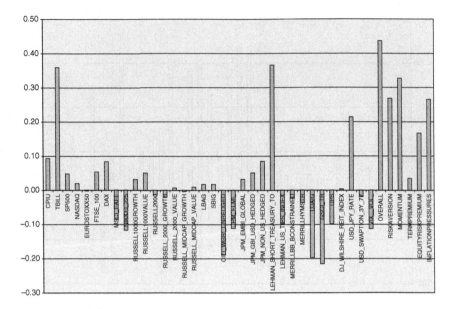

Figure 7.5 The third principal component of asset returns from 1999 through 2007 (monthly data). The vertical axis represents the coefficients of the principal components (or loadings) and is in normalized units of variance and shown for comparison purposes only. The vertical scale has no absolute significance. (*Source:* Author)

forecasts. In practice, we find the analytical framework that combines views and market forecasts with uncertainties in forecasts to be a powerful one. The Black-Litterman approach obtains better return forecasts. bayesian probability can be best stated as the following "theorem":

Posterior probability ∝ prior probability × likelihood function

$$(7.10)$$

Thus, intuitively, the probability distributions that are used for optimization in the Black-Litterman approach are posteriors, with the priors being equal to the views of the investor and the likelihood derived from an equilibrium argument. The Black-Litterman approach can be summarized by the following equation for the expected return (an $N \times 1$ vector), which is a blend of an equilibrium return and a view

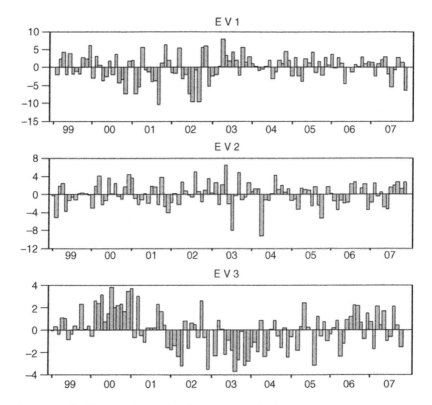

Figure 7.6 Time series of the three main principal component returns. Note the cyclical behavior. The vertical axis is normalized to units of variance. The vertical scale has no absolute significance. (*Source:* Author)

return:

$$E(R) = [(\tau\Sigma)^{-1} + P^T\Omega^{-1}P][(\tau\Sigma)^{-1}\Pi + P^T\Omega^{-1}Q] \quad (7.11)$$

Here, the first square bracket is normalization, Π is the implied excess return from the market $(N \times 1)$, Q is the view vector $K \times 1$, Ω is the diagonal covariance matrix of uncertainty in each view ($K \times K$ matrix) so that the inverse is the confidence level, P is the view-participation matrix $K \times N$ that identifies the assets on which the investor has views, and τ is a scalar.

To implement the approach,

- *Obtain* Π. First, estimate the risk-aversion coefficient λ by solving for the benchmark B (this sets the scale of returns):

$$\lambda = \frac{R_B - r_f}{\sigma_B^2} \qquad (7.12)$$

Now calculate implied excess equilibrium returns Π ($N \times 1$) by solving

$$\Pi = \lambda \Sigma w_m \qquad (7.13)$$

where λ (1×1) was computed in the last step, Σ ($N \times N$) is the covariance of the factor returns, and w_m ($N \times 1$) is the market capitalization. This step is frequently criticized because it assumes that the market weights are the optimal weights and that CAPM is a good description of reality.
- *Create blended returns.* Construct view portfolios and their confidence levels. In practice, the confidence levels are hard to quantify. One approach is to poll a number of investors and create a mean and a standard deviation from the poll results. Substitute in Eq. (7.11) to obtain the combined returns.
- *Optimize.* Perform new mean-variance optimization with these new combined returns in the mean-variance optimizer or one that incorporates higher moments.

Typically, views can be obtained by either ex ante considerations and macro forecasts or by using a building-blocks approach where each of the factor excess returns is forecast with confidence intervals around it. For instance, the view on a particular sector of the bond market would be a combination of the return from the risk-free rate, a duration-risk premium, and a corporate-risk premium. Black-Litterman makes return forecasts more robust but also creates some new challenges; the views on factor or asset returns now require a robust machinery for forecasting.

As an example, assume a simple portfolio of stocks and bonds. Assume that the correlation of returns is 0, stock volatility is 8 percent, and bond volatility is 5 percent. If we assume that the CAPM holds and that stocks are 75 percent of the market, with bonds being 25 percent of the market and the risk-aversion coefficient $\lambda = 10$ percent, then plugging into the CAPM equation gives an equilibrium expected excess return for stocks of 4.8 percent and bonds of 0.63 percent. Now we add a view that stocks will outperform bonds by only 2 percent. Inputting this into the Black-Litterman formula reduces returns for stocks to 3.56 percent and increases returns for bonds to 1.11 percent. Using these returns (and new volatilities from the Black-Litterman adjustment) gives the new optimal stock allocation to 55 percent and bond allocation to 44 percent, which is less than the market weights. What happens if we reduce the confidence in these forecasts to only 25 percent? Intuitively, we should expect the weightings to be a little close to the market weights. Indeed, that's what we find (stock returns go to 4.66 percent from 4.8 percent, and bond returns go from 0.63 percent to 0.68 percent). The optimal weights are now stocks 72.75 percent and bonds 23.25 percent.

While intellectually satisfying in its ability to interpolate systematically between the market implied returns and the view returns, the devil is in the details that go into Black-Litterman. One of the biggest limitations is that while assets might be in equilibrium, it is hard to believe that in a world where the derivatives markets are many times larger than the underlying assets, the risk factors are in equilibrium and amenable to accounting in the form required for equilibrium computations. I will not debate all the other challenges that the practical implementation using this methodology has faced, but conceptually, the approach is a big step forward in blending the views of the portfolio manager with those of the market. If nothing else, this conceptual victory makes it superior to simple mean-variance optimization with point forecasts of returns and a key tool in the arsenal of the allocator.

An alternative method that uses the bayesian elements of Black-Litterman but does not need the CAPM assumptions has been developed in Chatterjee and Woo [5]. The power of this approach is the ability to combine structural trades with fundamentals-based views without reference to market equilibrium. To outline this approach, assume that the carry-based structural distribution of prior returns is given by

$$R_t \approx N(\mu_t, \Sigma_t) \tag{7.14}$$

and the valuation views are given by

$$R_t \approx N(v_t, \Omega_t) \tag{7.15}$$

Then the combined posterior is given by the distribution

$$R_t | v_t \approx N(\mu_t^B, \Sigma_t^B) \tag{7.16}$$

where the posterior expected returns are

$$\mu_t^B = \mu_t + \Sigma_t(\Sigma_t + \Omega_t)^{-1}(v_t - \mu_t) \tag{7.17}$$

and the posterior covariance is

$$\Sigma_t^B = \Sigma_t - \Sigma_t(\Sigma_t + \Omega_t)^{-1}\Sigma_t \tag{7.18}$$

This provides us with all the elements to incorporate view returns along with yield or carry returns and may be used as a practical technique for constructing forward-looking portfolios.

Risk

In the context of asset allocation, the exercise of risk forecasting requires forecasting the evolution of the joint probability distribution of each risk factor, as well as each asset's idiosyncratic return. This is clearly a big task and without a simple solution. The first simplification used in practice is to summarize the dispersion about the mean using the second moment or the standard deviation, and the second simplification is to summarize the joint comovement using the linear correlation coefficient. We know that both these shortcuts are flawed if used blindly. For instance, using standard deviation as a proxy for volatility ignores the higher moments, and return distributions for many asset classes and factors (e.g., credit, liquidity) are notoriously fat tailed. When considering more than one asset, we immediately recognize that linear correlation estimates can be violated in periods of stress. Correlations are notoriously unstable. Stock-bond correlations have varied from highs of close to 80 percent at the beginning of this decade to recent ranges of close to −40 percent. If correlations are this unstable, how is one to use diversifying assets in the portfolio with any degreee of confidence? Again, a simple macroeconomic or factor approach can help. As demonstrated in papers by Li [24] and others, uncertainty of expected inflation is the main driving factor behind the longer-term correlations in stocks and bonds, so obtaining a better handle on the inflation-risk factor should precede forecasts of asset correlations.

The reader undoubtedly has heard about historical and realized volatility, GARCH, implied volatility estimates, and perhaps about multivariate GARCH, cointegration, and so on. Those involved in credit have heard about the copula approach to estimating and calibrating joint distributions. At the end of day, most of these tools end up having only a marginal amount of success in predicting risk. The reason simply is that these approaches, though mathematically sophisticated, lean on a combination of two semifatal errors: First, they use history (in most cases data that are readily available), and second, they assume that the market (wisdom of crowds) is generally accurate. While it would be hard to argue with the fact that in most cases it does not pay to take a diametrically opposite position to either of these

views, for risk-management purposes, it is critical to drop these two
assumptions and see what the impact of a significant event can be. This
aspect of risk management, which we call *tail risk management,* is the
hallmark of an asset-allocation program designed for long-term investment success. We have discussed this in this book previously, so we will
not belabor the point, but it is important to realize that some sacrifice of single-period returns in the form of purchased tail insurance,
constraints (which effectively reduce the excess return expectations),
or strategies that benefit from large deviations actually can result in
superior multiperiod risk returns. In other words, risk management
typically is thought of as incurring a cost on portfolio performance,
whereas the correct characterization is a long-term enhancement of the
return.

From Eq. (7.2) we can easily derive the realized variance (and
hence volatility) of the portfolio by squaring the returns and taking
the average. This naturally leads to the covariance matrix between the
returns as the relevant quantity that carries the information on volatility and comovement of assets. Using the factor-based approach of Eq.
(7.9), we see that the risk comes from a much richer set of sources.
The variance of the factor-based return process depends on the covariance of the factors. If the alphas are not really pure alphas but carry
hidden factor exposures, then the covariance between the explicit and
hidden factors also contributes to the risk. Thus a properly designed
hedge against the tails is really a hedge that insulates against simu-
lataneous negative realization of the factors to which the portfolio is
exposed. This observation can be used to our advantage—if tail risks
are systemic risks, and systemic risks are experienced as large-magnitude
shocks to factors, then the covariance between factors in periods of
stress can be used to supplement the portfolio with cheaper systemic
tail hedges.

Within the context of the key Eq. (7.9) we also can illustrate the
impact of leverage. Suppose that we "gear-up" the alpha exposures by

a multiplicative leverage factor L. Now the expected return is given by

$$E[r_P(t)] = \underbrace{L\alpha_P(t)}_{\text{Levered alpha}}$$

$$+ \underbrace{\sum_{i=1}^{n} \text{corr}[L\beta_{Pi}(t), F_i(t)]\sigma_{\beta_{Pi}(t)}\sigma_{F_i(t)}}_{\text{Levered factor timing}} \quad (7.19)$$

$$+ \underbrace{\sum_{i=1}^{n} E[L\beta_{Pi}(t)]E[F_i(t)]}_{\text{Levered risk premium}}$$

It is easy to see that when levering the alpha, the returns (both positive and negative) driven by the factor loadings are also magnified in proportion to the leverage. What this decomposition importantly illustrates is the trouble with levering alpha that is not really alpha but a beta in disguise. When factor volatility is high or timing frequency is high, the timing term can significantly impact portfolio returns if the leverage is employed at the wrong time (i.e., the selling of liquidity-driven "alpha" right before the summer 2007 crisis). In addition, leverage can magnify the "structural" value (last term) if the expected returns to the factor are of the same sign as the expected beta. If the signs are opposite (i.e., if a portfolio holds positive exposure to a factor with negative expected return), then this takes away from the portfolio returns.

Typically, investment portfolios use short-term strategies for alpha generation, cyclical strategies for factor timing, and structural or secular strategies for the risk-premium part. When the expected premium to certain factors becomes low or negative, it is critical for the investment manager to reduce the exposure to that factor. As discussed in detail earlier, there are three ways of doing this: First, the betas can be reduced directly; second, the betas can be hedged using other securities or combinations of options—in effect, the "bad betas" in tail events are reduced by buying protection that has the opposite sign of beta. Finally, strategies can be employed that mitigate the negative contribution from the timing term. For instance, a momentum strategy empirically has positive beta to liquidity events. In periods of liquidity shocks when the liquidity factor has negative realized returns, a structurally exposed portfolio can be insulated by having such a negatively correlated momentum strategy. A good example is provided by looking closely at the factor exposures of a traditional 60 percent stock and 40 percent bond portfolio, say, a combination of the MSCI Global Equity Index and the Barclays/Lehman Aggregate Index. In factor space and during periods of stress, the risk exposure from the equity factor is greater than 80 percent! In other words, such a portfolio has extremely high exposure to the equity beta factor. For insulating against some of this beta under a period of stress, we could either use reduced or maybe negative equity exposures (extremely hard to do with perfect foresight), purchase "insurance" that has a higher negative conditional equity factor beta in periods of stress, or use strategies that have a negatively correlated timing component to the equity beta. To systematically evaluate how much tail "insurance" is needed, we follow a systematic approach that can be applied regardless of market conditions: We input our portfolio's starting value, an amount we want to "insure" (i.e., losses below which we want to be hedged), annual cost (including time decay), and starting betas of our portfolio to the risk factors. We forecast, conditional on adverse events, excess returns and joint distribution for the factors as well as covariances. Finally, we observe market prices of positions that are positively correlated with the bad scenario. We obtain by simulation the net performance of the portfolio for different option choices and the distribution of the gap between the starting portfolio and the "insured" portfolio. This also yields the resulting beta of portfolio plus "insurance" to each factor exposure within acceptable bounds.

Constraints and Optimization

Contraints have a direct impact on both risk and reward. To illustrate this, let us go back to the return forecasting Eq. (7.9). Suppose that instead of the unconstrained problem, where we optimally select factor exposures and timing, we constrain the factors. There are two general types of constraints: The first type is the nonnegativity constraint, where the weights of securities $w_j \geq 0$, and the second one is where the weights are smaller than some maximum absolute value w_c. From Eq. (7.6), note that the first type of constraint can result in naked factor exposures that one might not desire. This easily can result, using Eq. (7.9), in both timing and risk-premium terms that have negative expected return contribution. The second type of constraint can best be explored by inserting the limiting value β^c in Eq. (7.9) (I use superscript c to signify constraints):

$$
\begin{aligned}
E[r_P(t)]^c = {}& \underbrace{\alpha_P(t)}_{\text{Pure alpha}} \\[2mm]
& + \underbrace{\sum_{i=1}^{n} \text{corr}[\beta_{P_i}^c(t), F_i(t)]\sigma_{\beta_{P_i}^c(t)}\sigma_{F_i(t)}}_{\text{Constrained factor timing}} \\[2mm]
& + \underbrace{\sum_{i=1}^{n} E[\beta_{P_i}^c(t)]E[F_i(t)]}_{\text{Constrained risk premium}}
\end{aligned}
\qquad (7.20)
$$

If expected exposure $|\beta^c| < |\beta|$ in all states of the world, then clearly the contribution from the risk-premium term is lower when the factor exposures and the factor returns are of the same sign. In other words, putting beta constraints on good structural strategies results in suboptimal returns. However, note that the benefit of constraints is that doing so can reduce risk when there is large forecast uncertainty in the factor returns. Once return and risk forecasts, as well as constraints, are obtained, an optimizer can solve for the appropriate allocations to the factors and hence to the assets, which are simply carriers of the factor exposures. What allocation scheme is used really should depend on the horizon and downside tolerance of the investment portfolio. For most long-term investment purposes, a mean-variance optimizer that is used as a tool to translate sensible return and risk forecasts (with errors in the forecast stage explicitly included) is good enough, as long as the results are tested against common sense. Sanity checking is probably the most important part of asset allocation. The basic question to ask is whether the final portfolio meets some objective criterion for success. This is probably the only point at which an optimizer is really needed. Assuming that we have an optimal portfolio of factor exposures and have a valid covariance matrix of factors, we can obtain the expected returns to each factor by "reverse optimization." This simply requires multiplying the inverse covariance matrix into the exposures.

Equity Risks in Bond Portfolios

Bond people like to think of bonds as a separate asset class from equities. While this is true in normal periods, the performance of fixed income markets in 2008 showed us that bonds have a lot of equity-market-driven liquidity risk in them. Until the Lehman bankruptcy, the equity market was living in its own world, but the default brought home in a hurry the truth that equity holders are ultimately taking the bulk of the enterprise risk. Since then, every bond class other than Treasuries have tracked the gyrations of the equity markets. Conceptually, this makes sense—equity markets are where the collective animal spirits live, and increasing risk aversion is experienced first hand when one meets equity markets in a freefall.

The well-known Merton model that links credit spreads to equities is indeed based on the relationship of both equities and bonds issued by a corporation to the underlying assets, and so the observation that a fall in the asset value of companies impacts both corporate stocks and bonds is hardly surprising. What is shocking is that so many asset classes that have nothing to do with corporations, and their assets have become so correlated with equities. Pure alpha strategies have shown little alpha and much equity market beta. Over the last couple years, a watchful investor generally could guess the daily direction of bond levels and yield-curve shape, currencies, commodities, and credit just by observing the changes in the equity market. This correlation of assets at the macro level has brought home the fact that much of the real risk of investments resides in the equity markets, and when the cuts from deleveraging get as close to the backbone of finance as they did last year, the equity market becomes the ultimate risk shock absorber. Even though the stock market itself remained fairly liquid through the crisis, falling equity prices are more likely than rising equity prices to result in falling liquidity of other asset classes. At the end of the day, in a levered economy in which assets are being supported by a diminishing equity base, each unit of falling equity prices very drastically magnifies the economy-wide leverage. If we are on a path of deleveraging that is not at its final resting place, then this "denominator effect" (where equity is the denominator, and the net assets are the numerator) will require a further downward adjustment of the numerator (i.e., of asset valuation broadly). Indeed, widely diversified asset portfolios show an uncanny lack of risk reduction owing to common risk factors. The benefit of asset-class diversification is not so much to reduce risk, they observe, but to provide sources of excess alpha when markets are stable.

The year 2008 created an explosive environment in which the destruction of the structured credit markets drastically simplified investing and asset allocation and called into question decades-old paradigms of asset-class diversification as a mechanism for risk reduction. Long-term investing lore says that a 60/30/10 (equity, bond, cash) mix is a stable long-term portfolio. There are other handy aids that preceded mean-variance optimizers and structured products, such as the best percentage allocation to equities in one's portfolio is 100 minus your age. In light of the fallacy of asset-class diversification, I believe that these rules of thumb are just as good (or maybe even better) than classic asset-allocation optimization as long as the percentage that is not in equities is really not exposed to the equity market. Alas, the major bond indices that represent the broad bond market have too much exposure to equity-market risk because a significant portion of these indices is composed of risk products such as mortgages and corporate bonds. One sees why we are in this situation—most bond indices have adopted the convention of market weighting; in other words, issuers that have large outstanding bond issues have a higher representation in the index. Let's think about this for a moment: Issuing bonds means borrowing. If a corporation borrows more and that borrowing has a bigger representation in an index, the index will have a lower average quality because larger borrowing is positively related to the probability and severity of default. Since the representative bond indices have a lot of equity or default risk mixed in, in periods of stress, the mix (60/30/10 or whatever) will behave as if it is almost completely equities.

By definition, the equity market beta of the stock market to itself is 1. The beta of any other security is the correlation of its returns times the ratio of the volatility of the asset to the volatility of the stock market. Thus, if a security such as a Treasury bond shows a beta of −0.10, this means, first, that its returns are negatively correlated with the stock market. On the other hand, high-yield bonds show an equity beta of almost 1; that is, not only are they positively correlated with the stock market, but they have volatility on the same order of magnitude as the equity market. One would only want to buy such a security if the compensation for holding the default risk exceeded the risk from the market volatility of the equity market by a wide margin. Many hedge funds and other absolute-return strategies turned out to be absolute-negative strategies in 2008 for similar reasons—they were short hidden equity or what is similar, liquidity risk. Higher equity beta should, in efficient markets, compensate with higher return, or so goes the CAPM, but higher beta also means higher drawdown and tail risk.

This all leads to the question of what can one do about it. Once uncorrelated and low-volatility assets become highly correlated with volatile markets, risk management requires nothing less than an aggressive control of the exposure to equity factor risk. Instead of deciding on the allocation to assets by percentage, we can do a much simpler exercise that starts with risk as the key decision variable. If you assume that equities will have a volatility of 30 percent over a long holding horizon, then a beta of 1 to equities in your portfolio means that you should be willing to tolerate a very high likelihood (almost 35 percent) of losing 30 percent of the value of your portfolio over the next year. One simple way to control risk is to look across your portfolio and dial the equity risk-factor beta down to a level of risk that you can tolerate. If you are unwilling to take no more than a 15 percent annual drawdown, you would scale your portfolio's beta down to 0.5 (0.5 × 30 percent = 15 percent). When the equity market is less volatile, revisit this risk allocation and forecast if prospective equity volatility is going to be low or high before increasing equity risk. Thus, if you assume that Treasuries have an equity beta of −0.10, cash and TIPS have an equity beta of 0, mortgages and municipal bonds have an equity beta of 0.25, corporate bonds have an equity beta of 0.50, and high-yield bonds have an equity beta of 1, then you would be comfortable getting some of your equity beta from equities and the rest from bonds. For example, if you put 58 percent of your risk in equities (100-age), that portion gives you an equity beta of 0.58, which is too large if a large drawdown is not tolerable. A safer bet would be to invest 30 percent in equities (with a beta of 0.3), 25 percent in a conservative mortgage or muni fund (with a beta contribution of 0.06), and the rest of the beta budget in corporate bonds (0.14 beta, or roughly 30 percent). The rest (15 percent) goes into cash and TIPS.

There are a few other ways of reducing portfolio equity beta: First, as we just illustrated, one can reduce exposure to assets that carry high equity beta by getting rid of them. The second way of reducing equity beta, if you just have to keep your current high-equity-beta portfolio, is by buying protection against further equity-market factor risk through "insurance," that is, via put options. The third way is to look for uncorrelated or negatively correlated securities such as Treasuries. Finally, you can use negatively correlated strategies: One that consistently works as a diversifier in crises has been momentum or trend following.

Portfolio Tail Risk

Standard deviation or volatility is not a very comprehensive measure of risk at the portfolio level for all horizons. This is primarily due to the inhererent difficulty in forecasting volatilities and correlations over long time horizons. Volatility only captures the normal fluctuations of asset prices, not the large deviation or tail events. Tail risk usually arises from the portfolio being short option-like features that are not captured by most mean-variance models. Our option-adjusted spread (OAS) models try to capture most contributions to OAS from factor risks, and a fraction of any excess OAS that remains is allocated to a "liquidity reserve." Factor risks can consist of level and shape changes of yield curves, changes of implied volatilities, changes in relative spreads of mortgages and corporates to Treasuries and swaps, changes in prepayment rates, fluctuations in currency rates, changes in tax rates, changes in inflation rates, and so on. Frequently, it is possible to structure trades that mitigate liquidity risk.

For a portfolio based on classic mean-variance analysis, what appears shocking at first sight to investors who assume that they would be shielded by "diversification" is how seemingly uncorrelated trades can get correlated. This is a direct consequence of the fact that not enough attention is paid to *liquidity* as perhaps the most important driver of mispricings in the market. We believe that while a portfolio's usual risk comes from normal fluctuations in market factors, it is liquidity that drives the large deviations. In this sense, being overly short liquidity is identical to being short a low-likelihood, high-negative-payoff option. When possible, we can try to buy securities that can cheaply reduce our exposure to liquidity risk.

To investigate the effect of negatively skewed strategies on the portfolio's risk, let us assume that we start with a portfolio that looks sufficiently normal, with an expected excess return of μ and volatility σ. Now let us add to this portfolio another trade and see what happens to the resulting statistics of the portfolio. We will assume that the new strategy can have only two outcomes, called the "up" and "down" outcomes.

If we assume that we invest a proportion α in the normally distributed portfolio and β in the binomial security, we can show that for the portfolio,[3] :

$$\text{Expected excess return} = \alpha\mu + \beta(r_u p + r_d(1 - p)) \qquad (7.23)$$

$$\text{Variance} = \alpha^2\sigma^2 + \beta^2(1 - p)p(r_u - r_d)^2$$

$$\text{Skewness} = \frac{\beta^3 p(1 - p)(1 - 2p)(r_u - r_d)^3}{(\alpha^2\sigma^2 + \beta^2(1 - p)p(r_u - r_d)^2)^{3/2}} \qquad (7.24)$$

Note from these results

- To allocate capital to the new trade over the normal trade must expect the product of r_u and p to be large, that is, a large expected return from the new trade.

---

[3]To derive this result note that the moment-generating function of convolved random variables is the product of their moment-generating functions, so convolving a weighted normal distribution and a weighted binomial distribution, as described in the text, we get

$$\text{Joint MGF} = \Psi(t) = \sum_{y=0,1} \int_{-\infty}^{\infty} e^{\alpha x + \beta r_u(\frac{r_d}{r_u}y)t} p^{1-y}(1 - p)^y \phi(x)dx \qquad (7.21)$$

which equals

$$\Psi(t) = pe^{(\alpha\mu + \beta r_u)t + \frac{1}{2}\alpha^2\sigma^2 t^2} + (1 - p)e^{(\alpha\mu + \beta r_d)t + \frac{1}{2}\alpha^2\sigma^2 t^2} \qquad (7.22)$$

from which differentiating $\Psi(t)$ with respect to t at $t = 0$ repeatedly we can get all the moments.

- Keeping all other things fixed, the expected "risk" or standard deviation of the portfolio scales linearly with the difference $r_u - r_d$ but as the square root of p. Thus the ability to forecast p is not as important as the ability to pick the "really good ones."
- What is perhaps most interesting is that the skewness (displayed in Equation 7.24) of the combined portfolio scales like the cube of the difference between the returns in the up-state r_u and the down-state r_d. If the strategy is one where the loss in the down state exceeds the gain in the up state (i.e. $r_d > r_u$), then the portfolio exhibits negative skewness. This negative skewness, when used in a utility-based portfolio allocation framework for a risk-averse investor, leads to a reduction in allocation of capital to the negatively skewed strategies.

Some approaches to manage tail risk rely heavily on value at risk. Value at risk (VaR) as a methodology of controlling tail risk is highly suspect owing to the unstable nature of correlations over long horizons. Recall how the value at risk of a portfolio is computed. First, start with a portfolio of n different strategies. Assume that the allocation of capital to strategy i is α_i. Also assume that the ith strategy has excess return $r_i - r_f$ ($/r_f$ is the risk-free rate). Now, the portfolio excess return is simply $r_p = \sum_{i=1}^{n}(r_i - r_f)$. Once we know what the distribution of the individual r_i is, we can theoretically construct the distribution of r_p. Then value at risk is simply the inverse cumulative density function of r_p for a specified confidence level. In other words, the user specifies that if a certain probability event happens (such as one in a hundred), then asks what is the corresponding loss in the portfolio over the horizon (i.e., the CDF of r_p for the 1 percentile tail). Note three important reasons why the simple VaR methodology can lead to drastic and misleading results:

- The underlying joint distribution of variables in the real world is not necessarily joint normal; that is, there is no guarantee that fat tails will be absent in the joint distribution. However, most VaR models are based on estimation of covariance matrices from an implicit assumption of joint normality of asset returns (for numerical efficiency). Hence, in reality, the user would find that large correlated moves will happen more frequently than predicted by the model. VaR as a risk-management tool fails grossly exactly when it is needed the most, that is, when fat-tail events of a multivariate portfolio occur.
- It is hard to base risk management on forecast covariance matrices when the number of securities involved gets large. Thus, practically, most VaR calculations are based on historically derived covariance matrices or VaR parameters. Since past history is no guarantee of future correlations and volatilities, basing risk management on historical VaR is dangerous.
- VaR and similar methodologies aggregate information, and this aggregation results in loss of granularity. Different methods of aggregation (which result from unstable covariance matrices) result in substantially different VaR outputs.

For most practical risk-management decisions, even though VaR and related measures are a quick ways to get a handle on outliers, they are less robust than factor-by-factor (disaggregated) risk measurement and risk limits.

Scaling

Perhaps the most important ingredient in managing any portfolio, and especially more so for leveraged portfolios, is to know when to add and when to reduce exposure to a position. The basic criterion for increasing the size of a trade or, for that matter, to introduce a new strategy into the portfolio is that the overall risk-reward profile should be higher after the change. Assuming that the Sharpe ratio is the measure of the risk versus reward trade-off of a portfolio, we would only add a new strategy if the result of adding it increased the overall portfolio Sharpe ratio.

Assume that we start with a portfolio that has ex ante excess return r_p and volatility σ_p to the horizon date. Then the Sharpe ratio of the portfolio is

$$S_p = \frac{r_p}{\sigma_p} \tag{7.25}$$

Let us now consider adding a new strategy with excess return r_n in weight w to the portfolio. The Sharpe ratio of the portfolio after adding the new trade will be

$$S_{p'} = \frac{wr_n + (1-w)r_p}{\sigma_{p'}} \tag{7.26}$$

where p' is the new portfolio. The volatility of the new portfolio is

$$\sigma_{p'} = \sqrt{w^2\sigma_n^2 + (1-w)^2\sigma_p^2 + 2w(1-w)\rho_{n,p}\sigma_n\sigma_p} \tag{7.27}$$

where $\rho_{n,p} = \rho$ is the correlation between the new trade and the old portfolio. The beta of the new strategy with respect to the new portfolio is

$$\begin{aligned}\beta_{n,p'} &= \frac{\text{cov}(n, p')}{\text{var}(p')} \\ &= \frac{w\sigma_n^2 + w(1-w)\rho\sigma_n\sigma_p}{w^2\sigma_n^2 + (1-w)^2\sigma_p^2 + 2w(1-w)\rho\sigma_n\sigma_p}\end{aligned} \tag{7.28}$$

The hurdle that the new strategy has to pass in order to be included into the portfolio is

$$r_n > r_{p'}\beta_{n,p} \tag{7.29}$$

and this also gives the optimal weight for inclusion in the portfolio. For instance, let us start with a portfolio that has excess return of 10 percent and volatility of 20 percent. To this portfolio, let us consider adding a strategy with excess return of 20 percent and volatility of 40 percent and with zero correlation with the original portfolio. Using the preceding equation, we find that the optimal allocation to the new trade is close to a third. Note that as correlation becomes negative, the hurdle rate falls.

Holdings under Leverage Constraints

To conclude this chapter, let's discuss what different investors with different leverage tolerances do to meet risk-return objectives. This example illustrates the inherent difficulty in a one-size-fits all risk management paradigm.

Let us assume that there are two different investors and three different fixed income securities. Investor Leveraging Larry (L) can use leverage, while investor Nonleveraging Nancy (N) cannot lever.

The three different securities are defined by the following characteristics (expressed as percentages in Table 7.3): (1) the expected excess return r_i, (2) the standard deviation or volatility of the excess return σ_i,

Table 7.3 Characteristics and Security Factor Exposures Available to Investors.

Security	Excess Return (r_i)	Standard Deviation (σ_i)	r_i/σ_i	d_i	c_i	m_i
S_1	1.5	1.8	0.83	0	0.25	0
S_2	1.0	1.2	0.83	8	0.0	0
S_3	2.0	3.0	0.66	0	0	5

(*Source:* Author)

(3) the Sharpe ratio r_i/σ_i, (4) duration exposure d_i, (5) the yield-curve steepening or flattening exposure (curve duration) c_i, and (6) a spread exposure m_i (e.g., mortgage OAS exposure).

We have close parallels to these three securities in capital markets. The first security can be thought of as a security that gives exposure to yield-curve steepening or flattening with no exposure to parallel shifts. The second security is akin to the 10-year part of the yield curve (with a duration of 8 years in our example, and no exposure to the steepening or flattening factor). The third security is an idealized "spread product" with no yield-curve exposure. We assume in this section that the securities are uncorrelated and carry independent factor exposures. None of the qualitative results depend on this assumption.

Suppose that both Larry and Nancy are given the objective that they need to minimize their portfolio volatility σ_P given a target portfolio return r_P. Now suppose we vary the return and ask Larry and Nancy to pick the most efficient portfolios to satisfy the return targets. We will define the best portfolio to be the one that minimizes the variance of the portfolio while simultaneously meeting the return target. Once w_1 and w_2 are found, the budget contraint $w_1 + w_2 + w_3 = 1$ fixes the third security w_3.

To summarize:

1. Define portfolio return $r_P = \sum_i w_i r_i$, where w_i are the security weights and r_i are the security excess returns. Similarly, define $\sigma_P^2 = \sum_i w_i^2 \sigma_i^2$ as the portfolio variance when the securities are uncorrelated.

2. Pick a portfolio return r_P, and minimize σ_P^2 to solve for w_i to get optimal weights w_i^*.

3. Multiply the vector of optimal factor weights w_i^* with the factor exposure matrix $f_{i,j}$ to obtain the portfolio factor exposure vector F_i.

Table 7.4 Portfolio Allocation and Risk Statistics for an Investor Who Can Leverage.

r_P	σ_P	w_1	w_2	d_P	c_P	m_P
1.0	1.16	0.12	0.94	7.5	0.03	−0.30
1.2	0.95	0.26	0.67	5.39	0.06	0.37
1.4	1.05	0.38	0.41	3.27	0.09	1.04
1.6	1.40	0.51	0.14	1.16	0.13	1.72
1.8	1.85	0.64	−0.12	−0.96	0.16	2.40
2.0	2.35	0.77	−0.38	−3.07	0.19	3.08
2.2	2.88	0.90	−0.65	−5.19	0.22	3.75
2.4	3.42	1.02	−0.91	−7.31	0.25	4.43

Note: The weight w_3 in the third security is determined by the budget constraint $w_1 + w_2 + w_3 = 1$.

(*Source:* Author)

Using this optimization algorithm, we compute Larry's selection of weights in Table 7.4 and observe the following:

- As return requirements increase, Larry begins to lever up on the first security, which requires him to short the second security. The budget constraint also forces him to lever up on the third security. The net result is that while the portfolio return increases, so does the portfolio variance.
- Since each security carries a factor exposure, increasing the demand for the first security at the expense of the second security makes the duration of the portfolio go negative. Demand and exposure to the third security also get driven up.

Now let us look at what Nancy's allocation is (she cannot lever) in Table 7.5:

- Since Nancy cannot lever, she has no way of getting a return beyond 2 percent for the portfolio, regardless of the mix she chooses.

**Table 7.5 Portfolio Allocation and Risk Statistics
for an Investor Who Cannot Leverage.**

r_P	σ_P	w_1	w_2	d_P	c_P	m_P
1.0	1.16	0.12	0.94	7.5	0.03	−0.30
1.2	0.95	0.26	0.67	5.39	0.06	0.37
1.4	1.05	0.38	0.41	3.27	0.09	1.04
1.6	1.40	0.51	0.14	1.16	0.13	1.72
1.7	1.61	0.57	0.01	0.10	0.14	2.06
1.8	1.94	0.40	0	0	0.1	3
1.9	2.43	0.20	0	0	0.05	4
2.0	3	0	0	0	0	5

Source: The weight w_3 in the third security is determined by the budget constraint $w_1 + w_2 + w_3 = 1$.

(*Source:* Author)

- As long as the required return is approxixmately 1.7 percent (or lower), both Larry and Nancy have the same allocations and factor exposures for their overall portfolio, but as soon as the required porfolio return increases beyond 1.7 percent, Nancy's constraint of not being able to lever increases her portfolio risk σ_P for the same level of portfolio return.
- Nancy ends up investing more in the highest-returning third security (which has the least attractive risk-reward characteristics).
- For the same return target, Nancy has a much larger factor exposure to the third factor.

The ability of some market participants to lever and the corresponding inability of other market participants to lever can lead to significant consequences for the market. If some fraction of participants can lever, and the remaining participants cannot lever, then the market equilibrium will be some mix of the optimal holdings of the levered and unlevered investors. Since a security cannot be in net negative demand, at equilbrium, some securities at best can be in zero net demand. In our example above, the second security is in zero net demand when return demands are higher than 1.8 percent. Note that the second security in our example is like the 10-year note. As demand for portfolio return increases, at a certain point, an optimizing investor will likely refuse to hold this security because it cannot simultaneously satisfy return maximization, risk minimization, and no leverage. The levered investor shorts it, and the unlevered investor refuses to own it. This leads to the security naturally being held by non-economically motivated investors. In other words, the residual holder of the duration-risk factor in our example is a nonoptimizing portfolio manager. Anecdotally, this could very well be a foreign holder of securities who is not optimizing his or her portfolio-simply in terms of short-term dollar risk-return trade-offs but in terms of some more general risk-reward trade-off.[4]

Observe further that if Larry actually goes to the allocation where his portfolio is net short duration (e.g., at required return of 2.4 percent he is net short 7.3 years' duration), his convexity exposure is very different from the convexity exposure of Nancy (who has net zero convexity). In equilibrium, the net negative convexity of the levered investor is being transferred to the nonoptimizing residual buyer of the duration exposure. A consequence of this is that if there is a large move away from market equilibrium, there can be a mad scramble for the unmatched factor exposure owing to risk-management constraints.

---

[4]In the case of some foreign holders of U.S. debt, this objective function might be the maintenance of the Bretton-Woods II paradigm. This mechanism allows for an export-led growth of the foreign economy by the dual mechanism of keeping the dollar artificially strong and U.S. long rates low and stimulative.

Epilogue

The drama of the crisis of 2007–2008 involved characters from all areas of the global economy. The ramifications of the unwind of leverage was felt in the financial industry, in goods and services industries, and eventually in households and even on sovereign balance sheets. Many lessons were learned. For financial market participants, the lessons were clear—leverage cuts both ways: When the going is good, it results in excess returns, but when the going gets bad, it can lead to ruin. For non-financial industry participants, the lesson was that in a levered economy even bricks-and-mortar production can get impacted by leverage. For individuals, the lesson was that even well-thought-out investment plans and diversified portfolios can be impacted by contagion and illiquidity and that the value of investment portfolios can go down more sharply than one can ascribe reasonable probabilities to.

Our discussion of fixed income investing has revolved around the central idea that excess return almost always arises from short option positions, either explicit or implicit, and thus that the risk arises from these options simultaneously increasing substantially in value and hence creating large portfolio losses. To control against such tail risks, we require an understanding of macroeconomics, the underlying risk factors, and the behavior of participants and the discipline to insure portfolios against large, severe losses. While it would be fantastic to have perfect option-pricing models for each of these implicit options, it is too hopeful to wait for such a utopia. But simply insulating portfolios through envisioning stresses can get one a long way toward creating robust portfolios.

The last crisis was probably not the final one in the annals of finance. Despite regulation and risk-control infrastructure, the demand for excess yield will allow for arbitrageurs to find new channels to take risk. Every investor needs to have the framework to think through the risk-versus-reward equation, take those where risk is well compensated in the context of their full portfolio and time horizon, and walk away from risks that are not adequately compensated. There are always other opportunities around the corner for the patient bond investor.

Hopefully the toolkit in this book provides the reader with the framework to make this independent evaluation of investment opportunities in the bond market.

References

1. "ABS CDOs: A primer," Lehman Brothers, November 2006.

2. A. Ang and Monika Piazzesi, "A no-arbitrage vector autoregression of term-structure dynamics with macroeconomic and latent variables," *Journal of Monetary Economics* 50(4): 2003, 745.

3. A. Ang, V. Bhansali, and Y. Xing, "Taxes on tax-exempt bonds," *Journal of Finance* Vol. 65, Issue 2, 2010, 565–601.

4. A. Bend, R. F. Engle, A. B. Voronov, "The Underlying Dynamics of Credit Correlations," 2007, available on SSRN.

5. A. Chatterjee and D. Woo, "Vector: The next generation of systematic currency trading," Barclays Capital, October 13, 2009.

6. A. Desclee, L. Dynkin, A. S. Gould, V. Konstantinovsky, B. Lu, and J. Rosten, "Replicating the Lehman Brothers Global Aggregate Index with liquid instruments," Lehman Brothers Fixed Income Research, 2005.

7. A. Lo and C. MacKinlay, "When are contrarian profits due to stock market over-reaction?" *Review of Financial Studies* 3: 1990, 175–206.

8. A. P. Attie and S. K. Roache, "Inflation hedging for long-term investors," IMF Working Paper, WP/09/90. April 2009.

9. B. Kopprasch, "A look at a variety of duration measures," *Yield Book*, Citigroup, 2004.

10. B. Tuckman, *Fixed Income Securities*, 2nd ed., Hoboken, NJ: Wiley, 2002.

11. E. Altman, "Current conditions in global credit markets," NMS Investment Management Forum, September 15, 2009.

12. F. Black and R. Litterman, "Asset allocation: Combining investors views with market equilibrium," *Fixed Income Research*, Goldman, Sachs & Company, September, 1990.

13. F. Black and R. Litterman, "Global asset allocation with equities, bonds, and currencies," *Fixed Income Research*, Goldman, Sachs & Company, October, 1991.

14. F. Black "Interest rates as options," *Journal of Finance*, 50(7): 1995, 1371–1376.

15. F. Black, and R. Litterman, "Global portfolio optimization," *Financial Analysts Journal*, September–October, 1992, 28–43.

16. F. Longstaff and A. Rajan, "An empirical analysis of the pricing of collateralized debt obligations," SSRN working paper, 2006.

17. G. Burghardt, T. Belton, M. Lane, and J. Papa, *The Treasury Bond Basis: An In Depth Analysis for Hedgers, Speculators and Arbitrageurs*. McGraw-Hill, 2005.

18. G. Miller, "Needles, haystacks and hidden factors," The Journal of Portfolio Management, Vol. 32, p. 2, 2006.

19. J. Cochrane and M. Piazzesi, "Bond risk premia," *American Economic Review*, 95(1): 2005, 138–160.

20. K. Jackwerth, "Option-implied risk-neutral distributions and risk aversion," Research Foundation of AIMR, 2004.

21. A. Khandani, A. W. Lo, "What happened to the quants in august 2007?," (November 4, 2007). Available at SSRN: http://ssrn.com/abstract=1015987.

22. L. Dynkin, A. Gould, J. Hyman, V. Konstantinovsky, and B. Phelps, *Quantitative Management of Bond Portfolios*. Princeton, NJ: Princeton University Press, 2007.

23. L. Martellini, P. Priaulet, and S. Priaulet, "Understanding the butterfly strategy," *Journal of Bond Trading and Management* 1(1): 2002, 1.

24. Li, Lingfeng, "Macroeconomic factors and the correlation of stock and bond returns," SSRN, 2002.

25. J. Liu and F. Longstaff, "Risk and return in fixed income arbitrage: Nickels in front of a steamroller?" UCLA, 2005.

26. A. Lo, "Where do alphas come from?: a new measure of the value of active investment management," SSRN, 2009. Available at http://ssrn.com/abstract=985127.

27. M. Baker and J. Wurgler, "Investor sentiment and the cross section of stock returns," *The Journal of Finance*, 61(4): 2006, 1645–1680.

28. M. Britten-Jones and S. M. Schaefer, "Non-linear Value at Risk", *European Finance Review* 2: 161, 1999.

29. M. Johannes and S. Sundaresan, "The impact of collateralization on swap rates," *Journal of Finance* 62(1): 2007, 383.

30. M. Leibowitz, "Structural betas: The key risk factor in asset allocation," Morgan Stanley Equity Research, June 2004.

31. R. C. Merton, (1974), "On the pricing of corporate debt: the risk structure of interest rates," *Journal of Finance*, 29, 449–70.

32. N. Jegadeesh and B. Tuckman, *Advanced Fixed Income Valuation Tools*. Hoboken, NJ: Wiley, 2000.

33. Ole E. Barndorff-Nielsen, 2004. "Power and bipower variation with stochastic volatility and jumps," *Journal of Financial Econometrics*, Oxford University Press, vol. 2(1), pages 1–37.

34. P. McCulley, and J. Fuerbringer, *Your Financial Edge*. Hoboken, NJ: Wiley, 2007.

35. Q. Dai and K. J. Singleton, "Specification analysis of term structure models," *Journal of Finance*, Vol. LV, No. 5, Oct 2000, p. 1943.

36. R. Bookstaber, *A demon of our own design: Markets, hedge funds and the perils of financial innovation*, Wiley, 2007.

37. R. Clarida, J. Gali, and M. Gertler, "Monetary policy rules and macroeconomic stability: Evidence and some theory," *Quarterly Journal of Economics* 113: 2000, 147–180.

38. R. Clarida, J. Gali, and M. Gertler, "The science of monetary policy: A new keynesian perspective," *Journal of Economic Literature*, XXXVII, Dec. 1999, 1661–1707.

39. R. Ingersoll, *Theory of Financial Decision Making*, 2nd ed., Hoboken, NJ: Wiley, 2002.

40. R. Michaud, *Efficient Asset Management*, Oxford, England: Oxford University Press, 1998.

41. Robert J. Greer, "What is an asset class, anyway?" *Journal of Portfolio Management*, Winter 1997.

42. Robert Litterman, and Jose A. Scheinkman, "Common factors affecting bond returns," *Journal of Fixed Income* 1: 1991, 54–61.

43. T. G. Andersen, T. Bollerslev, and F. Diebold, "Roughing it up: Including jump components in the measurement, modeling and forecasting of return volatility," Review of Economics and Statistics Vol. 89, 2007, 701–720.

44. V. Bhansali and M. B. Wise, "Forecasting portfolio risk in normal and stressed markets," *Journal of Risk* (4)1: 2001, 91–106.

45. V. Bhansali, M. Dorsten and M. B. Wise, "Asymmetric monetary policy and the yield curve," *Journal of International Money and Finance* 28(8): Dec. 2009, 1408–1425.

46. V. Bhansali, R. Gingrich, and F. Longstaff, "Systemic risk: What is the market telling us?," *Financial Analysts Journal*, 64(4): 2008, 16–24.

47. V. Bhansali, Y. Schwarzkopf, and M. B. Wise, "Modeling swap spreads in normal and stressed environments," *Journal of Fixed Income*, (18)4: 2009, 5–23.

48. V. Bhansali, "Putting economics (back) into quantitative models," *Journal of Portfolio Management*, 33(3): 2007, 63–76.

49. V. Bhansali, "Tail risk management," *Journal of Portfolio Management*, 34(4): 2008, 68–75.

50. V. Bhansali, "The P's of pricing and risk management revisited," *Journal of Portfolio Management*, 36(2): Winter 2010, 106–112.

51. V. Bhansali, "Volatility and the carry trade," *Journal of Fixed Income*, (17)3: 2007, 72–84.

52. W. Fung and D. A. Hsieh, "The risk in hedge fund strategies: Theory and evidence from trend followers," *Review of Financial Studies*, 14(2001), 313–341.

53. V. Bhansali and M. B. Wise, "How Valuable are the TALF Puts?" Journal of Fixed Income, Vol. 2, 2009, 71–75.

Index

A

Absolute risk aversion, 69
Affine models, 122–123
Alpha strategies, 262–263
Alphas:
    generation of, 5–6, 259–260
    separating betas from, 176, 237
Analytical tractability, 122–127
Arbitrage:
    fixed income, 108–111
    and model building, 127–130, 128t,
      129t
Asset allocation, 231–275
    constraints in, 260–261
    and equity risks, 262–266
    factor-based, 236–243
    leverage constraints in, 271–275,
      271t, 273t, 274t
    optimization in, 261–262
    and portfolio tail risk, 266–269
    and return forecasting, 243–256
    and risk factors, 234–236
    and risk forecasting, 256–260
    sanity checking in, 262
    scaling in, 269–271
Asset classes, 235–236
Asset swaps, 44–46
Asset-backed securities (ABSs), 47,
    51–52
Asset-class diversification, 21

B

Baker-Wurgler sentiment index,
    135–141, 136f–140f
Base correlations, 158–159
Bear duration, 9, 65, 208
Benchmarks, 191
Beta-adjusted durations, 163–167
Betas, 52–55
    computing, 52–53
    defined, 160
    equity, 264–266
    forecasting, 160–167
    long-term, 165–167
    replication of, 176
    separating alphas from, 176, 237
Black-Litterman approach, 250–256
Bootstrap approach, 229–230
Breakeven inflation rate, 18
Building blocks, 25–55

About the Author

Vineer Bhansali. Ph.D., managing director and portfolio manager at PIMCO, oversees PIMCO's quantitative investment portfolios. In addition, from 2000 he managed PIMCO's analytics department. Prior to joining PIMCO, he was a proprietary trader in the fixed-income trading group at Credit Suisse First Boston and in the fixed-income arbitrage group at Salomon Brothers in New York, and he served as head of the exotic and hybrid options trading desk at Citibank New York. The author of *Pricing and Managing Exotic and Hybrid Options and Fixed Income Finance: A Quantitative Approach*, he serves as an associate editor for the *International Journal of Theoretical and Applied Finance*. He received his Ph.D. in theoretical physics from Harvard University in 1992 and his bachelor's and master's degree in physics and engineering and applied sciences from Caltech in 1987. Bhansali lives in Laguna Beach, CA.

CPSIA information can be obtained
at www.ICGtesting.com
Printed in the USA
BVOW06*1059081217
502133BV00006B/15/P